Android™ Phones

FOR

DUMMIES®

A Wiley Brand

2nd Edition

Android™ Phones

FOR DUMMIES®

A Wiley Brand

2nd Edition

by Dan Gookin

FOR DUMMIES®

A Wiley Brand

Android™ Phones For Dummies® 2nd Edition

Published by: **John Wiley & Sons, Inc.,** 111 River Street, Hoboken, NJ 07030-5774, www.wiley.com

Copyright © 2014 by John Wiley & Sons, Inc., Hoboken, New Jersey

Published simultaneously in Canada

For general information on our other products and services, please contact our Customer Care Department within the U.S. at 877-762-2974, outside the U.S. at 317-572-3993, or fax 317-572-4002. For technical support, please visit www.wiley.com/techsupport.

Wiley publishes in a variety of print and electronic formats and by print-on-demand. Some material included with standard print versions of this book may not be included in e-books or in print-on-demand. If this book refers to media such as a CD or DVD that is not included in the version you purchased, you may download this material at http://booksupport.wiley.com. For more information about Wiley products, visit www.wiley.com.

Library of Congress Control Number: 2013946767

ISBN 978-1-118-72030-1 (pbk); ISBN 978-1-118-72029-5 (ebk); ISBN 978-1-118-72037-0 (ebk)

Manufactured in the United States of America

10 9 8 7 6 5 4 3 2 1

Contents at a Glance

Table of Contents

Introduction

*I*t may be a smartphone, but it makes you feel dumb. Don't worry: You aren't alone. As technology leaps ahead, it often leaves mortal humans behind. I mean, what's the point of owning the latest gizmo when the thing intimidates you to the point that you never use all its features? When that latest gizmo is a modern necessity, such as a cell phone, the problem becomes more complex because you always have the thing with you as a reminder.

Relax.

This book makes the complex subject of Android phones understandable. It's done with avuncular care and gentle hand-holding. The information is friendly and informative, without being intimidating. And yes, ample humor is sprinkled throughout the text to keep the mood light.

About This Book

I implore you: Do not read this book from cover to cover. This book is a reference. It's designed to be used as you need it. Look up a topic in the table of contents or the index. Find something about your phone that vexes you or something you're curious about. Look up the answer, and get on with your life.

Every chapter in this book is written as its own, self-contained unit, covering a specific topic about using an Android phone. The chapters are further divided into sections representing a task you perform with the phone or explaining how to get something done. Sample sections in this book include

- Accessing the onscreen keyboard
- Making a conference call
- Adding your phone to Google Voice
- Uploading a picture to Facebook
- Navigating to your destination
- Creating a mobile hotspot
- Dialing an international number
- Saving battery life

Every section explains a topic as though it's the first one you read in this book. Nothing is assumed, and everything is cross-referenced. Technical terms and topics, when they come up, are neatly shoved to the side, where they're easily avoided. The idea here isn't to learn anything. This book's philosophy is to help you look it up, figure it out, and get back to your life.

How to Use This Book

This book follows a few conventions for using your phone, so pay attention!

The main way to interact with the typical Android phone is by using its *touchscreen,* which is the glassy part of the phone as it's facing you. The physical buttons on the phone are called *keys.* These items are discussed and explained in Part I of this book.

Various ways are available to touch the screen, which are described in Chapter 3.

Chapter 4 covers typing text on an Android phone, which involves using something called the *onscreen keyboard.* Your phone may also feature a physical keyboard. Lucky you. When you tire of typing, you can dictate your text. It's all explained in Chapter 4.

This book directs you to do things on your phone by following numbered steps. Every step involves a specific activity, such as touching something on the screen; for example:

3. Choose Downloads.

This step directs you to touch the text or item on the screen labeled Downloads. You might also be told to do this:

3. Touch Downloads.

Because this book covers a variety of phones, alternative commands may be listed. One of them is bound to match something on your phone, or at least be close to what you see:

3. Touch the My Downloads command or the Downloads command.

In a few places, you might see text that's displayed on a computer. In these instances, the text is shown in a `monospace font`.

Various phone settings are turned off or on, as indicated by a box next to the setting. Touch this box on the screen to add or remove a check mark. When the check mark appears, as shown in the margin, the option is on; otherwise, it's off.

Some settings feature a master control, which looks like the on/off switch shown in the margin. Slide the button to the right to activate the switch, turning on a phone feature. Slide the button to the left to disable the feature. Some phone's feature the master control with the text On or Off.

Foolish Assumptions

Even though this book is written with the gentle hand-holding required by anyone who is just starting out or is easily intimidated, I have made a few assumptions.

I'm assuming that you're still reading the introduction. That's great. It's much better than getting a snack right now or checking to ensure that the cat isn't chewing through the TV cable again.

My biggest assumption: You have an Android phone. It can be any Android phone from any manufacturer supported by any popular cellular service provider in the United States. Because Android is an operating system (just like Windows for a PC), the methods of doing things on one Android phone are similar, if not identical, to doing things on another Android phone. Therefore, one book can pretty much cover the gamut of Android phones.

Like Windows, Android has versions. The Android versions covered in this book include Jelly Bean and Kit Kat, which are also known by the famous numbers 4.3 and 4.4, respectively. You can confirm which Android version your phone has by following these steps:

1. **At the Home screen, touch the Apps icon.**

2. **Open the Settings app.**

3. **Choose the About Phone item.**

   On some Samsung phones, you'll need to first touch the General tab atop the screen and then scroll down the screen to find an About Device item. Samsung phones can be a little different from other Android phones, and those differences are highlighted throughout this tome.

4. **Look at the item titled Android Version.**

   The number that's shown should be 4.3.*x*, or 4.4.*x* where the *x* is another number or maybe not even there are all.

Don't fret if these steps confuse you: Review Part I of this book, and then come back here. (I'll wait.)

More assumptions: You don't need to own a computer to use your Android phone. If you have a computer, great. The Android phone works well with both PCs and Macs. When directions are specific to a PC or Mac, the book says so.

Finally, this book assumes that you have a Google account. If you don't, find out how to configure one in Chapter 2. Having a Google account opens up a slew of useful features, information, and programs that make using your phone more productive.

How This Book Is Organized

This book has been sliced into six parts, each of which describes a certain aspect of the typical Android phone or how it's used.

Part I: Your Own Android

Part I serves as an introduction to your Android phone. Chapters cover setup and orientation and familiarize you with how the phone works. This part is a good place to start — plus, you discover things in this part that aren't obvious from just guessing how the phone works.

Part II: The Phone Part

Nothing is more basic for a phone to do than make calls, which is the topic of the chapters in Part II. As you may have suspected, your phone can make calls, receive calls, and serve as an answering service for calls you miss. It also manages the names of all the people you know and even those you don't want to know but have to know anyway.

Part III: Stay Connected

The modern cell phone is about more than just telephone communications. Part III explores other ways you can use your phone to stay in touch with people, browse the Internet, check your e-mail, do your social networking, exchange text messages, engage in video chats, and more.

Part IV: Amazing Phone Feats

Part IV explores the nonphone things your phone can do. For example, your phone can find locations on a map, give you verbal driving directions, take pictures, shoot videos, play music, play games, and do all sorts of wonderful things that no one would ever think a phone can do. The chapters in this part of the book get you up to speed on those activities.

Part V: Nuts and Bolts

The chapters in Part V discuss a slate of interesting topics, from connecting the phone to a computer, using Wi-Fi and Bluetooth networking, and taking the phone overseas and making international calls to customizing and personalizing your phone and the necessary chores of maintenance and troubleshooting.

Part VI: The Part of Tens

Finally, this book ends with the traditional *For Dummies* The Part of Tens, where every chapter lists ten items or topics. For your Android phone, the chapters include tips, tricks, shortcuts, and things to remember.

Icons Used in This Book

 This icon flags useful, helpful tips or shortcuts.

 This icon marks a friendly reminder to do something.

 This icon marks a friendly reminder *not* to do something.

 This icon alerts you to overly nerdy information and technical discussions of the topic at hand. Reading the information is optional, though it may win you a pie slice in *Trivial Pursuit.*

Where to Go from Here

Thank you for reading the introduction. Few people do, and it would save a lot of time and bother if they did. Consider yourself fortunate, although you probably knew that.

Your task now: Start reading the rest of the book — but not the whole thing, and especially not in order. Observe the table of contents and find something that interests you. Or look up your puzzle in the index. When these suggestions don't cut it, just start reading Chapter 1.

My e-mail address is dgookin@wambooli.com. Yes, that's my real address. I reply to every e-mail I receive, especially when you keep your question short and specific to this book. Although I enjoy saying "Hi," I cannot answer technical support questions, resolve billing issues, or help you troubleshoot your phone. Thanks for understanding.

My web site is www.wambooli.com. This book has its own page on that site, which you can check for updates, new information, and all sorts of fun stuff. Visit often:

www.wambooli.com/help/android/phones/

Bonus information for this title can be found online. You can visit the publisher's website to find an online cheat sheet at

www.dummies.com/cheatsheet/androidphones

Supplemental online material has been created for this book. That supplemental stuff can be found at

www.dummies.com/extras/androidphones

Updates to this book might someday be found at

www.dummies.com/extras/androidphones

Enjoy this book and your Android phone!

Part I
Your Own Android

getting started
with

Your Android

Phone

In this part . . .

✔ Get started with Android phones.

✔ Work through the setup of your Android phone.

✔ Learn how to use your Android phone.

✔ Discover parts of the Android phone.

Have a Little Android

*I*t may have a funky name, like a character in a science fiction novel or a sports hero. Or it can simply be a fancy number, perhaps with the letter *X* thrown in to spice it up. No matter what, the phone you own is an *Android* phone because it runs the Android operating system. Before getting into more detail, let me specify that the adventure you're about to undertake begins with removing the thing from the box and getting to know your new smartphone.

Liberation and Setup

The phone works fastest when you remove it from its box. The procedure differs depending on whether you're a technology nut or someone desperate to make a phone call. I prefer to gingerly open the box, delicately lifting the various flaps and tenderly setting everything aside. I even savor the smell of industrial solvent. If you prefer, you can just dump everything on the tabletop. But be careful: Your phone may be compact, but it's not cheap.

Several useful items might be found loitering inside your Android phone's box. Some of them are immediately handy, and others you should consider saving for later. Even if you've already opened the box and spread its contents across the table like some sort of tiny yard sale, take a few moments to locate and identify these specific items:

- ✔ The phone itself, which may be fully assembled or in pieces
- ✔ Papers, instructions, a warranty, and perhaps a tiny, useless *Getting Started* pamphlet
- ✔ The phone's battery, which might already be installed inside the phone
- ✔ The phone's back cover, which might already be on the phone
- ✔ The charger/data cable or USB cable
- ✔ The charger head, which is a wall adapter for the charger/data cable
- ✔ Other stuff, such as a SIM card; or if the SIM card is already installed, the SIM card holder, SIM insertion tool, or other scary electronic tidbits

The phone itself may ship with a clingy, static, plastic cover over its screen, back, or sides. The plastic thingies might tell you where various features are located or how to install the battery. You can remove all plastic, clingy sheets at this time. Check the rear camera to confirm that you've removed the plastic thingy from its lens.

In addition to the items described in the preceding list, you might have received a bonus package of goodies from whoever sold you the phone. If the outfit is classy, you have a handy little tote bag with perhaps the Phone Company's logo on it. Inside the bag, you might find these items:

- ✔ A microSD card to use as the phone's removable storage
- ✔ A smart-looking, leatherette belt-clip phone holster
- ✔ A micro-USB car charger
- ✔ A car windshield mount
- ✔ Headphones
- ✔ Screen protectors
- ✔ A phone case
- ✔ A desktop dock or multimedia station
- ✔ Even more random pieces of paper

You can safely set aside all this stuff until you put the phone together. I recommend keeping the instructions and other information as long as you own the phone: The phone's box makes an excellent storage place for that stuff — as well as for anything else you don't plan to use right away.

If anything is missing or appears to be damaged, immediately contact the folks who sold you the phone.

✔ The phone's box contains everything you need to use the phone. Anything extra you buy merely enhances the phone-using experience.

✔ See the later section "Adding accessories" for a description of various goodies you can obtain for the typical Android phone.

Phone Assembly

Most Android phones come disassembled in their boxes. The primary thing you must install is the battery. The phone's back cover must then be attached. Only if your phone has no removable battery does it come fully assembled, and even then it may have a SIM or microSD card (memory) that you must install. The following sections offer a general idea of how everything fits together.

Oftentimes, the people who sell you the phone assemble the thing for you. That's a plus. Even so, it helps to be familiar with how to open your phone, access its guts, and reassemble it. Such knowledge will come in handy later, for example, should you need to replace the battery or access some other internal phone doohickey.

Opening the phone

If you've just received your phone, it might already be in an opened state. If so, skip to the next section for information on installing the battery.

The process of opening the phone involves removing its back cover in one of two general ways:

✔ Use your thumbs to slide the back cover up (or down) and lift it off the phone.

✔ Insert a thumbnail into a slot on the phone's top or edge, and pop off the back cover.

In either case, the phone is facing away from you when you pop off the back cover.

After the cover is removed, set it aside. You're now ready to add or remove items from the phone's cramped interior.

- ✔ Don't fret if you hear a clicking or popping sound when you pop off the back cover; this type of noise is expected when you remove a cover that doesn't slide off.

- ✔ Not every Android phone has a removable back cover. If yours doesn't, that's fine, but it also means your phone lacks a removable or replaceable battery.

Installing the battery

The most common thing to install in a new Android phone is the battery. The battery is supplied separately inside the box. Unless the friendly folks at the Phone Store installed the battery for you, it's your job to stick it inside your new phone.

Before installing the battery, ensure that you don't first need to install other items in your phone. For example, on some phones the microSD may be installed internally. The card must be inserted before the battery is installed.

Obey these steps to stick the battery into your phone:

1. **If necessary, remove the battery from its plastic bag.**

2. **Remove the phone's back cover, as discussed in the preceding section.**

3. **Orient the battery.**

The battery goes in only one way, but because of its shape, it can be oriented improperly.

Look for an arrow or for written directions on the battery or inside the phone to find a hint to the proper orientation.

4. **Place the battery in the phone so that the contacts on the battery match the ones on the connector inside the phone.**

Figure 1-1 illustrates an example of inserting the battery into an Android phone.

5. **Insert the battery the rest of the way, as though you're closing the lid on a tiny box.**

When the battery is properly installed, it lies flush with the back of the phone.

Battery

Contacts

Figure 1-1: Sticking the battery in your phone.

After the battery is installed, your next step is to charge it. See the later section "Charge the Battery."

Removing the battery

Removing the phone's battery is uncommon but sometimes necessary. One reason would be to replace the battery with a better model or to access a microSD card or SIM card obscured by the battery inside the phone. Another, albeit sad, reason is that removing the battery is often the only way to regain control over a phone run amok.

To remove the battery, follow these steps:

1. **Remove the phone's back cover and set it aside.**

2. **Locate the "lift here" or "pull" tab on or around the battery.**

3. **Lift the battery out of the phone.**

   Just as you insert the battery, removing the battery works like opening the lid on a tiny box.

Set the battery aside.

If you're replacing the battery, store the original inside a nonmetallic box in a dark, dry location. If you need to dispose of the battery, do so properly; batteries are classified as hazardous waste and should not be placed in the trash.

Installing the SIM card

A *SIM card* identifies your phone on a digital cellular network. Before you can use the phone, the SIM card must be installed.

If the kind people at the Phone Store haven't installed the SIM card, you must do so yourself. Follow these steps:

1. **Remove the SIM card from its container.**

   For a 4G LTE SIM card, pop the card out of the credit-card-size holder.

2. **Insert the SIM card into the SIM card slot.**

   On some phones, the SIM card is inserted internally. In that case, remove the phone's back cover and, if necessary, remove the battery to access the SIM card slot.

   On other phones, the SIM slot is found on the device's outer edge. You must open the tiny SIM slot cover and insert the SIM card into the slot. This procedure may require a special pointy-thing that came with your phone; insert the pointy-thing into the hole by the SIM slot cover to open the cover. Insert the SIM card directly into the slot, or first place the card into a SIM card carrier and then insert it.

   The SIM card is shaped in such a way that it's impossible to insert improperly. If the card doesn't slide into the slot, reorient the card and try again.

3. **If necessary, replace the battery and the phone's back cover.**

   You're done.

The good news is that you seldom, if ever, need to remove or replace a SIM card.

- ✔ Don't lose that SIM-card-cover-opening doohickey, also known as the pointy-thing. Keep it in the phone's box for long-term storage.

- ✔ SIM stands for subscriber identity module. SIM cards are required for GSM cellular networks as well as for 4G LTE networks.

Understanding the microSD card

Many Android phones feature two types of storage: internal and removable. Removable storage comes in the form of a memory card. For Android phones, the microSD form factor is used.

If your phone accepts a microSD card, it may not have come with one. That means you'll have to purchase a microSD card and install it all by yourself.

A microSD card comes in a capacity rated in gigabytes (GB), just like most media storage or memory cards. Common microSD card capacities are 8GB, 16GB, and 32GB. The maximum size allowed in your phone depends on its design; some older phones cannot read higher-capacity microSD cards. When you're in doubt, get the 16GB size.

Installing the microSD card

After obtaining a microSD card for your phone, install it by obeying these directions:

1. **If necessary, remove the phone's back cover.**

   Most newer phones have the microSD card slot on the phone's outside edge. It's covered by a flexible door or hatch. If your phone features such a slot, you do not need to remove the phone's back cover.

2. **Locate the slot into which you stick the microSD card.**

   When the microSD card is installed internally, you may find its slot behind or somehow obscured by the battery.

3. **Insert the microSD card into the slot.**

   The card goes in only one way. If you're fortunate, a little outline of the card illustrates the proper orientation. If you're even more fortunate, your eyes will be good enough to see the tiny outline.

   You may hear a faint clicking sound when the card is fully inserted.

4. **Reinstall the battery (if necessary), and reassemble the phone.**

If the phone is on, you may see a prompt on the touchscreen with information about the card. And, yes, it's okay to insert the microSD card while the phone is on. However, if you need to remove the phone's battery to install the card, well, the phone is going to be off.

Removing the microSD card

To remove the microSD card, follow these steps:

1. **Turn off the phone.**

   Regardless of whether or not the microSD card is installed by removing the phone's back cover, this operation works best when you power off the phone. Specific power-off directions are found in Chapter 2.

2. **Open the little hatch covering the microSD card slot.**

3. **Using your fingernail or a bent paperclip, gently press the microSD card inward a tad.**

   The microSD card is spring-loaded, so pressing it in pops it outward.

4. **Pinch the microSD card between your fingers and remove it completely.**

After you've removed the card, you can replace it or close up the back cover and continue using the phone without a microSD card.

- A microSD card is teensy! If you remove it from your phone, keep it in a safe place where you won't lose it. Never stick the microSD card into your ear.

- You can purchase microSD card adapters to allow the card's data to be read by a computer, by either a standard SD memory slot or the USB port.

- If you're upgrading to a new Android phone, simply remove the microSD card from the old phone and install it in the new one. By doing so, you instantly transfer your pictures, music, and videos.

- Your phone works with or without a microSD card installed.

- Refer to Chapter 20 for more information on storage.

- GB is an abbreviation for gigabyte, which is one billion characters of storage. One gigabyte is enough storage for about an hour of video, or a week's worth of music, or a year's worth of photographs. It's a lot of storage.

- SD stands for *Secure Digital*. It is but one of about a zillion different media card standards.

Closing the phone

When you're done with phone surgery, you need to close up the patient. Specifically, you must reinstall anything you removed — battery, SIM card, microSD card — and reattach the back cover.

The back cover affixes itself to the phone in the reverse manner in which it was removed. Do one of the following:

- Position the cover over any slots or tab holes, and then use your thumbs to slide the back cover up (or down) to secure it on the phone.

- Position the cover directly over the back of the phone, and then press it gently on all sides to seal it shut.

When the back cover is on properly, you should see no gaps or raised edges. If the cover doesn't seem to go on all the way, try again. Never force it!

Charge the Battery

The phone's battery may have enough oomph in it to run the setup-and-configuration process at the Phone Store. If so, count yourself lucky. Otherwise, you need to charge the phone's battery. Don't worry about flying a kite and waiting for a lightning storm. Instead, follow these steps:

1. **If necessary, assemble the charging cord.**

   Connect the charger head (the plug thing) to the USB cable that comes with the phone. They connect in only one way.

2. **Plug the charger head and cable into a wall socket.**

3. **Plug the phone into the USB cable.**

   The charger cord plugs into the micro-USB connector, found at the phone's side or bottom. The connector plugs in only one way.

As the phone charges, a notification light on the phone's front side may glow or you may see a charging battery graphic on the touchscreen. Such activity is normal.

The phone may turn on when you plug it in for a charge. That's okay, but read Chapter 2 to find out what to do the first time the phone turns on. You also may need to contact your cellular provider for additional setup instructions the first time you turn on the phone.

- I recommend fully charging the phone before you use it.

- You can use the phone while it's charging, although the phone won't turn on if the battery is too low.

- You can charge the phone in your car, using what was once called a cigarette lighter. Simply ensure that your car-phone-charger device features the proper connector for your phone or is designed for use with your cell phone brand.

✔ The phone also charges itself whenever it's plugged into a computer by way of a USB cable. The computer must be on for charging to work.

✔ Cell phones charge more quickly when plugged into the wall than into a computer's USB port or a car adapter.

✔ Unlike the old NiCad batteries, you don't need to worry about fully discharging your phone before recharging it. If the phone needs a charge, even when the battery is just a little low, feel free to do so.

✔ Many Android phones use the micro-USB connector. This connector has a flat trapezoid shape, which makes it different from the mini-USB connector, which is squat and slightly larger and used primarily on evil cell phones.

Android Phone Orientation

First impressions are everlasting. Your Android phone is, no doubt, a new thing. It's also something that will grow to become an important part of your life. Now is not the time to botch your introduction!

Finding things on your phone

I think it's cute when people refer to things that they can't name as a *doodad* or *thingamabob*. Cute, but inaccurate. Take a gander at Figure 1-2, which illustrates common things found on the front and back of a typical Android phone.

Not every item shown in the figure may be in the exact same spot on your phone. For example, the Power/Lock key might be found on the top of the phone, not the side.

The terms referenced in Figure 1-2 are the same as the terms used elsewhere in this book and in whatever scant Android phone documentation exists. Here are the highlights:

Power/Lock key: The Power/Lock key could be called the phone's on/off button, but it's not. That's because the key does more than just turn on or off the phone. Chapter 2 covers the details.

Volume key: The phone's volume control is two buttons in one. Press one end of the key to set the volume higher; the other end sets the volume lower. This key might also be used to control the zoom function when using the phone as a camera.

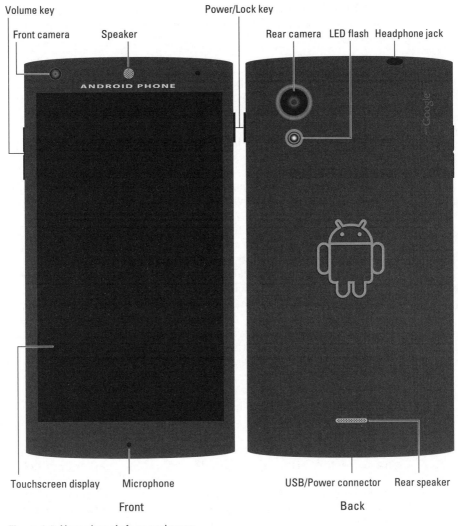

Figure 1-2: Your phone's face and rump.

Touchscreen display: The main part of the phone is its *touchscreen* display. It's a see-touch thing: You look at the display and also touch it with your fingers to control the phone. That's where it gets the name *touch*screen.

Front camera: The phone's front-facing camera is typically found above the touchscreen. It's used for taking self-portraits as well as for video chat. Not every Android phone features a front-facing camera.

Speaker(s): The primary phone speaker is located top center on the phone. One or more additional speakers might also be found on the phone's backside.

Microphone: Somewhere on the bottom of the phone, you'll find the microphone. It's usually tiny, about the diameter of a pin. Don't stick anything into the hole! A second, noise-cancelling microphone might also be found on the back of the phone.

Headphone jack: On the top of the phone, or high up on one of the sides, you find a hole where you can connect standard headphones.

Rear camera: The rear camera is found on the phone's back. It may be accompanied by one or two LED flash gizmos.

USB/Power connector: This important jack is usually located on the phone's bottom edge, right in the center, although some phones may place the connector on the side. Whatever the location, use the USB/Power connector to attach the phone's USB cable. That cable is used both to charge the phone as well as to communicate with a computer. Charging the phone is covered in this chapter; see Chapter 20 for information on sharing files with a computer.

Beyond the features shown in Figure 1-1, you'll find a variety of buttons, holes, connectors, and other important doodads on your phone. The location of these items varies. They include:

SIM card cover: This spot is where the phone's SIM card is inserted, although some phones may use an internal SIM card, as described in the earlier section "Installing the SIM card."

Media card slot: Lift the cover on this slot to add or remove a microSD memory card. See the "Installing a microSD card" section, earlier in this chapter.

HDMI connector: This connector allows the phone to use an external HDMI monitor or TV set to show movies, watch slide shows, or do other interesting things. Not every Android phone has an HDMI connector.

Home key: Some phones, such as those in the Samsung Galaxy line, feature a physical button called the Home key. This key is found below the touchscreen.

Not shown in Figure 1-2 is a physical keyboard, found on a few Android phone models. The keyboard might be below the touchscreen, or it might slide out or flip up. See Chapter 4 for additional information on the keyboard.

Take a moment to locate all the items mentioned in this section, as well as shown in Figure 1-2, on your own phone. It's important that you know where they are.

- ✔ Some Android phones may also show navigation icons or keys just below the touchscreen. See Chapter 3 for more information.
- ✔ A few Android phones feature a pointing device, such as a trackball or a teensy joystick. This device can be used for editing text, navigating links on a web page, or choosing items on the screen.
- ✔ The Galaxy Note line of phones feature a pointing device in the form of a digital stylus called an S Pen.
- ✔ The main microphone is found on the bottom of the phone. Even so, it picks up your voice loud and clear. You don't need to hold the phone at an angle for the microphone to work.

Using earphones

You don't need to use earphones to get the most from your Android phone, but it helps! If the nice folks who sold you the phone tossed in a pair earphones, that's wonderful! If they didn't, well then, they weren't so nice, were they?

The most common type of cell phone earphones are the *earbud* style: You set the buds into your ears. The sharp, pointy end of the earphones, which you don't want to stick into your ear, plugs into the phone.

Between the earbuds and the sharp, pointy thing, you might find a doodle on which a button sits. The button can be used to mute the phone or to start or stop the playback of music when the phone is in its music-playing mode.

You can also use the doodle button to answer the phone when it rings.

A teensy hole that's usually on the back side of the doodle serves as a microphone. The mic allows you to wear the earphones and talk on the phone while keeping your hands free. If you gesture while you speak, you'll find this feature invaluable.

- ✔ You can purchase any standard cell phone headset for use with your phone. Ensure that the headset features a microphone; you need to both listen and talk on a phone.
- ✔ Some headsets feature extra doodle buttons. These headsets work fine with your phone, though the extra buttons may not do anything specific.
- ✔ The earbuds are labeled R for right and L for left.

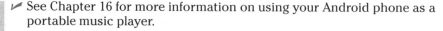

✔ See Chapter 16 for more information on using your Android phone as a portable music player.

✔ Be sure to fully insert the earphone connector into the phone. The person you're talking with can't hear you well when the earphones are plugged in only part of the way.

✔ You can also use a Bluetooth headset with your phone, to listen to a call or some music. See Chapter 19 for more information on Bluetooth.

✔ Fold the earphones when you put them away, as opposed to wrapping them in a loop. Put the earbuds and connector in one hand, and then pull the wire straight out with the other hand. Fold the wire in half and then in half again. You can then put the earphones in your pocket or on a tabletop. By folding the wires, you avoid creating something that looks like a wire ball of Christmas tree lights.

Adding accessories

Beyond earphones, you can find an entire Phone Store full of accessories and baubles that you can obtain for your Android phone. The variety is seemingly endless, and the prices, well, they ain't cheap.

Docking station

A *docking station* is a heavy base into which you can set your phone. The most basic model simply props up the phone so that you can easily see it. I use the basic docking station on my nightstand, where my Android phone serves as my alarm clock. (See Chapter 17.)

More advanced docking stations offer HDMI output, USB connections, and perhaps even a laptop-size screen and keyboard.

Car mount

If you plan to use the phone while driving, a car mount is a must-have item. It provides a cradle into which you set your Android phone. It may also have a cable you can use to charge the phone while you drive. That way, the phone is handy and visible for making calls, listening to music, finding navigation instructions, or undertaking other interesting activities while you perilously navigate the roads.

Inductive charging coil

Though it sounds like a bogus technical term from the old *Star Trek* TV show, an inductive charging coil is a new technology you can really use. Basically, the coil replaces the battery and back cover so that you can wirelessly charge your phone. Not every Android phone manufacturer provides the inductive charging coil as an option.

HDMI cable

If your Android phone features an HDMI connector, you can obtain an HDMI cable. Using the cable, your phone can throw its sound and image onto a computer monitor or TV screen. It may sound like a silly thing at first, but I've used the HDMI cable on my Android phones so that the whole family can sit around our large-screen TV and enjoy rented movies. See Chapter 17 for more information about renting movies on your phone.

A Home for Your Phone

I've been in more than one older home that features a special vault in the wall, into which the phone was set. Later on, phones just sat on tables or were affixed directly to the wall. Then came the cordless era, when phones were stored in couch cushions. Today's cell phones? They end up everywhere! They do, that is, unless you read my handy advice on where to store the phone, as described in this section.

Toting your Android phone

The compactness of the modern cell phone makes it perfect for a pocket or even the teensiest of party purses. And its well-thought-out design means you can carry your phone in your pocket or handbag without fearing that something will accidentally turn it on, dial Mongolia, and run up a heck of a cell phone bill.

Your Android phone most likely features a proximity sensor, so you can even keep the phone in your pocket while you're on a call. The proximity sensor disables the touchscreen, which ensures that nothing accidentally gets touched when you don't want it to be touched.

- Though it's okay to place the phone somewhere when you're making a call, be careful not to touch the phone's Power/Lock key (refer to Figure 1-2). Doing so may temporarily enable the touchscreen, which can hang up a call, mute the phone, or do any of a number of undesirable things.

- You can always store your phone in one of a variety of handsome carrying case accessories, some of which come in fine Naugahyde or leatherette.

- Don't forget when the phone is in your pocket, especially in your coat or jacket. You might accidentally sit on the phone, or it can fly out when you take off your coat. The worst fate for any cell phone is to take a trip through the wash. I'm sure your phone has nightmares about it.

Storing the phone

I recommend that you find a single place for your phone when you're not taking it with you: on top of your desk or workstation, in the kitchen, on the nightstand — you get the idea. Phones are as prone to being misplaced as are your car keys and glasses. Consistency is the key to finding your phone.

Then again, your phone rings, so you can always have someone else call your cell phone to help you locate it.

- ✔ Any of the various docking stations makes a handsome, permanent location for your Android phone.

- ✔ I store my phone on my desk, next to my computer. Conveniently, I have the charger plugged into the computer so that the phone remains plugged in, connected, and charging when I'm not using it.

- ✔ Phones on coffee tables get buried under magazines and are often squished when rude people put their feet on the furniture.

- ✔ Avoid putting your phone in direct sunlight; heat is bad news for any electronic gizmo.

- ✔ Do not put your phone in the laundry (see the preceding section). See Chapter 23 for information on properly cleaning the phone.

2

Initial Android Duties

I t would be delightful if your Android phone were smart enough to pop out of the box, say "Hello," and immediately know everything about you. It doesn't, of course. That introduction is still necessary and it requires some careful attention. It's all part of the initial setup and configuration process that happens when you first turn on the phone. And if you haven't yet turned on your phone, this chapter helps with that ordeal as well as the turning off and phone-locking procedures.

Verizon Wireless
Charging (86%)

Hello, Phone

Modern, technical gizmos lack an on–off switch. Instead, they feature a power button. In the case of your Android phone, the button is called the *Power/ Lock* key. This key is used in several ways, some of which may not be obvious or apparent. That's why I wrote this section.

Turning on your phone for the first time

The very first time you turn on your phone is a special occasion. It's when setup and configuration happens, a necessary process for a device as advanced as an Android phone. The good news is that you need to endure this ordeal only once. In fact, if the phone has already been set up and configured, skip to the next section, "Turning on the phone."

The specifics for the setup and configuration differ depending on the phone's manufacturer as well as the cellular provider. Odds are pretty good that the people at the Phone Store helped you through the initial setup process. If not, read the generic Android phone setup process outlined in this section, and see the notes at the end of the section for details that may apply to your specific phone.

1. Turn on the phone by pressing the Power/Lock key.

You may have to press it longer than you think. When you see the phone's logo on the screen, you can release the key.

It's okay to turn on the phone while it's plugged in and charging.

2. Answer the questions presented.

You'll be asked to select options for some if not all of the following items:

- Select your language
- Activate the phone on the cellular network
- Choose a Wi-Fi network (can be done later)
- Set the time zone
- Sign into your Google account
- Add other online accounts
- Set location information

When in doubt, just accept the standard options as presented to you during the setup process.

To fill in text fields, use the onscreen keyboard. Or use the physical keyboard, if your phone has one. See Chapter 4 for keyboard information.

Other sections in this chapter, as well as throughout this book, offer information and advice on these settings. You can't screw up anything at this point; any selection you make can be changed later.

Having a Google account is important to the setup process. See the later section, "Account Setup."

3. After each choice, touch the Next button or icon.

The Next icon may resemble a large right-pointing triangle, as shown in the margin.

4. Touch the Finish button.

The Finish button appears on the last screen of the setup procedure.

The good news is that you're done. The better news is that you need to complete this setup only once on your Android phone. From this point on, starting the phone works as described in the next few sections.

After the initial setup, you're taken to the Home screen. Chapter 3 offers more Home screen information, which you should probably read right away, before the temptation to play with your new phone becomes unbearable.

- ✔ Some AT&T phones require you to use the AT&T Read2Go app to complete your phone's setup process. You'll need to use a computer at the same time you use your phone to complete the process. If you have any concerns, please visit the AT&T wireless store for assistance.

- ✔ Additional information on connecting your phone to a Wi-Fi network is found in Chapter 19.

- ✔ Location items relate to how the phone knows its position on planet Earth. I recommend activating all these items to get the most from your Android phone.

- ✔ It's not necessary to use any specific software provided by the phone's manufacturer or your cellular provider. For example, if you don't want a Samsung account, you don't need to sign up for one; skip that step.

- ✔ By setting up your Google account, you coordinate whatever information you have on the Internet with your new Android phone. This information includes your e-mail messages and contacts on Gmail, appointments on Google Calendar, and information and data from other Google Internet applications.

- ✔ See the later sidebar "Who is this Android person?" for more information about the Android operating system.

Turning on the phone

To turn on your Android phone, press and hold the Power/Lock key. After a few seconds, you'll feel the phone vibrate slightly and then see the phone's startup animation, logo, or hypnotic brainwashing image. Release the Power/Lock key; the phone is starting.

Eventually, you'll see the phone's unlock screen. The standard *slide* lock is illustrated in Figure 2-1, along with other variations for unlocking an Android phone.

To unlock the phone, swipe the touchscreen as illustrated in Figure 2-1. In most cases, the phone is unlocked by touching a padlock icon. While keeping your finger down, slide your finger across the phone's touchscreen. Other phones use similar techniques, as illustrated in the figure.

Once the phone unlocks, you can begin using it.

- ✔ The phone may provide animation during the unlocking process to assist you. Pay attention to it if you find yourself confused.

- ✔ You probably won't be turning on your phone much in the future. Instead, you'll simply be unlocking it. See the next section.

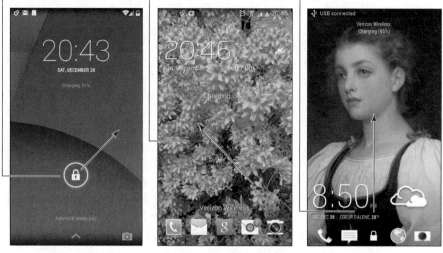

Slide the lock icon outward   Swipe a line anywhere across   Slide upward from the bottom
    the touchscreen   of the screen

Generic Android   Samsung   HTC One

Figure 2-1: Unlocking an Android phone.

Unlocking the phone

Most of the time, you don't turn your phone on and off. Instead, you lock and unlock it. To unlock and use the phone, press the Power/Lock key. A quick press is all that's needed. The phone's touchscreen comes to life, and you see the unlocking screen.

The standard slide lock is shown in Figure 2-1. For more security, you may have to work one of several different unlocking screens, three of which are illustrated in Figure 2-2.

The pattern lock is perhaps the most popular, although not the most secure, screen lock. To unlock the phone, trace your finger over the dots along a preset pattern, as illustrated in Figure 2-2.

The PIN lock requires that you type a secret number to unlock the phone. Touch the Return icon, shown in the margin, to accept the PIN.

The password lock is the most secure. It requires that you type a multicharacter password to unlock the phone. Touch the onscreen keyboard's Done button to accept the password.

Whether or not you see one of these lock screens depends on how the phone's security has been configured. Specific directions for setting and removing screen locks are found in Chapter 22.

| Pattern | PIN | Password |

Figure 2-2: Common Android unlocking screens.

- It isn't necessary to unlock the phone for an incoming call. For information on receiving phone calls, see Chapter 5.

- For additional information on working with the onscreen keyboard, see Chapter 4.

- Other types of screen locks are available beyond those shown in Figure 2-2. For example, the face unlock screen works when you hold up the phone and gaze onto the touchscreen. If the phone recognizes you, it unlocks. The availability of this lock screen, as well as others, depends on your phone's manufacturer as well as cellular provider.

- See the later section "Locking the phone" for information on manually locking the phone.

- When your phone is playing music, which it can do while it's locked, information about the song may appear on the lock screen (not shown in Figure 2-2). Touch the information to see controls to play and pause or to skip to the next or previous song. See Chapter 16 for more information on using an Android phone as a portable music player.

Unlocking and running an app

Some phones may allow for startup apps to adorn the lock screen, such as the icons shown in the center and right examples in Figure 2-1. When the Slide screen lock is set, you can unlock the phone and immediately start one of those apps. To do so, touch an app icon and swipe the screen. The phone unlocks and the chosen app starts automatically.

Who is this Android person?

Just like a computer, your phone has an operating system. It's the main program in charge of all the software, or apps, inside the phone. Unlike on a computer, however, Android is a mobile device operating system, designed primarily for use in cell phones and tablets.

Android is based on the Linux operating system, which is also a computer operating system, though it's much more stable and bug-free than Windows, so it's not as popular. Google owns, maintains, and develops Android, which is why your online Google information is synced with the phone.

The Android mascot, shown here, often appears on Android apps or hardware. He has no official name, though most folks call him Andy.

Account Setup

Your Android phone can be home to your various online incarnations. That includes your e-mail accounts, online services, social networking, subscriptions, plus other digital personas. I recommended adding those accounts to your phone as you continue the setup and configuration process.

Obtaining a Google account

It's possible to use your Android phone without a Google account, but you'd be missing out on a buncha features. So if you don't already have a Google account, drop everything (but not this book) and follow these steps to obtain one:

1. **Open the computer's web browser program.**

2. **Visit the main Google page at** www.google.com.

   Type **www.google.com** into the web browser's address box.

3. **Click the Sign In link or button.**

   Another page opens, where you can log in to your Google account, but you don't have a Google account, so:

4. **Click the link to create a new account.**

   The link is typically found below the text boxes where you would log in to your Google account. As I write this chapter, the link is titled Create an Account.

5. **Continue heeding the onscreen directions until you've created your own Google account.**

Eventually, your account is set up and configured. I recommend that you log off and then log on to Google, just to ensure that you did everything properly. Also consider creating a bookmark for your account's Google page: Pressing Ctrl+D or Command+D does the job in just about any web browser.

Continue reading in the next section for information on synchronizing your new Google account with your Android phone.

✔ A Google account is free. Google makes zillions of dollars by selling Internet advertising, so it doesn't charge you for your Google account or any of the other fine services it offers.

✔ The Google account gives you access to a wide array of free services and online programs. They include Gmail for electronic messaging, Calendar for scheduling and appointments, and an account on YouTube, along with Google Finance, blogs, Google+, Hangouts, and other features that are also instantly shared with your phone.

Adding accounts to your phone

You don't have to add all your online accounts during the phone's initial setup and configuration process. If you skipped those steps, or when you have more accounts to add, you can easily do so. With your phone turned on and unlocked, follow these steps:

1. Go to the Home screen.

The Home screen is the main screen on your phone. You can always get there by touching the Home icon, found at the bottom of the touchscreen.

2. Touch the Apps icon.

The Apps icon is found at the bottom of the Home screen. It looks similar to the icon shown in the margin, although it has many variations. See Chapter 3 for the variety.

After touching the Apps icon you see the apps drawer, which contains all the apps (also called applications or programs) installed on your Android phone.

3. Choose the Settings icon to start the Settings app.

You may have to swipe the apps drawer screen a few times, paging through the various apps, to find the Settings icon. If you're having trouble, see Chapter 3 for specifics on how you swipe the screen.

The Settings app allows you to access internal options, controls, and settings for configuring your Android phone. The Accounts heading in the Settings app lists all accounts currently associated with your phone. You should see your Google account plus other accounts listed. The last item in the list is a command, Add Account.

4. Choose the Add Account item.

If you don't see an Add Account item on the main Settings app screen, look for an item titled Accounts & Sync. Choose that item to view the accounts associated with your phone, and then touch the Add icon, shown in the margin, to add a new account.

5. Choose an account to add from the list that appears.

Don't worry if you don't see the exact type of account you want to add. You may have to install a specific app before an account appears. Chapter 18 covers installing new apps on your phone.

6. Follow the directions on the screen to sign into your account.

The steps that follow depend on the account. Generally speaking, you sign in using an existing username and password.

You can continue adding accounts by repeating these steps. When you're done, touch the Home icon to return to the Home screen.

- ✔ See Chapter 10 for details on adding e-mail accounts to your Android phone.

- ✔ Chapter 12 covers social networking on your phone. Refer there for specific information on adding Facebook, Twitter, and other accounts.

Goodbye, Phone

You can dismiss your Android phone in several ways, only one of which involves an unblemished goat and a full moon. Fortunately, that's the least popular method. The other two are covered in this section.

Locking the phone

To lock your Android phone, press and release the Power/Lock key. The touchscreen display turns off and the phone is locked.

- ✔ You can lock the phone while you're making a call. Simply press and release the Power/Lock key. The call stays connected, but the display is disabled.

- ✔ You can continue talking on the phone while it's locked; press it against your cheek or (if you have headphones) put it in your pocket. When the phone is locked, your face and pocket are in no danger of accidentally hanging up the call or muting it.

- ✔ Your Android phone will probably spend most of its time locked.

- ✔ Locking does not turn off the phone; you can still receive calls while the phone is somnolent. The phone continues to play music while it's locked, and any set timers or alarms will sound. See Chapter 17 for information on setting timers and alarms; Chapter 16 covers playing music.

Controlling the lock timeout

Your Android phone automatically locks itself after a given period of inactivity. Typically, after 1 minute of not touching the phone, the screen dims and then the phone locks. You can control that duration by following these steps:

1. **At the Home screen, touch the Apps icon.**

2. **Open the Settings app.**

3. **Choose Display.**

   This item might instead be titled Display, Gestures & Buttons.

4. **Choose the Sleep or Screen Timeout item.**

5. **Choose a timeout value from the list that's provided.**

   The standard value is 1 minute.

6. **Touch the Home icon to return to the Home screen.**

The lock timer measures inactivity. When you don't touch the screen or press a key, the timer starts ticking. A few seconds before the time-out value you set (refer to Step 5), the touchscreen dims. Then it turns off. The phone is locked. If you touch the screen before then, the sleep timer is reset.

Turning off the phone

To turn off your phone, obey these steps:

1. **Press and hold down the Power/Lock key.**

   When you see the Phone Options menu, shown in Figure 2-3, you can release the key.

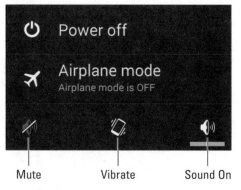

Figure 2-3: The Phone Options menu.

2. Choose the Power Off item.

A confirmation message appears, although some phones may instantly turn themselves off.

3. Touch the OK button.

The phone turns itself off.

The phone doesn't receive calls when it's turned off. Likewise, any alarms or reminders you've set won't sound when the phone is off.

✔ Calls received while the phone is off are routed instead to voicemail. See Chapter 7 for more information on voicemail.

✔ The phone can be charged while it's off.

✔ The Phone Options menu may show additional commands, such as Restart, Sleep, or Kid Mode. The volume control commands, shown at the bottom of the menu in Figure 2-3, might not be available on all phones.

The Android Tour

Decades ago, the more powerful the computer, the more buttons, knobs, and dials it had. Those room-sized computers that ran the 1960 census were powerful. They had hundreds of switches and controls. Back then it would have been easy to assume that a powerful computer of the future would have thousands of switches and controls. The reality is far different.

Today, smart devices like your Android phone are basically bereft of buttons. Despite its seemingly endless capabilities, your phone is a simple device. The touchscreen is the main control. That's probably not what folks expected back in the 1960s, and it's probably not what you expect today. Therefore, I present this chapter to help you get up to speed on how to operate that advanced gizmo, the Android cell phone.

Basic Operations

Your Android phone's capability to frustrate you is only as powerful as your fear of the touchscreen and how it works. After you clear that hurdle, understanding how your phone works becomes easier.

Manipulating the touchscreen

The touchscreen works in combination with one or two of your fingers. You can choose which fingers to use, or whether to be adventurous and try using the tip of your nose, but touch the touchscreen you must. Here are some of the many ways you manipulate your phone's touchscreen:

Touch: In this simple operation, you touch the screen. Generally, you're touching an object such as an icon or a control. You might also see the term *press* or *tap*.

Long-press: Touch and hold down on part of the screen. Some operations, such as moving an icon on the Home screen, begin with the long-press. In fact, that icon-moving operation is called a *long-press drag*.

Swipe: When you swipe, you start with your finger in one spot and then drag it to another spot. Usually, a swipe is up, down, left, or right, which moves something in the direction you swipe your finger. A swipe can be fast or slow. It's also called a *flick* or a *slide*.

Double-touch: Touch the screen in the same location twice. A double-touch can be used to zoom in on an image or a map, but it can also zoom out. Because of the double-tap's dual nature, I recommend using the pinch and spread operations instead.

Pinch: A pinch involves two fingers, which start out separated and then are brought together. The pinch is used to zoom out on an image or a map. This move may also be called a *pinch close*.

Spread: In the opposite of a pinch, you start with your fingers together and then spread them. The spread is used to zoom in. It's also known as a *pinch open*.

Rotate: Use two fingers to twist around a central point on the touchscreen, which has the effect of rotating an object on the screen. If you have trouble with this operation, pretend that you're turning the dial on a safe.

You can't manipulate the touchscreen while wearing gloves, unless they're gloves specially designed for use with electronic touchscreens, such as the gloves that Batman wears.

Exploring the navigation icons

Below the touchscreen on your Android phone dwell a series of icons. They can appear as part of the touchscreen itself, or on some phones they may be part of the bezel or even physical buttons. These are the navigation icons and they serve specific functions.

Traditionally you'll find three navigation icons:

Back: The Back icon serves several purposes, all of which fit neatly under the concept of "back." Touch the icon once to return to a previous page, dismiss an onscreen menu, close a window, hide the onscreen keyboard, and so on.

Home: No matter what you're doing on the phone, touching this icon displays the Home screen.

Recent: Touching the Recent icon displays a list of recently opened or currently running apps. The list scrolls up and down, so when it's too tall for the screen, just swipe it with your finger to view all the apps. Choose an app from the list to switch to that app. To dismiss the list of recently used apps, touch the Back icon. See the later section "Switching apps" for more info.

Your phone may not use the same icons for Back, Home, and Recent as shown in the margin. Some phones offer subtle variations. You may even find additional icons below the touchscreen, but the three traditional Android navigation icons are Back, Home, and Recent.

- On Android phones without a Recent icon, press and hold the Home icon to see the recent apps list.

- Some Android phones may feature an Answer icon below the touchscreen. Touch that icon to answer an incoming call.

- Beyond Back, Home, and Recent, perhaps the most common icon found below the touchscreen is Menu. Touch this icon or press the Menu button to display a pop-up menu from which you can choose commands. If nothing happens when you touch the Menu icon, no pop-up menu is available.

- The Menu icon is essentially the same thing as the Action Overflow icon. See the section "Using common icons" elsewhere in this chapter.

- A Search icon might be found below the touchscreen. Touch this icon to start a phone or web search.

- The three navigation icons may hide themselves when some apps run. In most cases, the icons are still there but are invisible.

- The Back icon may change its appearance to the down caret, shown in the margin. Touch this icon to hide the onscreen keyboard, dismiss the recent app list, or other actions similar to those of the Back navigation icon.

Setting the volume

The Volume key is found on the side of the phone. Press the top part of the key to raise the volume. Press the bottom part to lower the volume.

As you press the Volume key, a graphic appears on the touchscreen to illustrate the relative volume level, as shown in Figure 3-1. You can also use the graphic to set the volume, as shown in the figure.

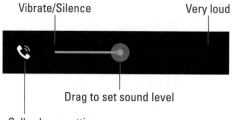

Vibrate/Silence   Very loud

Drag to set sound level

Call volume setting

Figure 3-1: The volume controls graphic.

The Volume key controls whatever noise the phone is making when you use it: When you're on a call, the volume controls set the level of the call. When you're listening to music or watching a video, the volume controls set the media volume.

✔ When the volume is set all the way down, the phone is silenced. Click the Volume key down one more notch to place the phone into vibration mode.

✔ The Volume key works even when the phone is locked. That means you don't need to unlock the phone to adjust the volume when you're listening to music.

✔ The volume can be preset for the phone or its media, alarms, and notifications. See Chapter 22 for more information.

"Silence your phone!"

You cannot be a citizen of the twenty-first century and not have heard the admonition "Please silence your cell phones." The quick way to obey this command with your Android phone is to keep pressing the bottom part of the Volume key until the phone vibrates. You're good to go.

You can also silence the phone by pressing and holding the Power/Lock key. From the Phone Options menu, choose the Mute or Vibrate option. (Refer to Figure 2-3 in Chapter 2 to see the Phone Options menu.) Note every phone features a Mute option on its Phone Options menu.

Some phones may feature a Sound quick action. Touch that icon to mute or vibrate the phone. See the later section "Accessing quick actions" for details.

- When the phone is silenced, a Silenced icon appears on the status bar.

- When the phone is in vibration mode, a Vibration icon appears on the status bar.

- The sample icons shown in the margin are only examples of how the Silenced and Vibration icons might look.

- You make the phone noisy again by reversing the directions in this section. Most commonly, touching the "louder" side of the Volume key restores the phone's sound.

- The phone doesn't vibrate if you've turned off that option. See Chapter 22.

Changing the orientation

Android phones feature an *accelerometer* gizmo. It's used by various apps to determine in which direction the phone is pointed or whether you've reoriented the phone from an upright to a horizontal position.

The easiest way to see how the vertical-horizontal orientation feature works is to view a web page on your phone. Obey these steps:

1. **Start your phone's web browser app.**

   The browser's app icon can be found on the Home screen or, if not there, in the apps drawer. The icon may be named Internet, Browser, or Web. The Chrome app is also a web browser.

   After the web browser app starts, it displays a web page. If not, browse to a web page so that you have something visual on the screen.

2. **Tilt the phone to the left.**

   As shown in Figure 3-2, the web page switches itself to the horizontal or landscape orientation. For some applications, it's truly the best way to see things.

3. **Tilt the phone upright again.**

   The web page redisplays itself in its original, upright mode.

The rotation feature may not work for all apps, especially games that present themselves in one orientation only.

- See Chapter 11 for more information on using your phone to browse the web.

- The Home screen may or may not switch between portrait and landscape orientations.

✔ Some phones feature a quick action setting that locks the orientation. See the later section, "Accessing quick actions."

✔ A useful application for demonstrating the phone's accelerometer is the game *Labyrinth.* You can purchase it at the Google Play Store download a free version, *Labyrinth Lite.* See Chapter 18 for more information on the Google Play Store.

Portrait   Landscape

Figure 3-2: Vertical and horizontal orientations.

Home Screen Chores

The Home screen is where you start your Android day. It's the location from which you begin common phone duties, including starting apps. Knowing about the Home screen is an important part of understanding your Android phone.

 To view the Home screen at any time, touch the Home icon found at the bottom of the touchscreen. Some phones feature a physical Home button or key, which performs the same duties as the Home icon.

Exploring the Home screen

The generic Android Home screen is shown in Figure 3-3. The image shown in the figure is doubtless a lot more boring than your phone's Home screen. But the generic Home screen helps you identify some basic points of interest.

Wallpaper

Status bar

Notifications

Phone status

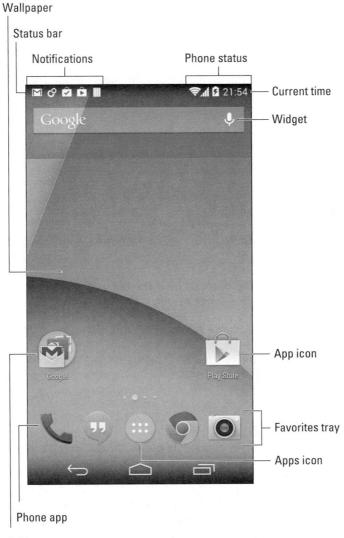

Current time

Widget

App icon

Favorites tray

Apps icon

Phone app

Folder

Figure 3-3: The Home screen.

Status bar: The top of the Home screen is a thin, informative strip that I call the *status bar*. It contains notification icons and status icons plus the current time.

Notifications: The notification icons come and go, depending on what happens in your digital life. For example, a new notification icon appears when you receive a new e-mail message or have a pending appointment. The "Reviewing notifications" section, later in this chapter, describes how to deal with notifications.

Phone status: Icons on the right end of the status bar represent the phone's current condition, such as the type of network it's connected to, its signal strength and battery status, as well as whether the speaker is muted or the phone is connected to a Wi-Fi network, for example.

App icons: The meat of the meal on the Home screen plate are the app icons. Touching an app icon runs a program, or *app.* These icons may be referred to as *launcher icons* in some Android documentation.

Widgets: These teensy programs can display information as well as let you control the phone, manipulate a feature, access an app, or do something purely amusing.

Folders: Multiple apps can be stored in a folder. Touch the folder to see a pop-up window listing all the apps.

Wallpaper: The background image you see on the Home screen is the wallpaper.

Favorites tray: The lineup of icons near the bottom of the screen contains slots for popular apps. Not every phone features a favorites tray.

Phone app: You use the Phone app to make calls. It's kind of a big deal.

Apps icon: At the bottom of the Home screen is the Apps icon. Touching this icon displays the apps drawer, which lists all apps installed on your phone. See the later section "Finding an app in the apps drawer" for details. This icon might also be referred to as the *launcher.*

Ensure that you recognize the names of the various parts of the Home screen. These terms are used throughout this book and in whatever other scant Android phone documentation exists. Directions for using the Home screen gizmos are found throughout this chapter.

- ✔ The Home screen is entirely customizable. You can add and remove icons, add widgets and shortcuts, and even change wallpaper images. See Chapter 22 for more information.

- ✔ Touching part of the Home screen that doesn't feature an icon or a control does nothing — unless you're using the *live wallpaper* feature. In that case, touching the screen changes the wallpaper in some way, depending on the wallpaper that's selected. You can read more about live wallpaper in Chapter 22.

Accessing multiple Home screens

The Home screen is more than what you see. It's actually an entire street of Home screens, with only one Home screen *panel* displayed at a time.

To switch from one panel to another, swipe the Home screen left or right. The currently displayed Home screen can be determined by looking at the Home screen index, shown in Figure 3-4.

Swipe Home screen panels left and right

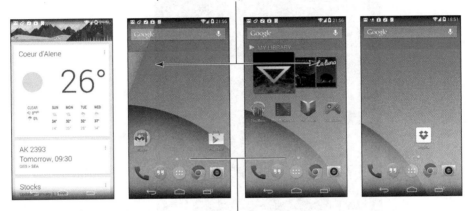

Google Now   Home screen index

Figure 3-4: The Home screen index.

When you touch the Home icon, you're returned to the last Home screen panel you viewed. To return to the main Home screen panel, touch the Home icon a second time.

- ✔ You might be able to see an overview of all Home screen panels by double-touching the Home icon.
- ✔ The number of Home screen panels left and right varies, depending on the phone. I've seen Android phones with as few as three panels and some with up to seven.
- ✔ The Home screen panel on the far left might be the Google Now app on some phones, such as the one shown in Figure 3-4.
- ✔ Adding, removing, and managing Home screen panels are tasks covered in Chapter 22.

Reviewing notifications

Notifications appear as icons at the top left of the Home screen, as illustrated earlier, in Figure 3-3. To review them, you pull down the notifications drawer by dragging your finger from the top of the screen downward. The notifications drawer is illustrated in Figure 3-5.

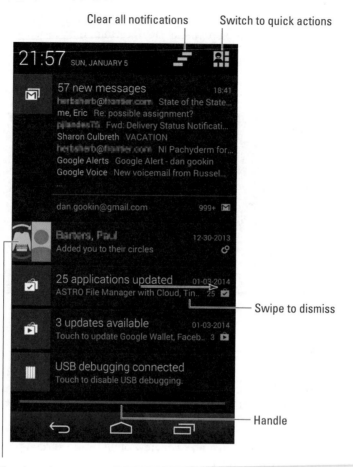

Clear all notifications   Switch to quick actions

Swipe to dismiss

Handle

Touch to view

Figure 3-5: Reviewing notifications.

Touch a notification to deal with it. What happens next depends on the notification, but most often the app that generated the notification appears, such as Gmail when you touch a new message notification. You might also be given the opportunity to deal with whatever caused the notification, such as a calendar appointment.

Dismiss an individual notification by sliding it to the right or left. To dismiss all notifications, touch the Clear icon, illustrated in Figure 3-5 and shown in the margin. On some phones, the Clear icon may be labeled with the word *Clear*.

When you're done looking, you can slide the notifications drawer up again: Touch the notifications drawer handle and drag your finger up the screen. Or, if you find this process frustrating (and it can be), touch the Back icon.

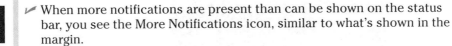

- If you don't deal with notifications, they can stack up!

- When more notifications are present than can be shown on the status bar, you see the More Notifications icon, similar to what's shown in the margin.

- Notification icons disappear after you choose or dismiss their notifications.

- Some ongoing notifications cannot be dismissed. For example, a USB connection notification stays active until the USB cable is disconnected.

- Dismissing some notifications doesn't prevent them from appearing again in the future. For example, notifications to update your programs continue to appear, as do calendar reminders.

- Some apps, such as Facebook and Twitter, don't display notifications unless you're logged in. See Chapter 12.

- The phone plays a sound, or *ringtone,* when a new notification floats in. You can choose which sound plays; see Chapter 22 for more information.

- Notification icons appear on the screen when the phone is locked. You must unlock the phone before you can drag down the status bar to display notifications.

Accessing quick actions

The flip side of the notifications drawer is the quick actions drawer, shown in Figure 3-6. This drawer lists icons that provide access or shortcuts to common phone features. You can review the icons to check the phone's status, or touch an icon to get more information or change a setting.

To view the quick actions drawer, touch the Quick Actions icon when viewing the notifications drawer (refer to Figure 3-5). Likewise, you can switch back to the notifications drawer by touching the Notifications icon, shown in Figure 3-6.

Dismiss the quick actions drawer by touching the Back or Home icon.

- The Settings icon in the quick actions drawer provides instant access to the Settings app, a popular place to visit as you learn about your Android phone.

- Some phones may refer to quick actions as *quick settings.*

- On some Android phones, quick actions may appear as a row of icons along the top of the notifications drawer.

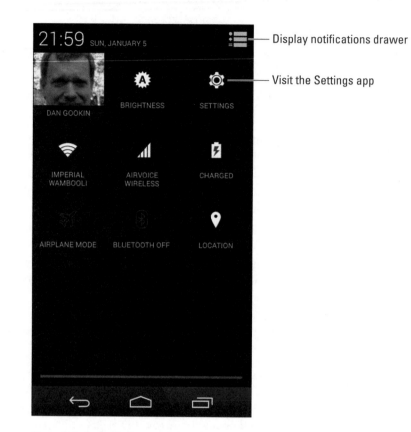

Figure 3-6: Android phone quick actions.

Using the Car Home screen

Your Android phone may also feature an alternative Home screen, provided for the scary proposition of using the phone while driving an automobile. The Car Home screen, designed to be easy to see at a glance, offers you access to the phone's more popular features without distracting you too much from the priority of piloting your car.

✏ The Car Home screen appears automatically when your Android phone is nestled into a car mount phone holder accessory, discussed in Chapter 1.

✏ Car Home may also appear as an app in the apps drawer.

✏ See Chapter 14 for information on using your Android phone for navigation, a handy feature available directly from the Car Home screen.

The World of Apps

The Android operating system can pack thrill-a-minute excitement, but it's probably not the only reason you purchased the phone. No, an Android phone's success lies with the apps you obtain. Knowing how to deal with apps is vital to being a successful, happy Android phone user.

Starting an app

It's cinchy to run an app on the Home screen: Touch its icon. The app starts.

- ✔ App is short for *application*. It's another word for *program* or *software*.

- ✔ Not all apps appear on the Home screen, but they all appear when you display the apps drawer. See the later section, "Finding an app in the apps drawer."

Quitting an app

Unlike a computer, you don't need to quit apps on your Android phone. To leave an app, touch the Home icon to return to the Home screen. You can keep touching the Back icon to back out of an app. Or you can touch the Recent icon to switch to another running app.

- ✔ Some apps feature a Quit or Exit command. But for the most part, you don't quit an app on your phone like you quit an app on a computer.

- ✔ If necessary, the Android operating system shuts down apps you haven't used in a while. You can directly stop apps that have run amok, as described in Chapter 18.

Wonderful widgets

Like apps, widgets appear on the Home screen. To use a widget, touch it. What happens after that depends on the widget and what it does.

For example, the YouTube widget lets you peruse videos. The Calendar widget shows a preview of your upcoming schedule. A Twitter widget may display recent tweets. Other widgets do interesting things, display useful information, or give you access to the phone's settings or features.

New widgets are obtained from the Google Play Store, just like apps. See Chapter 18 for information. Also see Chapter 22 for details on adding widgets to the Home screen.

Finding an app in the apps drawer

The place where you find all apps installed on your Android phone is the *apps drawer*. Even though you can find launcher icons (app shortcuts) on the Home screen, the apps drawer is where you need to go to find *everything*.

To view the apps drawer, touch the Apps icon on the Home screen. This icon has a different look to it, depending on your Android phone. Figure 3-7 illustrates various looks to the Apps icon, though more varieties may exist.

Figure 3-7: Apps icon varieties.

After you touch the Apps icon, you see the apps drawer. Swipe through the icons left and right or up and down across the touchscreen.

To run an app, touch its icon. The app starts, taking over the screen and doing whatever magical thing the app does.

✔ As you add new apps to your phone, they appear in the apps drawer. See Chapter 18 for information on adding new apps.

✔ Some phones allow apps in the apps drawer to be grouped into folders. Such a folder is shown in the margin. To access apps in the folder, touch the icon. Not every phone has this feature.

✔ The apps drawer displays apps alphabetically. On some phones, you can switch to a nonalphabetical viewing grid. With that feature active, it's possible to rearrange the apps in any order you like.

✔ For apps that you use all the time, consider creating launcher icons or shortcuts on the Home screen. Chapter 22 describes how.

Switching apps

The apps you run on your phone don't quit when you dismiss them from the screen. For the most part, they stay running. To switch between running apps, or any app you've recently opened, touch the Recent icon. Choose the app to switch to from the list displayed, similar to what's shown in Figure 3-8.

Scroll the list of recent apps up and down to peruse the entire list. If you can't find the app you're looking for, start it as you normally would, either from the Home screen or apps drawer.

✔ For Android phones without a Recent icon, press and hold down the Home icon to see recent apps.

✔ Some Android phones feature a Task Manager app that lets you not only view and switch to apps but also close some apps.

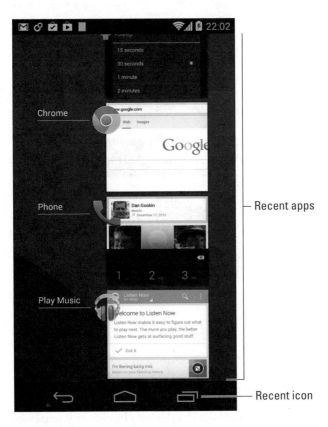

Figure 3-8: Recently opened apps.

Understanding Android apps

Most Android apps feature a similar design. This design provides consistency between the apps, plus it helps you to quickly learn new apps, where to find features, and generally how to get around.

Figure 3-9 shows a typical app. One common feature to look for is the app icon, found in the upper-left corner of the screen. To the left of the icon is the Navigation Drawer icon; touch it to see the navigation drawer, as shown in the figure.

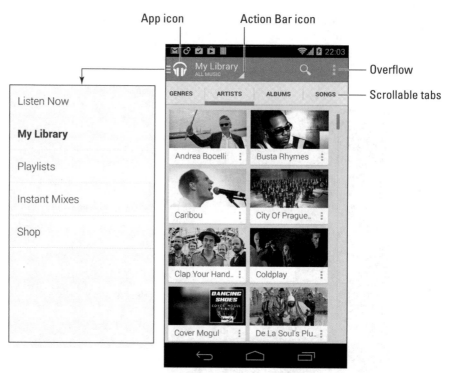

Figure 3-9: A typical Android app.

Use the navigation drawer to peruse top-level items in an app, such as message boxes for an e-mail app, social networking categories, or features found in the Maps app.

To close the navigation drawer, touch the app icon in the upper-left corner of the screen.

Another common app feature is scrollable tabs, also shown in Figure 3-9. The tabs highlight various categories. Touch a tab to choose a category and display its contents. Some tabs can be scrolled left or right by swiping your finger.

Also see the next section for icons commonly found in Android apps.

Using common icons

In additional to the navigation icons, various other icons appear while you use your Android phone. These icons serve common functions in your apps as well as in the Android operating system. Table 3-1 lists the most common icons and their functions.

Table 3-1		Common Icons
Icon	*Name*	*Function*
	Action Bar	Displays a pop-up menu. This teensy icon appears in the lower-right corner of a button or picture.
	Add	Adds or creates an item. The plus symbol (+) may be used in combination with other symbols, depending on the app.
	Back	Returns to the previous screen, cancels an onscreen menu, or dismisses the onscreen keyboard.
	Close	Closes a window or clears text from an input field.
	Delete	Removes one or more items from a list or deletes a message.
	Done	Dismisses an action bar, such as the text-editing action bar.
	Edit	Lets you edit an item, add text, or fill in fields.
	Home	Displays the Home screen.
	Microphone	Lets you use your voice to dictate text.
	Action Overflow	Displays an app's menu or list of commands.
	Recent	Pops up a list of recently opened or currently running apps.
	Refresh	Fetches new information or reloads.
	Search	Searches the phone or the Internet for some tidbit of information.

(continued)

Table 3-1 *(continued)*

Icon	Name	Function
	Settings	Adjusts options for an app.
	Share	Shares information stored on the phone via e-mail, social networking, or other Internet services.
	Star	Flags a favorite item, such as a contact or web page.

Various sections throughout this book give examples of using the icons. Their images appear in the book's margins where relevant.

 On some phones, the Gear icon, shown in the margin, is also used to represent settings. In fact, some phones use both the Settings icon in Table 3-1 and the Gear icon to represent the Settings command.

4

Text to Type, Text to Edit

*Y*ou may be surprised by the amount of typing you do on an Android phone. Although I seriously doubt that anyone would consider writing the Great American Novel, you will end up typing text messages, composing e-mail, and taking notes as part of your daily phone duties. To help with those tasks, your phone features an onscreen keyboard. It also provides for voice dictation. You can even edit text on the touchscreen just you would on a word processor. If you find all that stuff overwhelming, you're reading the right chapter.

Keyboard Mania

Whenever text input is required, your Android phone displays an onscreen keyboard. Don't let it freak you out. If it does, read this section to become more familiar with the amazing feat of typing on a touchscreen.

Accessing the onscreen keyboard

The onscreen keyboard appears on the bottom part of the touchscreen. It shows up any time your phone demands text as input, such as when you type an e-mail, write something on the web, or compose a drunken midnight Facebook status update.

Figure 4-1 illustrates the typical Android keyboard, which is called the Google keyboard. The onscreen keyboard you see on your phone may look subtly different, but it's basically the same tool. Also, be aware that certain keys may change their function depending on what you're typing. This feature can be useful but disconcerting.

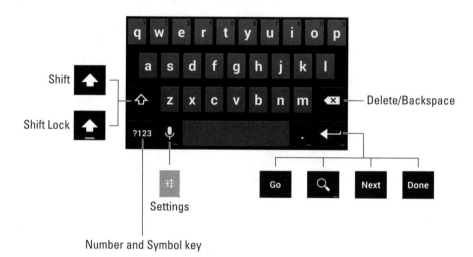

Figure 4-1: The onscreen keyboard.

In Figure 4-1, the onscreen keyboard is shown in alphabetic mode. You see keys from A through Z in lowercase. You also see a Shift key for producing capital letters, and a Delete key, which works to backspace and erase.

The Enter key changes its look depending on what you're typing. Five variations are shown in Figure 4-1. Here's what each one does:

Enter/Return: Just like the Enter or Return key on a computer keyboard, this key ends a paragraph of text. It's used mostly when filling in long stretches of text or when multiline input is needed.

Go: This action key directs the app to proceed with a search, accept input, or perform another action.

Search: You see the Search key when you're searching for something. Touching the key starts the search.

Next: This key appears when you're typing information into multiple fields. Touching this key switches from one field to the next, such as when typing a username and password.

Done: This key appears whenever you've finished typing text in the final field of a screen that has several fields. Sometimes it dismisses the onscreen keyboard, sometimes not.

The large key at the bottom center of the onscreen keyboard is the Space key. The keys to the left and right may change depending on the context of what you're typing. For example a www or .com key may appear to assist in typing a web page or an e-mail address. Other keys may change as well, although the basic alphabetic keys remain the same.

TIP

- ✔ To display the onscreen keyboard, touch any text field or spot on the screen where typing is permitted.

- ✔ To dismiss the onscreen keyboard, touch the Back icon. This icon may appear as in the margin or as a down-pointing chevron.

- ✔ The keyboard reorients itself when you rotate the phone. The onscreen keyboard's horizontal orientation is wide so you might find it easier to use.

Working the built-in keyboard

A handful of Android phones feature a real keyboard, either right below the touchscreen or somehow hidden behind it. You can use the physical keyboard to perform your cell phone typing duties in addition to or instead of the onscreen keyboard.

Generally speaking, the physical keyboard looks like a mini-version of the standard QWERTY keyboard found on computers. The keys are color-coded, with one color for standard keys and a second color for alternative (ALT or SYM) keys.

A bonus to having the physical keyboard is that it often comes with direction keys: up, down, right, and left, plus maybe even an Activate or OK key. Using these keys is covered later in this chapter, in the section "Text Editing."

Choosing another keyboard

Some phones may feature keyboard varieties in addition to the ones on the Google keyboard shown in Figure 4-1. To view which types of keyboards might be available, heed these steps:

1. **At the Home screen, touch the Apps icon.**

2. **Open the Settings app.**

3. **Choose Language & Input.**

   On some phones, the item may read Language & Keyboard. On some Samsung phones, the Language and Input item is found by first touching the Controls tab atop the Settings app screen.

The Language & Input screen shows the variety of keyboards available under the heading Keyboard and Input Methods. You should see Google Keyboard as well as Google Voice Typing. Any other available keyboards also appear in this list.

To use a keyboard exclusively, choose it from the list and remove the check marks by other keyboards.

- ✔ Some keyboard variations are installed via apps obtained at the Google Play Store. See Chapter 18 for information on the Play Store.

- ✔ The XT9 keyboard works like a phone dialpad. It interprets your typing based on numbers typed. For example, you type **43556** and the phone interprets it as *hello.*

- ✔ The ABC keyboard also works like a phone dialpad, but it interprets numbers differently than the XT9 keyboard. For example, to type *hello,* press **44 33 555 555 666**. This method may seem awkward, but it's designed for people who are used to typing this way on a phone keypad.

- ✔ You can quickly access keyboard settings by long-pressing the Microphone key on the keyboard. Choose the Settings key that appears to display the Input Options menu. From that menu, choose Google Keyboard Settings.

The Ol' Hunt-and-Peck

Trust me: No one touch-types on a cell phone. No one. Not even the most lithe and swift preteen texting fiend manages to spew forth cryptic prose without keeping one or more eyes on the phone. So don't feel bad if you can't type on your Android phone as fast as you can on a computer. On the phone, everything is hunt-and-peck.

Typing one character at a time

The onscreen keyboard is pretty easy to figure out: Touch a letter to produce the character. It works just like a computer keyboard in that respect. As you type, the key you touch is highlighted. The phone may give a wee bit of feedback in the form a faint click or vibration.

- ✔ To type in all caps, press the Shift key twice. The Shift key may appear highlighted, the shift symbol may change color, or a colored dot may appear on the key, all of which indicates that Shift Lock is on.

- ✔ Press the Shift key again to turn off Shift Lock.

- ✔ People generally accept the concept that composing text on a phone isn't perfect. Don't sweat it if you make a few mistakes as you type text messages or e-mail, though you should expect some curious replies about unintended typos.

- ✔ Above all, it helps to *type slowly* until you get used to the onscreen keyboard.

- ✔ When you make a mistake, touch the Delete key to back up and erase.

- ✔ A blinking cursor on the touchscreen shows where new text appears, which is similar to how typing text works on your computer.

 ✔ When you type a password, the character you type appears briefly, but for security reasons, it's then replaced by a black dot.

 ✔ See the later section, "Text Editing," for more details on editing your text.

Accessing special characters

You're not limited to typing only the symbols you see on the alphabetic keyboard (refer to Figure 4-1). The onscreen keyboard has many more symbols available, which you can see by touching the Number and Symbol key.

The Number and Symbol key may be labeled ?123 or 12# or sometimes SYM. Touching this key gives you access to additional keyboard layouts, examples of which are shown in Figure 4-2.

Show alpha keyboard

Show symbol keyboard

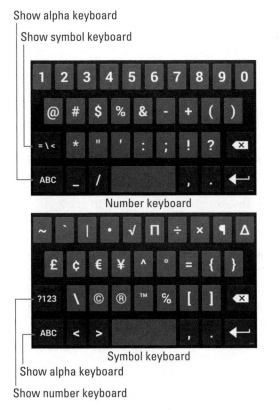

Number keyboard

Symbol keyboard

Show alpha keyboard

Show number keyboard

Figure 4-2: Number and symbol keyboards.

The keys on these layouts may have labels different from what's shown in the figure. For example, you might use the 1/2 or 2/2 key to switch between two sets of symbol keyboards. To return to the standard alpha keyboard (refer to Figure 4-1), touch the ABC key.

You can access special character keys from the main alphabetic keyboard, providing you know a secret: Long-press (touch and hold down) a key. When you do, you see a pop-up palette of additional characters, similar to the ones shown for the A key in Figure 4-3.

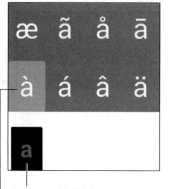

Press and hold down

Then drag your finger over a character to select it

Figure 4-3: Special symbol pop-up palette thing.

Choose a character from the pop-up palette by keeping your finger down and sliding over the key you want. Or choose the highlighted key (the **à** in Figure 4-3) by lifting your finger from the touchscreen. (If you accidentally type a special character, just touch the Delete key to erase it.)

- ✔ Not every character sports a special pop-up palette.

- ✔ Extra characters are available in uppercase as well; press the Shift key before you long-press on the onscreen keyboard.

- ✔ Accessing special characters on a physical phone keyboard is done in a number of ways. Generally speaking, look for a colored key that you access by pressing the SYM or ALT key. Activating this combination displays a palette of symbols on the touchscreen. Choose the symbol from the palette.

Typing quickly by using predictive text

Many Android phones sport a predictive text feature, which displays words the phone thinks you're about to type before you type them. For example, you might type **abo** and a list of words starting with *abo* appears: *above, about, abode,* and so on. Touch a word to choose it.

As you use predictive text, it may even suggest the next word to type. For example, in Figure 4-4, I typed the word *I.* The keyboard then suggested the words *have, am,* and *can.* Long-pressing the word *am* displayed the pop-up list of 15 other suggestions. Choose a word to insert it in your text.

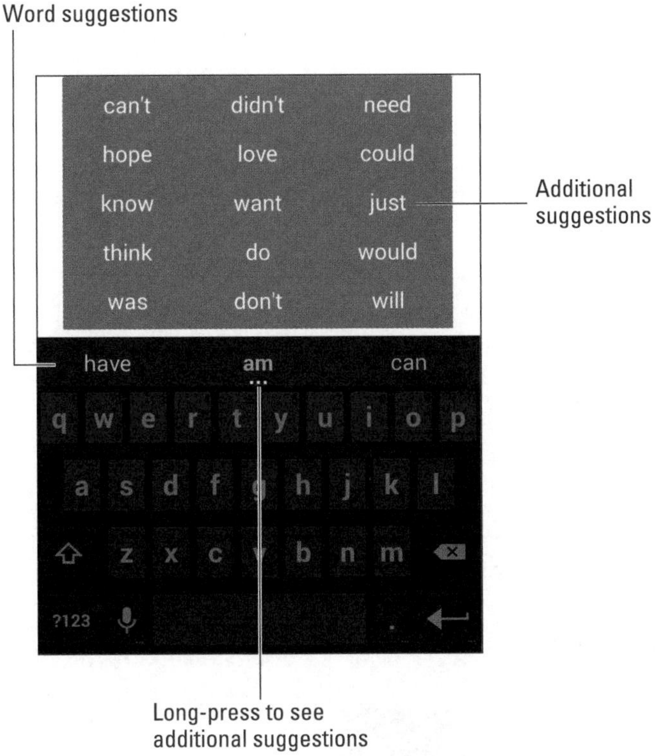

Word suggestions

Additional suggestions

Long-press to see additional suggestions

Figure 4-4: Predictive text in action.

When the desired word doesn't appear, continue typing: The predictive text feature begins making suggestions based on what you've typed so far. Touch the right word when it appears.

To ensure that the predictive text has been activated on your phone, follow these steps:

1. **At the Home screen, touch the Apps icon.**

2. **Open the Settings app.**

3. **Choose Language & Input.**

4. **Touch the Settings icon by Google Keyboard.**

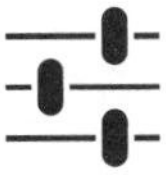

   The Settings icon is shown in the margin.

   The Google Keyboard Settings screen appears.

5. Ensure that a check mark appears by the Next-Word Suggestions item.

This item may be titled Show Suggestions.

When you type a word that the phone doesn't recognize, you might be prompted to add the word to the phone's dictionary. (Yes, the phone has a dictionary.) Choose that option. Also see Chapter 24 for more information about the phone's dictionary and spell-checking feature.

Adding gesture typing

If you're really after typing speed, consider using gesture typing. It allows you to type words by swiping your finger over the onscreen keyboard, like mad scribbling but with a positive result.

To make sure that this feature is enabled, follow Steps 1 through 4 in the preceding section to view the Google Keyboard Settings screen. Place a check mark by the Enable Gesture Typing item. While you're at it, ensure that all the items in the Gesture Typing section are enabled; a check mark should be found by each one.

You use gesture typing by dragging your fingers over letters on the keyboard. Figure 4-5 illustrates how the word *hello* would be typed in this manner.

Dynamic floating preview

Start swiping here

Lift your finger here

Trace each letter

Figure 4-5: Using gesture typing to type *hello.*

The gesture typing feature may not be active when you need to type a password or for specific apps on the phone. When it doesn't work, use the onscreen keyboard one letter at a time.

Google Voice Typing

Your Android phone has the amazing capability to interpret your utterances as text. It works almost as well as computer dictation in science fiction movies, though I can't seem to find the command to destroy Alderaan.

Activating voice input

The phone's voice input feature is officially known as Google Voice Typing. To ensure that this feature is active, obey these steps:

1. **At the Home screen, touch the Apps icon.**
2. **Open the Settings app.**
3. **Choose Language & Input.**

   This command may be titled Input & Language on some phones.
4. **Ensure that the item Google Voice Typing has a check mark.**

   If not, touch that item to activate Google Voice Typing.

Your primary clue that voice input is active is the Microphone icon found on the keyboard. If you can see that icon, you're good.

Dictating text

Talking to your phone really works, and works quite well, providing that you touch the Microphone key on the keyboard and properly dictate your text.

After touching the Microphone key, you see a special window at the bottom of the screen, similar to what's shown in Figure 4-6. When the text Tap to Speak or Speak Now appears, dictate your text; speak directly at the phone.

As you speak, the Microphone icon on the screen flashes. The flashing doesn't mean that the phone is embarrassed by what you're saying. No, the flashing merely indicates that your words are being digested.

Google Voice typing active   Google Voice typing paused

Figure 4-6: Google Voice typing.

The text you utter appears as you speak. To pause, touch the Tap to Pause text on the screen. To use the keyboard, touch the Keyboard icon just to the left of the Microphone icon, shown in Figure 4-6, right.

- The first time you try voice input, you might see a description. Touch the OK button to continue.

- The better your diction, the better your results.

- You cannot use Google Voice Typing to edit text. Text editing still takes place on the touchscreen, as described in the section, "Text Editing."

- Speak the punctuation in your text. For example, you would say, "I'm sorry comma and it won't happen again" to produce the text `I'm sorry, and it won't happen again`.

- Common punctuation you can dictate includes the comma, period, exclamation point, question mark, and colon.

- You cannot dictate capital letters. If you're a stickler for such things, you'll have to go back and edit the text.

- Dictation may not work without an Internet connection.

Uttering s**** words

Your Android phone features a voice censor. It replaces those naughty words you might utter, placing the word's first letter on the screen, followed by the appropriate number of asterisks.

For example, if *spatula* were a blue word and you uttered *spatula* when dictating text, the dictation feature would place `s******` on the screen rather than the word *spatula*.

Yeah, I know: silly. Or "s****."

Your Android phone knows a lot of blue terms, including the infamous "Seven Words You Can Never Say on Television," but apparently the terms *crap* and *damn* are fine. Don't ask me how much time I spent researching this topic.

See Chapter 24 if you really want the phone to take naughty dictation.

Text Editing

You probably won't do a lot of text editing on your Android phone. Well, no major editing, such as for a term paper or ransom note. From time to time, however, you may find yourself wanting to fix a word. It's usually a sign that you're over 25; kids no longer seem to care about editing text.

Moving the cursor

The first part of editing text is to move the cursor to the right spot. The *cursor* is that blinking, vertical line where text appears. Then you can type, edit, or paste, or simply marvel that you were able to move the cursor hither and thither.

On most computing devices, you move the cursor by using a pointing device. If your Android phone features a pointing device, such as a thumb ball or arrow keys on a physical keyboard, you can use that device to move the cursor while you edit text. Otherwise, your finger performs the cursor-moving task.

To move the cursor, simply touch the spot on the text where you want to place the cursor. To help your precision, a cursor tab appears below the text, as shown in the margin. You can move that tab with your finger to move the cursor around in the text.

After you move the cursor, you can continue to type, use the Delete key to back up and erase, or paste in text copied from elsewhere.

✔ You may see a pop-up by the cursor tab containing a Paste command button. That button is used to paste text, as described in the later section, "Cutting, copying, and pasting."

✔ You can also move the cursor around by dragging your finger over the onscreen keyboard. This trick doesn't work when the gesture typing feature is activated. See the section "Adding gesture typing" earlier in this chapter.

Selecting text

Selecting text on an Android phone works just like selecting text in a word processor: You mark the start and end of a block. That chunk of text appears highlighted on the screen. How you get there, however, can be a mystery — until now!

Start selecting by long-pressing the text or double-tapping a word. Upon success, you see a chunk of text selected, as shown in Figure 4-7.

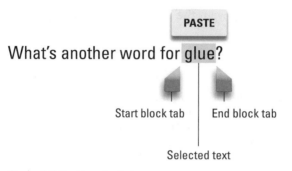

Figure 4-7: Text is selected.

Drag the start and end markers around the touchscreen to define the selected text.

When text is selected, a contextual action bar appears atop the screen. The standard Android version of the action bar appears in Figure 4-8, although your phone may sport an action bar with a different look. Either way, you use the action bar to deal with the selected text.

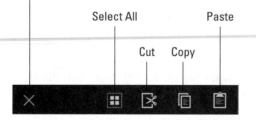

Figure 4-8: Contextual action bar for text selection.

After you select the text, you can delete it by touching the Delete key on the onscreen keyboard. You can replace the text by typing something new. Or you can cut or copy the text. See the next section, "Cutting, copying, and pasting."

To cancel text selection, touch the Cancel (X) icon on the action bar, or just touch anywhere on the touchscreen outside of the selected block.

✔ When your phone has a physical keyboard with cursor keys or a control pad, you can hold down the Shift key and use the direction keys or cursor pad to select text.

✔ Text selection on a web page works similarly to selecting text elsewhere. The primary difference is that the action bar lacks a command to cut the text.

Cutting, copying, and pasting text

Selected text is primed for cutting or copying, which works just like it does in your favorite word processor. After you select the text, choose the proper command from the contextual action bar, which looks like a toolbar atop the touchscreen.

The action bar lists several commands. Icons commonly found on the bar as shown in Table 4-1. For example, to copy the text, choose the Copy command; to cut text, choose Cut.

Table 4-1		Text Selection Action Bar Commands
Icon	**Name**	**Function**
✕	Close	Dismiss the action bar and deselect the text.
⊞	Select All	Select all the text.
✂	Cut	Cut the selected text to the clipboard.
▤	Copy	Copy the selected text to the clipboard.
▥	Paste	Paste any previously cut or copied text at the cursor's position.
⦡	Share	Share the selected text.
🔍	Search	Search the Internet for the selected text.

Just like on your computer, cut or copied text on your phone is stored in a clipboard. To paste any previously cut or copied text, move the cursor to the spot where you want the text pasted.

✔ A quick way to paste text is to touch the Paste command button above the cursor tab. To see that button, touch anywhere in the text. Not every phone features a Paste command above the cursor tab.

✔ Some phones feature a Clipboard app, which lets you peruse, review, and select previously cut or copied text or images. You might even find a Clipboard key on the onscreen keyboard.

✔ You can paste text only into locations where text is allowed. Odds are good that if you see the onscreen keyboard, you can paste text.

Part II
The Phone Part

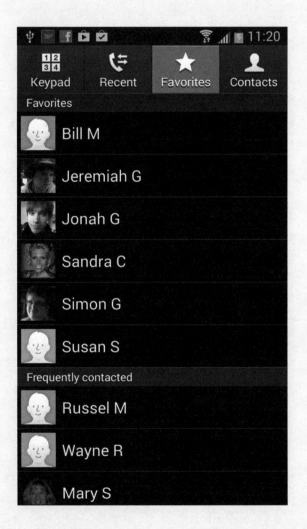

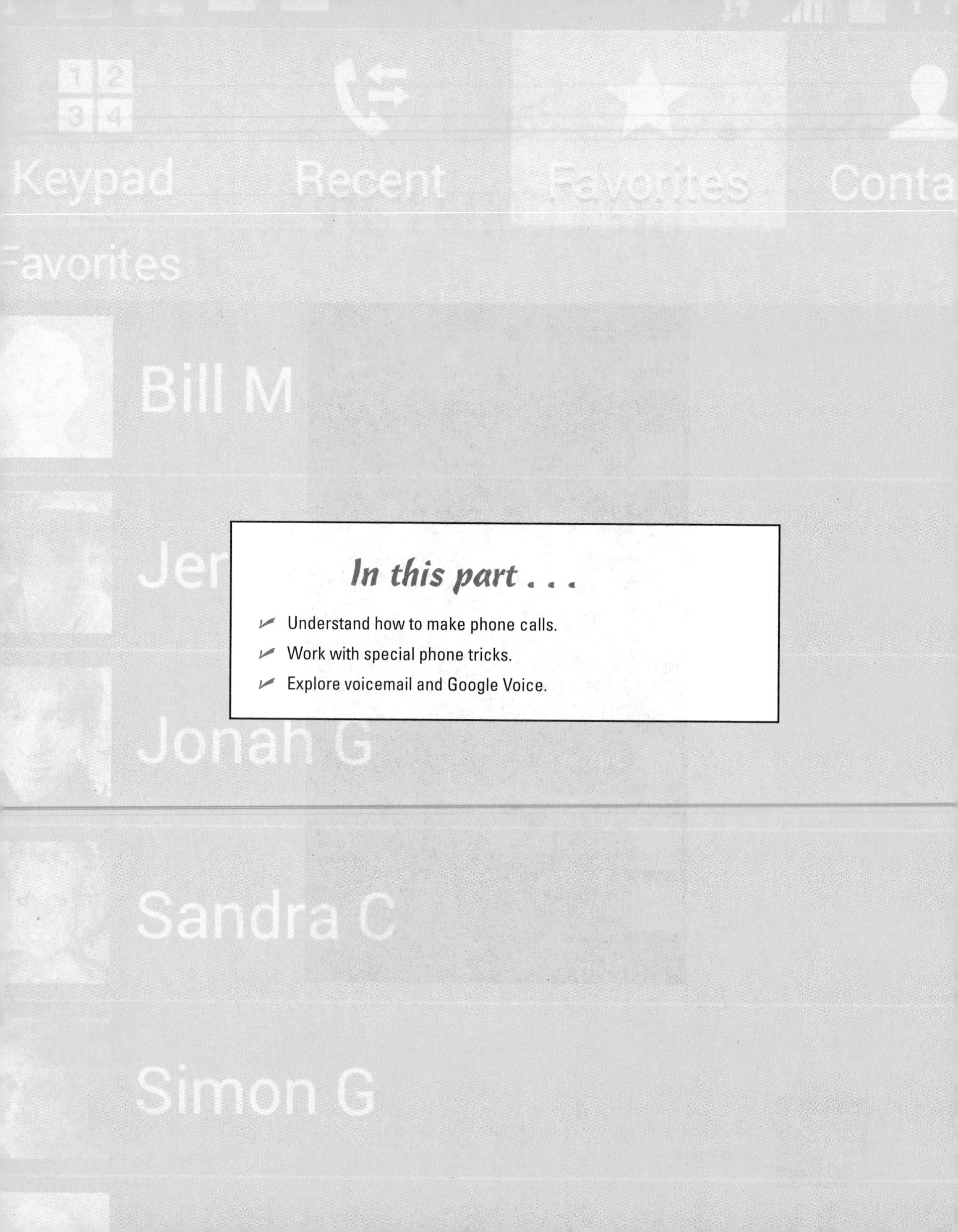

Keypad   Recent   Favorites   Conta

Favorites

Bill M

Je

Jonah G

Sandra C

Simon G

In this part . . .

- ✔ Understand how to make phone calls.
- ✔ Work with special phone tricks.
- ✔ Explore voicemail and Google Voice.

5

It's a Telephone

*T*he patent for the telephone was awarded to Alexander Graham Bell in 1876. Telephone-like devices existed before then, and a host of nine-teenth-century scientists worked on the concept. But Bell beat them all to the patent office, so he gets the credit. And it took many more years for people to patent other, ancillary inventions, including the busy signal (1878), the notion of a second line for teenage girls (1896), and the extension cord, which allowed for simultaneously talking and pacing (1902).

Making phone calls may seem simple enough, but if you've never used an Android phone, it may be an utterly new experience for you. Therefore, I wrote this chapter with some tips, suggestions, and worthy points, all covering that most basic of cell phone functions: making phone calls.

Reach Out and Touch Someone

Until they perfect teleportation, making a phone call is truly the next best thing to being there. Or, to copy another Phone Company slogan, you can use your Android phone to "reach out and touch someone." It all starts by punching in a number or calling someone from the phone's address book. This section explains how it works.

Making a phone call

To place a call on your phone, heed these steps:

1. **Touch the Phone app on the Home screen.**

   The dialing operation on an Android phone is handled by an app. The official Android name for the app is Phone, although your phone may call it the Dialer app. Regardless of the name, the app sports a phone handset icon, similar to what's shown in the margin.

2. **If necessary, display the dialpad.**

   The typical Phone app has several screens, including call history or recent calls, favorites, and contacts, similar to what's shown in Figure 5-1.

   To view the dialpad, touch the Dialpad icon, shown in Figure 5-1.

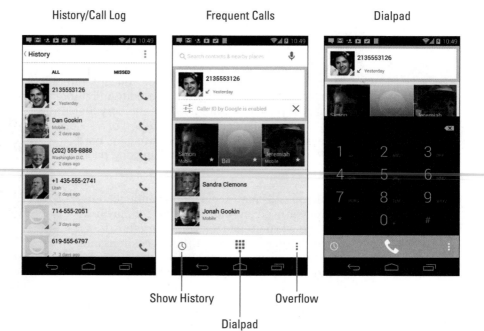

History/Call Log   Frequent Calls   Dialpad

Show History   Overflow

Dialpad

Figure 5-1: The Phone app.

The Phone app's dialpad screen is where you place phone calls. Figure 5-2 shows the layout of the default Android phone dialer.

3. Type the number to call.

Use the keys on the dialpad to type the number. If you make a mistake, touch the Delete icon, labeled in Figure 5-2, to back up and erase.

As you dial, you may hear the traditional touch-tone sound as you type the number.

The phone may display matching contacts as you type a number. You can choose one of those contacts to complete the number for faster dialing.

Signal strength

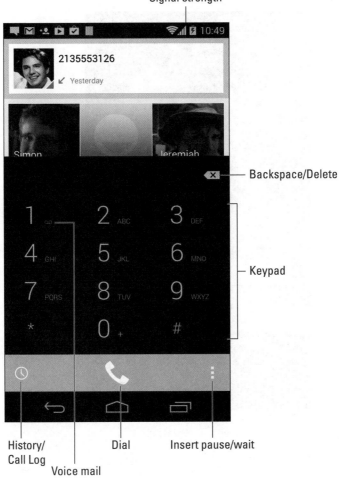

Figure 5-2: The dialpad screen.

4. **Touch the Phone handset icon to place the call.**

As the phone attempts to make the connection, two things happen:

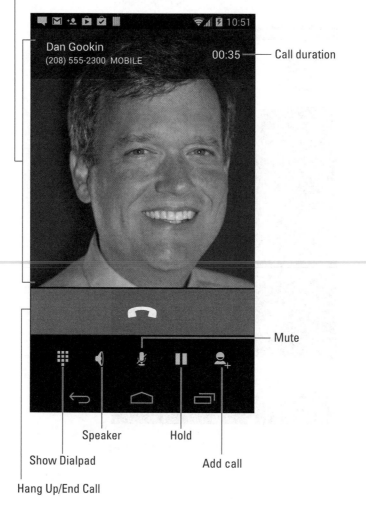

- First, the Call in Progress notification icon appears on the status bar. The icon is a big clue that the phone is making a call or is actively connected.

- Second, the screen changes to show the number you dialed, similar to Figure 5-3. When the recipient is in the phone's address book, the contact's name, photo, and social networking status (if available) may also appear.

Contact info

Call duration

Mute

Speaker

Hold

Show Dialpad

Add call

Hang Up/End Call

Figure 5-3: A successful call.

Even though the touchscreen is pretty, at this point you need to listen to the phone: Put it up to your ear, or listen using earphones or a Bluetooth headset.

5. **When the person answers the phone, talk.**

What you say is up to you, though it's good not to just blurt out unexpected news: "I just ran over your cat" or "I think I just saw your daughter on the back of a motorcycle, leaving town at inappropriately high speeds."

Use the phone's Volume buttons (on the side of the device) to adjust the speaker volume during the call.

6. **To end the call, touch the End Call icon.**

The phone disconnects. You hear a soft *beep,* which is the phone's signal that the call has ended. The call-in-progress notification goes away.

You can do other things while you're making a call: Touch the Home icon to run an app, read old e-mail, check an appointment, or do whatever. Activities such as these don't disconnect you, although your cellular carrier may not allow you to do other things with the phone while you're on a call.

To return to a call after doing something else, swipe down the notifications at the top of the screen and touch the notification for the current call. You return to the connected screen, similar to the one shown in Figure 5-3. Continue yapping. (See Chapter 3 for information on reviewing notifications.)

✔ If you're using earphones, you can press the phone's Power/Lock key during the call to turn off the display and lock the phone. I recommend turning off the display so that you don't accidentally mute or end the call.

✔ You can connect or remove the earphones at any time during a call. The call is neither disconnected nor interrupted when you do so.

✔ You can't accidentally mute or end a call when the phone is placed against your face; a sensor in the phone detects when it's close to something, and the touchscreen is automatically disabled.

✔ Don't worry about the phone's microphone being too far away from your mouth; it picks up your voice just fine.

✔ To mute a call, touch the Mute icon, shown in Figure 5-3. The Mute status icon (like the one shown in the margin or something similar) appears as the phone's status atop the touchscreen.

✔ Touch the Speaker icon to be able to hold the phone at a distance to listen and talk, which allows you to let others listen and share in the conversation. The Speaker status icon appears when the speaker is active.

✔ Don't hold the phone to your ear when the speaker is active.

✔ If you're wading through one of those nasty voicemail systems, touch the Dialpad icon, labeled in Figure 5-3, so that you can "Press 1 for English" when necessary.

✔ See Chapter 6 for information on using the Add Call and Hold icons.

✔ When using a Bluetooth headset, connect the headset *before* you make the call.

✔ If you need to dial an international number, press and hold down the 0 (zero) key until the plus sign (+) appears. Then input the rest of the international number. Refer to Chapter 21 for more information on making international calls.

✔ You hear an audio alert whenever the call is dropped or the other party hangs up. The disconnection can be confirmed by looking at the phone, which shows that the call has ended.

✔ You cannot place a phone call when the phone has no service; check the signal strength (refer to Figure 5-2). Also see the nearby sidebar, "Signal strength and network nonsense."

✔ You cannot place a phone call when the phone is in airplane mode. See Chapter 21 for information.

Signal strength and network nonsense

One of your Android phone's most important status icons is the Signal Strength icon. It appears in the upper-right corner of the screen, next to the Time and Battery Strength status icons.

The Signal Strength icon features the familiar bars, rising from left to right. The more bars, the better the signal. An extremely low signal is indicated by zero bars. When there's no signal, you may see a red circle with a line through it (the International No symbol) over the bars.

When the phone is out of its service area but still receiving a signal, you see the Roaming icon, which typically includes an *R* near or over the bars. See Chapter 21 for more information on roaming.

Your phone may also show a Network icon. This icon represents to which type of digital cellular network the phone is connected. Here are some of the different network types:

✔ **1X, E, EDGE,** or **GSM:** These are the original (slow) mobile networks. You may still see icons for these networks when faster networks aren't available.

✔ **3G:** This icon represents the third-generation network, which is presently the second-fastest network.

✔ **4G, 4G LTE, H+,** or **HSPA:** This icon represents the fastest current-generation cellular data network.

Also see Chapter 19 for more information on the network connection and how it plays a role in your phone's Internet access.

✔ The call-in-progress notification is useful. When you see this notification, the phone is connected to another party. To return to the phone screen, swipe down the status bar and touch the phone call's notification. You can then touch the End Call icon to disconnect or put the phone to your ear to hear who's on the line.

Dialing a contact

Your Android phone also serves as an address book. One of the key times that you use that address book is to dial phone numbers associated with your friends flung far and wide. Here's how it works:

1. **Start the People or Contacts app.**

   It's found on the Home screen. If not, check the apps drawer.

2. **Scroll the list of contacts to find the person you want to call.**

   To rapidly scroll, you can swipe the list with your finger or use the index on the side of the screen.

3. **Touch the contact you want to call.**

   In some cases, choosing the contact instantly dials that person. Other times, you may have to choose the phone number to call or touch a Phone icon to dial the contact.

At this point, dialing proceeds as described earlier in this chapter.

✔ The phone's address book may be directly accessibly from the Phone app. Look for a tab, button, or link to the contacts list. The link might be found at the bottom of the frequent contacts list. You might also find access to the address book from a command on the Action Overflow or Menu icon.

✔ See Chapter 8 for more details on how to use the phone's address book.

Calling a favorite

A special contact category in the phone's address book is favorites. A *favorite* is someone you call frequently or whose information you need to have handy. To call a favorite, choose the Favorites tab in the Phone app, similar to what's shown in Figure 5-4. Touch a favorite contact to either dial that person directly or to display their contact information, and then choose the number to dial.

The favorites (or frequent calls list) might be visible from the main Phone app screen (refer to Figure 5-1, center).

See to Chapter 8 for information on how to make one of your contacts a favorite.

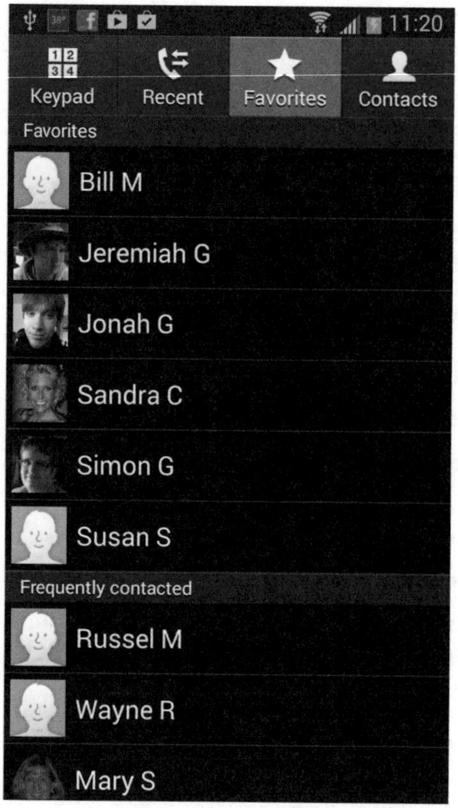

Figure 5-4: The favorites screen.

It's the Phone!

Who doesn't enjoy getting a phone call? It's an event! Never mind that it's the company that keeps calling you about lowering the interest rate on your credit cards. The point is that someone cares enough to call. Truly, the cell phone ringing can be good news, bad news, or mediocre news, but it provides a little drama to spice up an otherwise mundane day.

Receiving a call

Several things can happen when you receive a phone call on your Android phone:

- ✔ The phone rings or makes a noise signaling you to an incoming call.
- ✔ The phone vibrates.

✔ The touchscreen reveals information about the call, as shown in Figure 5-5.

✔ The car in front of you explodes in a loud fireball as your passenger screams something inappropriately funny.

That last item happens only in Bruce Willis movies. The other three possibilities, or a combination thereof, are your signals that you have an incoming call. A simple look at the touchscreen tells you more information, as illustrated in the top half of Figure 5-5.

The techniques for answering your phone depend on the phone. The unadulterated Android method is to slide the Answer icon to the right to answer, to the left to decline the call, or up to reply with a text message. These actions are illustrated in Figure 5-5.

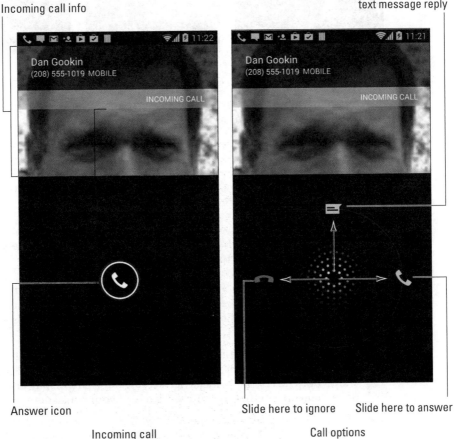

Figure 5-5: You have an incoming call.

Your phone may deal with an incoming call differently than what's shown in Figure 5-5. Figure 5-6 illustrates a few other varieties. Generally speaking, you slide the Answer icon one way to answer and the other way to ignore the call.

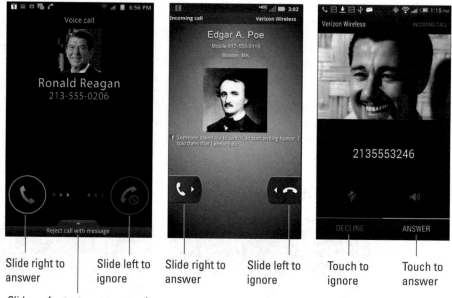

Slide right to answer   Slide left to ignore   Slide right to answer   Slide left to ignore   Touch to ignore   Touch to answer

Slide up for text message reply

Figure 5-6: Other ways to answer a call.

When you choose to answer the call, place the phone to your ear or, if a headset is attached, use it. Say "Hello," or, if you're in a grouchy mood, say "What?" loudly.

Touch the End Call button to hang up when you're done with the call. If the other party hangs up first, the call ends automatically.

- The phone always stops whatever you're doing — surfing the web, playing a game, answering e-mail — to display the incoming call screen. If the phone is locked, the touchscreen wakes up and displays the incoming call screen.

- The contact's picture (refer to Figures 5-4 and 5-5) appears only when you've assigned a picture to the contact. Otherwise, a generic contact image shows up. The contact's social networking information may also appear, depending on whether the contact is one of your social networking pals.

- If you're using a Bluetooth headset, you touch the control on the headset to answer your phone. See Chapter 19 for more information on using Bluetooth gizmos.

> ✔ The sound you hear when the phone rings is known as the *ringtone*. You can configure your phone to play a number of ringtones, depending on who is calling, or you can set a universal ringtone. Ringtones are covered in Chapter 6.

> ✔ If you receive a call while you're on the phone, you can choose to answer the call separately, place the original caller on hold, or create a conference call. See Chapter 6 for information on juggling multiple calls.

> ✔ See Chapter 22 for information on setting the incoming call volume.

> ✔ See the "Rejecting a call with a text message" section for information on the text message reply feature.

Dispensing with an incoming call

Several options are available when you don't want to receive an incoming call.

The first option is just to ignore the call; let the phone ring. The missed call shows up on the phone's recent calls list. See the later section, "Who Called Who When?"

The second option is to ignore the call but blissfully silence the ringing. To do so, touch the Volume key. The call continues to ring through, but you can't hear it. The call shows up as missed on the phone's recent calls list.

The third option is to dismiss the call: On some phones, slide the Answer icon to the Ignore or Dismiss icon. On other phones you simply slide an Ignore icon across the screen. The phone stops ringing. Calls you choose to ignore don't show up as missed calls on the phone's recent calls list. (See the later section "Dealing with a missed call.")

A final option is to ignore the call but reply with a text message. See the next section.

In all cases, when you don't answer the phone, the call is sent to voicemail. See Chapter 7 for information on voicemail.

Rejecting a call with a text message

I'm quite fond of the text message rejection method. Rather than just dismiss a call, you can reply to the call with a text message. Choose the Text Message icon or drawer when dismissing a call, shown in Figures 5-5 and Figure 5-6, respectively. Then select a text message, similar to what's shown in Figure 5-7.

After you choose a text message, the incoming call is dismissed. In a few cellular seconds, the person who called receives the message.

Figure 5-7: Text message rejection selection.

To review or change the preset text messages, heed these steps:

1. **Touch the Action Overflow or Menu icon while using the Phone app.**

2. **Choose the Settings command, and then choose Call Settings.**

   On some Samsung phones, the Call Settings screen is accessed from the Settings app; choose the Device tab, and then choose the Call item.

3. **Choose the Quick Responses item.**

   This item might also be titled Set Up Call Rejection Messages.

Choose a message to edit its text. Deleting a message's text effectively removes that response from the list.

 To add a new message, touch the Add icon. On some phones, the Add command might be found on the Action Overflow menu, or you can touch a blank item in the message list to add a new rejection message.

✔ Not every phone is a cell phone. Sending a text message to Aunt Suzie's landline phone just won't work.

✔ See Chapter 9 for more information on text messages.

Dealing with a missed call

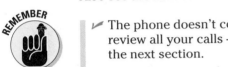

The notification icon for a missed call looming at the top of the screen means that someone called and you didn't pick up. Here's what you can do:

1. **Display the notifications.**

   See Chapter 3 for details on how to deal with notifications.

2. **Touch the missed call notification.**

   You see a list of missed calls. The list shows who called, with more information displayed when the phone number matches someone in your contacts list. Also shown is how long ago the person called.

3. **Touch an entry in the call log to return the call.**

Also see the next section for more information on the call log.

✔ The phone doesn't consider a call you've dismissed as being missed. To review all your calls — incoming, outgoing, dismissed, and missed — see the next section.

✔ Some phones may display a Call Back icon below the missed call notification. Touch that icon in the notifications drawer to instantly return the call.

Who Called Who When?

Your Android phone keeps track of all your phone calls — incoming, outgoing, missed, and so on. It's something I refer to as the call log, although on your phone it may be referenced as Recent Calls or Call History. The place to look is in the Phone app.

Figure 5-8 shows what the phone's call history can look like. To see that item, touch the Recent or History icon from the main Phone app screen.

Scroll through the list to examine recent calls. The list is sorted so that the most recent calls appear at the top of the list. Information appears associated with each call, such as the date and time, call duration, and whether the call was incoming, outgoing, missed, or ignored.

To see more details about the call, choose its item in the list. You can also phone someone back by choosing an item; touch the phone number or Phone icon to return the call.

Outgoing call

Missed call   Show only missed calls

Incoming call   Touch to call

Figure 5-8: The call log.

✔ Tabs at the top of the call history (refer to Figure 5-8) let you sort the list by all calls or only missed calls. Not every phone's call history has this feature.

✔ Sometimes you can sort the list of recent calls by touching the Action Overflow icon, shown in the margin. Choose a sorting command from the menu that appears.

✔ Using the call log is a quick way to add a recent caller as a contact: Simply touch an item in the list, and choose Add to Contacts from the call details screen. See Chapter 8 for more information about contacts.

✔ Remove an item from the call log by long-pressing its entry. Choose the Remove command from the pop-up menu. When a pop-up menu doesn't appear, choose the recent call from the list to display more details. Touch the Action Overflow icon and choose the command Remove from Call Log.

✔ To clear the call log, touch the Action Overflow icon. Choose either the Clear List or Delete All command to wipe clean the call log.

✔ On some phone, touch the Menu icon or button instead of the Action Overflow icon to see a list of commands.

More Telephone Things

A phone call was a phone call, and that's pretty much all that phones did until the 1980s. Around that time, the government started breaking up the old Bell System. Coincidentally, new features began to appear on the commonplace, mortal telephone: call waiting, speed dial, three-way calling, and eventually caller ID. Such things were breathtaking improvements to the plain old telephone, but for today's cell phone they're commonly included — and at no extra charge.

Your Android phone is capable of a great many feats, all of which were once considered extras — *expensive* extras — beyond standard telephone service. This chapter describes that potential. Whether your phone sports all the fancy features depends on how willing your cellular provider is to supply them.

Super Dialing Tricks

Any mere mortal can use the Phone app on an Android phone to key in a number. To take your dialing skills up a notch, consider some of the special tricks carefully explained in this section.

Assigning numbers to speed dial

Not every Android phone features speed dial. To see whether yours does, heed these steps:

1. **Start the Phone app.**

   The Phone app icon is found on the Home screen.

2. **Display the dialpad.**

3. **Touch the Action Overflow icon.**

   If you don't see the Action Overflow icon on the screen, touch the Menu icon. When you can't find either icon, the Phone app most likely lacks a speed dial feature.

4. **Choose Speed Dial or Speed Dial Setup.**

   Most carriers configure number 1 as the voicemail system's number. The remaining numbers, 2 through 9, are available to program.

5. **Touch an unused or blank item in the list, or touch the Add icon.**

   The item may say Add Speed Dial or Not Assigned as opposed to being blank.

6. **Choose a contact to speed-dial.**

7. **Repeat Steps 5 and 6 to add more speed dial contacts.**

When you're done adding numbers, press either the Back or Home icon to exit the speed dial screen.

Using speed dial is simple. Summon the Phone app and display the dialpad. Long-press a number on the dialpad. When you release your finger, the speed dial number is dialed.

Adding pauses when dialing a number

Unlike the ancient telephone, dialing a number on an Android phone isn't an interactive process: You type the number and then touch a Phone icon to dial. The number is instantly spewed into the phone system. If you need to pause the number as it's dialed, you need to know the secret pause dialing command.

To insert a pause or wait prompt into a phone number, follow these steps:

1. **Type the number to dial.**

2. **When you need to insert a pause, touch the Action Overflow icon.**

   On some phones, touch the Menu icon to see the pop-up menu shown in Figure 6-1.

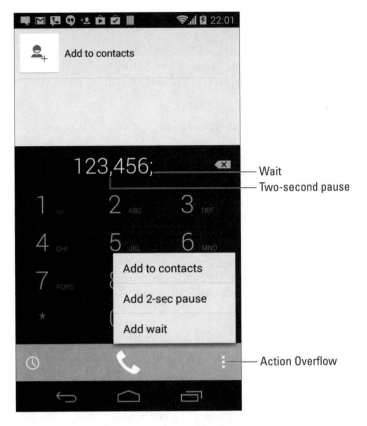

Figure 6-1: Inserting a pause into a phone number.

3. Choose the proper command to insert a pause into the number dialed.

The Add 2 Second Pause command inserts a comma (,) into the number. When the phone dials the comma, it waits for two seconds and then dials the rest of the number.

The Add Wait command inserts a semicolon (;) into the number. When the phone dials the semicolon, a prompt is displayed.

4. Continue composing the number.

When you're done, dial the number. When the comma (,) is encountered, the phone pauses two seconds, then dials the rest of the number. When the semicolon (;) is encountered, the phone prompts you to continue. Touch the Yes or OK button to continue dialing the rest of the number.

The comma (,) and semicolon (;) can also be inserted into the phone numbers you assign contacts. See Chapter 8 for information on contacts and the phone's address book.

Multiple Call Mania

As a human being, your brain limits your ability to hold more than one conversation at a time. Your phone's brain, however, lacks such a limitation. It's entirely possible for an Android phone to handle more than one call at a time.

Putting someone on hold

It's easy to place a call on hold using your Android phone — as long as your cellular provider hasn't disabled that feature. Simply touch the Hold icon. Refer to Figure 5-3 in Chapter 5 for the Hold icon's location on the call-in-progress screen.

To "unhold" the call, touch the Hold icon again. The icon may change its look, for example, from a pause symbol to a play symbol.

Fret not if your phone lacks the Hold icon. Rather than hold the call, mute it: Touch the Mute icon on the call-in-progress screen. That way, you can sneeze, scream at the wall, or flush the toilet and the other person will never know.

Receiving a new call when you're on the phone

You're on the phone, chatting it up. Suddenly, someone else calls you. What happens next?

Your phone alerts you to the new call, perhaps by vibrating or making a sound. Look at the touchscreen to see what's up with the incoming call, similar to what's shown in Figure 6-2.

You have three options:

- **Answer the call.** Touch the green Answer icon to answer the incoming call. The call you're on is placed on hold.
- **Send the call directly to voicemail.** Touch the Ignore icon. The incoming call is sent directly to voicemail.
- **Do nothing.** The call eventually goes into voicemail.

When you choose to answer the call and the call you're on is placed on hold, you return to the first call when you end the second call. Or you can manage the multiple calls, as described in the next section.

Incoming call info

You're already on the line

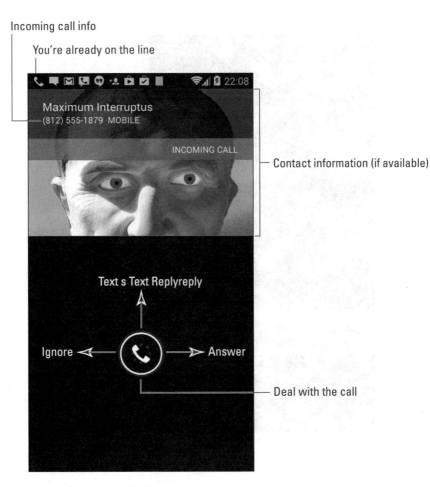

Contact information (if available)

Deal with the call

Figure 6-2: Suddenly, there's an incoming call!

Juggling two calls

After you answer a second call, as described in the preceding section, your phone is working with two calls at once. In this situation, you can speak with only one person at a time; juggling two calls isn't the same thing as participating in a conference call.

Some Android phones feature a multicall screen, similar to what's shown in Figure 6-3. The screen lists the calls you're working on and lets you easily switch between them in a visual manner, as shown in the figure.

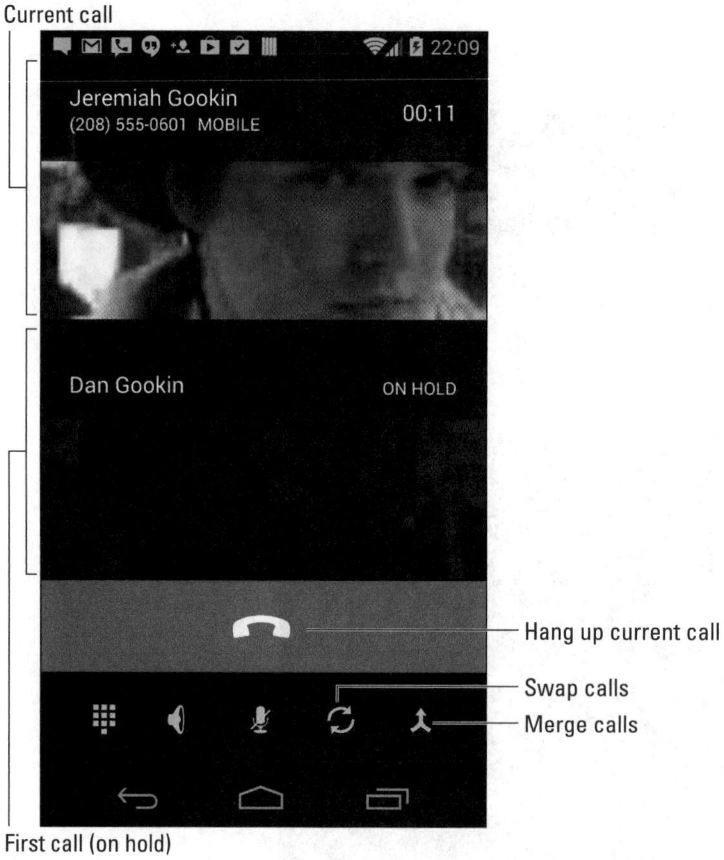

Current call

Jeremiah Gookin
(208) 555-0601 MOBILE   00:11

Dan Gookin   ON HOLD

———— Hang up current call

———— Swap calls
———— Merge calls

First call (on hold)

Figure 6-3: The multicall screen.

Your options for dealing with multiple calls include the following:

 Swap/Switch Calls: To switch between callers, touch the Swap or Switch Calls icon on the touchscreen. Every time you touch that icon, the conversation switches to the other caller and the current person is put on hold.

 Merge Calls: To combine all calls so that everyone is talking (three people total), touch the Merge Calls icon. This icon may not be available should the merge feature be suppressed by your cellular provider.

End Call: To end a call, touch the End Call icon, just as you normally do.

After one call ends, the conversation returns to the other caller. You can then proceed to talk — discuss the weather, the local sports team, whatever — until you hang up or another call interrupts you.

✏ The number of different calls your phone can handle depends on your carrier. For most subscribers in the United States, your phone can handle only two calls at a time. In that case, a third person who calls you either hears a busy signal or is sent directly into voicemail.

✏ If the person on hold hangs up, you may hear a sound or feel the phone vibrate when the call is dropped.

✏ When you touch the End Call icon using an Android phone on the Verizon network, both calls may appear to have been disconnected. That's not the case: In a few moments, the call you didn't disconnect "rings" as though the person is calling you back. No one is calling you back, though: The phone is simply returning you to that ongoing conversation.

Making a conference call

Unlike someone interrupting a conversation by making an incoming call, a *conference call* is one you set out to make intentionally: You make one call and then *add* a second call. Touch an icon on the phone's touchscreen and then everyone is talking. Here's how it works:

1. **Phone the first person.**

2. **After the call connects and you complete a few pleasantries, touch the Add Call icon.**

   The Add Call icon is shown in the margin. (It can be seen also in Figure 5-3, in Chapter 5.) After touching that icon, or a similar icon, the first person is put on hold.

3. **Dial the second person.**

   You can use the dialpad or choose the second person from the phone's address book or the recent calls log.

   Say your pleasantries and inform the party that the call is about to be merged.

4. **Touch the Merge or Merge Calls icon.**

   The two calls are now joined: The touchscreen says *Conference Call,* and the End Last Call icon appears. Everyone you've dialed can talk to and hear everyone else.

5. **Touch the End Call icon to end the conference call.**

   All calls are disconnected.

When several people are in a room and want to participate in a call, you can always put the phone in speaker mode: Touch the Speaker icon on the ongoing call screen.

Your Android phone may feature the Manage icon while you're in a conference call. Touch this icon to list the various calls, to mute one, or to select a call to disconnect.

Forward Calls Elsewhere

You have a choice for dealing with incoming calls. You can ignore them, silence the ringer, banish them to e-mail, or admit defeat and answer. You can also choose to automate the process by forwarding one or all incoming calls.

Forwarding phone calls

Call forwarding is the process by which you reroute an incoming call. For example, you can send all your calls to the office while you're on vacation. Then you have the luxury of having your cell phone and still making calls but freely ignoring anyone who calls you.

The options for call forwarding on your phone can be set by using either the Android operating system itself or the controls set up by your cellular provider.

Call forwarding may affect your phone's voicemail service. See Chapter 7 for details.

Forward calls using Android settings

To confirm that call-forwarding options can be set by using the Android operating system, follow these steps:

1. **Open the Phone app.**

2. **Touch the Action Overflow icon.**

   On some phones, touch the Menu icon instead to see a list of commands.

3. **Choose Settings or Call Settings.**

   The Call Settings command might be found on a second screen; choose Settings first, and then choose Call Settings. Eventually you'll see the call settings screen.

4. **Choose Call Forwarding.**

   If the option isn't available, use your cellular carrier to forward calls as described in the next section.

5. Choose one of the following options:

- *Always Forward:* All incoming calls are sent to the number you specify; your phone doesn't even ring. This option overrides all other forwarding options.

- *Forward When Busy:* Calls are forwarded when you're on the phone and choose not to answer. This option is normally used to send a missed call to voicemail, although you can forward to any number.

- *Forward When Unanswered:* Calls are forwarded when you choose not to answer the phone. Normally, the call is forwarded to your voicemail.

- *Forward When Unreached:* Calls are forwarded when the phone is turned off, out of range, or in airplane mode. As with the two previous settings, this option normally forwards calls to voicemail.

6. Set the forwarding number.

Or you can edit the number that already appears. For example, you can type your home number for the Forward When Unreached option so that your cell calls are redirected to your home number when you're out of range.

7. Touch Enable or OK.

The Call Forwarding status icon appears atop the touchscreen whenever you've activated an Android operating system forwarding option.

To disable call forwarding, touch the Disable icon when you're given the opportunity to type a forwarded phone number (refer to Step 6).

Forward calls by using your cellular provider

Some Android phones are forced to use the forwarding methods provided by the cellular provider rather than by the Android operating system. For example, the cellular provider Verizon in the United States, uses the call forwarding options described in Table 6-1.

Table 6-1	Verizon Call Forwarding Commands	
To Do This	*Input First Number*	*Input Second Number*
Forward unanswered incoming calls	*71	Forwarding number
Forward all incoming calls	*72	Forwarding number
Cancel call forwarding	*73	None

So, to forward all calls to (714) 555-4565, you input ***727145554565** and touch the green Phone icon on your Android phone. You hear only a brief tone after dialing, and then the call ends. After that, any call coming into your phone rings at the other number.

You must disable call forwarding to return to normal cell phone operations: Dial ***73.**

Sending a contact directly to voicemail

You can configure your phone to forward any of your phone's address book contacts directly to voicemail. It's a great way to deal with a pest! Follow these steps:

1. **Touch the Apps icon on the Home screen.**

2. **Open the People or Contacts app.**

   You need to access the phone's address book, so if it uses a name other than People or Contacts, open that app.

3. **Choose a contact.**

   Use your finger to scroll the list of contacts until you find the annoying person you want to eternally banish to voicemail. Display that person's contact information on the touchscreen.

4. **Touch the Action Overflow icon.**

   On some phones, touch the Menu icon instead to see a pop-up list of commands.

5. **Depending on your phone, choose one of the following commands:**

   - All Calls to Voicemail
   - Add to Reject List
   - Options, and then touch the square next to the Incoming Calls option

When the contact has been banished, you'll never receive another call from that person. Instead, you'll get a voicemail notification, but only if the caller chose to leave you a message.

To "unbanish" the contact, repeat these steps but in Step 5 deselect the option: Remove the check mark or choose the Remove from Reject List command.

- This feature is one reason you might want to retain contact information for someone with whom you never want to have contact.

- See Chapter 8 for more information on contacts.

- Also see Chapter 7, on voicemail.

Fun with Ringtones

I confess: Ringtones can be lots of fun. They uniquely identify your phone's jingle, especially when you forget to mute your phone and you're hustling to turn the thing off because everyone in the room is annoyed by your *We Will Rock You* ringtone.

On your Android phone, you can choose which ringtone you want. You can create your own ringtones or use snippets from your favorite tunes. You can also assign ringtones for individual contacts. This section explains how it's done.

Choosing the phone's ringtone

To select a new ringtone for your phone, or to simply confirm which ringtone you're using, follow these steps:

1. **At the Home screen, touch the Apps icon.**

2. **Open the Settings app and then choose Sound.**

3. **Choose Phone Ringtone or Ringtone.**

   If a ringtone app is installed, you may see a menu that asks you which source to use for the phone's ringtone. Choose Media Storage or Android System, and then touch the Just Once button. (See Chapter 24 for details on the Always/Just Once decision.)

4. **Choose a ringtone from the list that's displayed.**

   Scroll the list. Tap a ringtone to hear its preview.

5. **Touch OK to accept the new ringtone, or touch Cancel to keep the phone's ringtone as is.**

You can also set the ringtone used for notifications: In Step 3, choose the command Default Notification Sound or Notification Ringtone.

Text messaging ringtones are set from the Text Messaging or Hangouts app. See Chapter 9.

Setting a contact's ringtone

Ringtones can be assigned by contact so that when your annoying friend Larry calls, you can have your phone yelp like a whiny puppy. Here's how to set a ringtone for a contact:

1. **Open the People or Contacts app.**

   The app may be found on the Home screen, or it can be located in the apps drawer.

2. **From the list, choose the contact to which you want to assign a ringtone.**

3. **Locate the Ringtones command.**

    Touch the Action Overflow or Menu icon and choose the Ringtone or Set Ringtone command. On some phones, you may have to edit the contact to see a Ringtone command or category.

4. **If prompted, choose the app to supply the ringtone.**

    For example, you may see a prompt that lists various ringtone apps, including the phone's Media Storage app and the Zedge app. Choose the app, and then touch Just Once or Always. See Chapter 24 for information on the difference between those options.

5. **Choose a ringtone from the list.**

    It's the same list that's displayed for the phone's ringtones.

6. **Touch OK to assign the ringtone to the contact.**

Whenever the contact calls, the phone rings using the ringtone you've specified.

To remove a specific ringtone for a contact, repeat the steps in this section but in Step 5 choose Default Ringtone. (It's found at the top of the list of ringtones.) This choice sets the contact's ringtone to be the same as the phone's ringtone.

Also see Chapter 8 for information on banishing a specific contact directly to voicemail.

7

Leave Your Message at the Tone

*V*oicemail is nothing new. Way back when, it was called "Can you take a message?" The person taking the message was only as reliable as such persons can be. Teenagers? They didn't take the best messages. Therefore, concerned telephone scientists developed answering machines. Those gizmos eventually morphed into the voicemail system, which is merely a fancier term for *answering machine* or *an electronic gizmo that takes a message.* See? Nothing is new.

Your phone doesn't really have a voicemail system. Nope, that's the job of your cellular provider. It's the same, boring voicemail system they offer to all their cell phone customers, even customers who have non-Android phones or those dreaded non-smartphones, or dumb-phones. That choice isn't the end of your voicemail options, however, as this chapter cleverly describes.

oicemail   📞   ▷

Marie Antoinette
(211) 555-1793
Received: 14:12 (9 secs)

Hi Dan, **This is Mary. Please call me back. I**
someone **to talk to bye.**

Boring Carrier Voicemail

The most basic, and most stupid, form of voicemail is the free voicemail service provided by your cell phone company. This standard feature has few frills and nothing that stands out differently for your nifty Android phone.

Carrier voicemail picks up missed calls as well as calls you thrust into voicemail. A notification icon, looking similar to the one shown in the margin, appears whenever someone leaves you a voicemail message. You can use the notification to dial into your carrier's voicemail system, listen to your calls, and use the phone's dialpad to delete messages or repeat messages or use other features you probably don't know about because no one ever pays attention to them.

Setting up carrier voicemail

If you haven't yet done it, set up voicemail on your phone. I recommend doing so even if you plan on using another voicemail service, such as Google Voice. That's because carrier voicemail, despite all my grousing, remains a valid and worthy fallback option when those other services don't work.

Even if you believe your voicemail to be set up and configured, consider churning through these steps, just to be sure:

1. **Open the Phone app.**

2. **Touch the Action Overflow icon and then choose the Settings command.**

   On some phones you need to touch the Menu icon to access the Settings command.

3. **On the settings screen, choose Call Settings.**

4. **On the call settings screen, choose Voicemail or Voicemail Service.**

5. **Choose My Carrier, if it isn't chosen already.**

   Or, if it's the only option, you're set.

When the My Carrier option is chosen, the phone number listed for voicemail is your carrier's voicemail service. You can confirm that number by choosing the Setup or Voicemail Settings command on the voicemail screen.

After performing the steps in this section, call the carrier voicemail service to finish the setup: Set your name, a voicemail password, a greeting, and various other steps as guided by your cellular provider's cheerful robot.

✔ If your Android phone features speed dial, long-pressing the 1 key on the dialpad connects you with your carrier's voicemail service.

✔ Some versions of the Phone app feature a Voicemail icon on the dialpad. Use it to quickly connect to your carrier's voicemail service.

✔ Your phone may also feature a Voicemail app, which you can use to collect and review your messages.

✔ Complete your voicemail setup by creating a customized greeting. If you don't, you may not receive voicemail messages, or people may believe that they've dialed the wrong number.

Retrieving your messages

When you have a voicemail message looming, the New Voicemail notification icon appears on the status bar, similar to the one shown in the margin. You can either pull down this notification to connect to the voicemail service or dial into the voicemail service by long-pressing the 1 key on the Phone or Dialer app's dialpad.

What happens next depends on how your carrier has configured its voicemail service. Typically, you have to input your PIN or password, and then new messages play or you hear a menu of options. My advice: Look at the phone so that you can see the dialpad, and touch the Speaker icon so that you can hear the prompts.

In case you need to remember the prompts, you can write them down here:

Press _____ to listen to the first message.

Press _____ to delete the message.

Press _____ to skip a message.

Press _____ to hear the menu options.

Press _____ to hang up.

While you're at it, in case you ever forget your voicemail password, write it down here:

_____

The Wonders of Google Voice

Perhaps the best option I've found for working with voicemail is something called Google Voice. It's more than just a voicemail system: You can use *Google Voice* to make phone calls in the United States, place cheap international calls, and perform other amazing feats. In this section, I extol the virtues of using Google Voice as the voicemail system on your Android phone.

✔ Even when you choose to use Google Voice, I still recommend setting up and configuring the boring carrier voicemail, as covered earlier in this chapter.

✔ With Google Voice configured as your phone's voicemail service, your voicemail messages arrive in the form of a Gmail message. The message's text is a transcription of the voicemail message.

✔ Better than reading a Gmail message is receiving a Google Voice message by using the Google Voice app. See the section "Using the Google Voice app."

✔ You may need to reset Google Voice after using call forwarding. That's because Google Voice relies upon forwarding unanswered or dismissed calls. See Chapter 6 for more information on call forwarding.

Configuring Google Voice

You need to create a Google Voice account on the Internet before you configure your Android phone for use with Google Voice. Start your adventure by visiting the Google Voice home page at `http://voice.google.com`. I recommend using a computer to complete these steps:

1. **If necessary, sign in to your Google account on the Google Voice web page.**

   You use the same account name and password that you use to access your Gmail.

2. **Accept the terms of service, if prompted.**

3. **Choose to use your existing mobile number.**

4. **Type your cell phone's number if prompted.**

   Google Voice checks for availability.

5. **Select the option to use Google Voice Lite.**

   Upon success, the Verify Your Phone step appears on the computer's screen. Google Voice calls your phone and prompts you to type a two-digit number, shown on the screen.

6. **Click the Call Me Now button.**

   Google Voice dials your phone to confirm the number.

7. **Answer the incoming call.**

   You might want to display the keypad and use the speaker while you're on this call.

8. **Use the keypad to type the number on the computer screen.**

   On my computer's screen, I see the number 10. I type that number on my Android phone to confirm my account.

9. **Use your phone to configure Google Voice.**

   You'll set your name and a greeting — typical voicemail stuff.

10. **On the computer, type and confirm a PIN number.**

    The PIN is used to access Google Voice via your phone. Again, this process is typical for setting up any voicemail account.

11. **On your phone, dial the phone number displayed on the computer's screen.**

    It's going to be a long, complex, weird-looking number. Type it exactly as shown. Effectively, you're programming the phone to forward unanswered calls to the Google Voice service.

    A confirmation message appears briefly on the phone, indicating that the action was successful.

12. **On the computer screen, click the Continue button.**

    You're done.

A Google Voice access number appears on the computer screen. Write that number here for future reference:

My Google Voice access number: (_____) _____ - _____

I also recommend creating a contact for your Google Voice access number. Create the new contact per the directions in Chapter 8. And while you're at it, consider bookmarking the Google Voice website on your computer.

Although this step configures a Google Voice account, you still need to program your phone to use Google Voice as its voicemail service. That's best accomplished by installing the Google Voice app. See the later section, "Using the Google Voice app."

 Google Voice offers a host of features: international dialing, call forwarding, and other stuff I am not aware of and, honestly, am quite afraid of. It's possible, however, merely to use Google Voice as a voicemail service, which is what I recommend.

Adding a second line to Google Voice

When you already have a Google Voice account, you add your new Android phone's number to the list of phone numbers already registered for Google Voice. Here's how that's done:

1. **Visit the Google Voice web page on the Internet at** voice.google.com.

    This process works best using a computer.

2. **Click the Gear icon in the upper-right corner of the Google Voice home page, and choose the Settings command from the menu.**

    The Settings command may change its location in a future update to the Google Voice web page. If so, the purpose of this step is to access the settings screen, where you register phone numbers for use with Google Voice.

3. **Click the Add Another Phone link.**

4. **Work the steps to verify your phone for use with Google Voice.**

   As this book goes to press, the steps involve typing a name for the phone, such as My Nexus 5, and then typing the phone's number, including the area code.

   Eventually, Google Voice needs to phone your cell phone.

5. **When Google Voice calls your cell phone, use the dialpad on your phone to type the code number you see on your computer's screen.**

   After confirming the code number, you see your Android phone listed as a registered phone — but you're not done yet.

6. **Click the Activate Voicemail link.**

   You must activate your phone for it to work with Google Voice. This step is the most important one in adding your number to Google Voice!

7. **On your phone, dial the number you see on your computer screen, or otherwise obey the instructions to forward your busy, unanswered, or unreachable calls to the Google Voice number.**

   Refer to Chapter 6 for more information on call forwarding options.

8. **On your computer screen, click the Done button.**

Your Android phone is now registered for use with Google Voice.

Using the Google Voice app

Google Voice transcribes your voicemail messages, turning the audio from the voicemail into a text message you can read. The messages all show up eventually in your Gmail inbox, just as though someone sent you an e-mail rather than left you voicemail. It's a good way to deal with your messages, but not the best way.

The best way to handle Google Voice is to use the Google Voice app, available from the Google Play Store, although you may find a copy already dwelling in the phone's apps drawer. (See Chapter 18 for details on obtaining apps at the Google Play Store.)

After the Google Voice app is installed, you have to work through the setup, which isn't difficult: The goal is to switch over the phone's voicemail number from the carrier's voicemail system to Google Voice. Eventually, you see the app's main interface, which looks and works similarly to an e-mail program. You can review your messages or touch a message to read or play it, as illustrated in Figure 7-1.

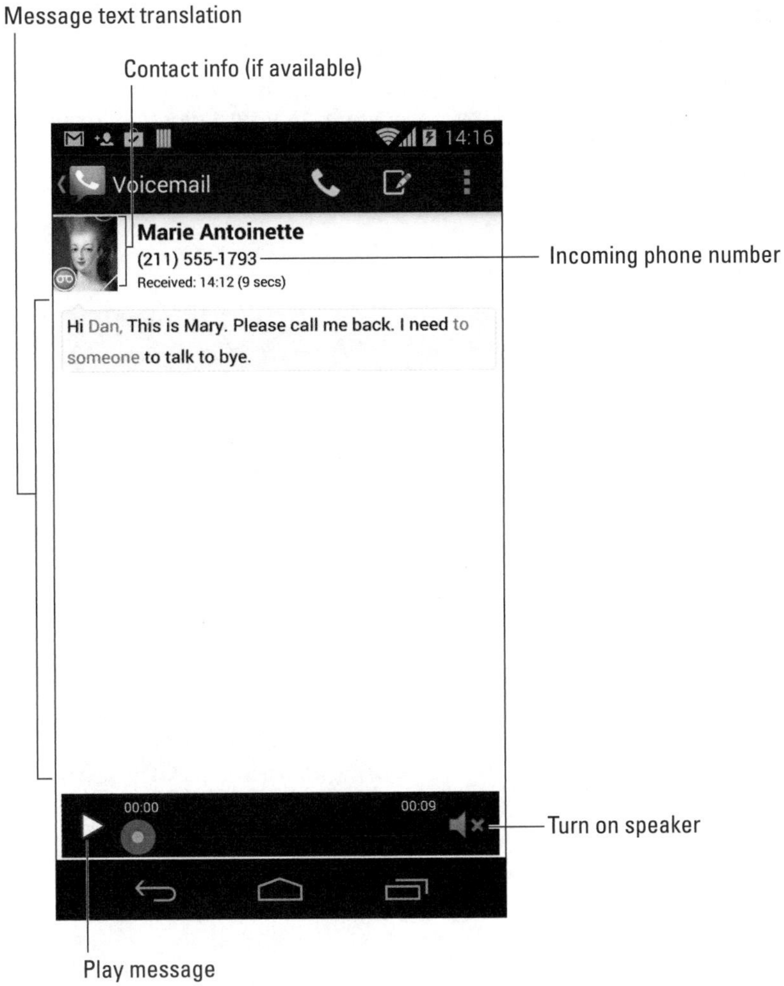

Message text translation

Contact info (if available)

Marie Antoinette
(211) 555-1793 ———————————— Incoming phone number
Received: 14:12 (9 secs)

Hi Dan, This is Mary. Please call me back. I need to
someone to talk to bye.

00:00   00:09 ◀× ——— Turn on speaker

Play message

Figure 7-1: Voicemail with the Google Voice app.

 When new Google Voice messages come in, you see the Google Voice notification icon, as shown in the margin. To read or listen to the message, pull down the notifications and choose the item labeled Voicemail from *whomever*.

✓ With Google Voice installed, you see two notices for every voicemail message: one from Google Voice and another for the Gmail message.

 ✓ The Google Voice app works only after you acquire a Google Voice account and add your Android phone's number to that account. See the earlier section, "Configuring Google Voice."

- ✔ The text translation feature in Google Voice is at times astonishingly accurate and at other times not so good.

- ✔ The text *Transcript Not Available* appears whenever Google Voice is unable to create a text message from your voicemail or whenever the Google Voice service is temporarily unavailable.

Part III
Stay Connected

Learn how to work with contact groups at www.dummies.com/extras/
androidphones.

In this part . . .

- Use the address book.
- Try text messaging.
- Send Gmail and e-mail.
- Discover the web on a cell phone.
- Connect with social networking.
- Dig into text, voice, and video chat.

8

The Address Book

In This Chapter

▶ Examining your phone's contacts

▶ Sorting and searching contacts

▶ Creating contacts

▶ Getting a contact from a map search

▶ Editing contact information

▶ Putting a picture on a contact

▶ Working with favorites

▶ Deleting contacts

*O*nce upon a time, humans went to the trouble of memorizing phone numbers. They didn't commit everyone's number to memory, just a few key contacts. So if a kid were stranded at the bowling alley, he could phone Mom's workplace, Grandpa, or even a neighbor lady to ask for a lift.

Today, memorizing phone numbers is pretty much a thing of the past. That's because your Android phone adeptly stores all that information. The task is handled by the phone's address book app, which also conveniently stores e-mail addresses, physical addresses, and even random information such as birthdays or anniversaries. It's indispensable.

PHONE

202-456-1111

ƆME

The People You Know

The phone's address book is accessed from a number of apps, such as Gmail, Email, and Hangouts. The address book app might be named People or Contacts. People is the stock Android name; Samsung phones tend to use Contacts. Your phone might even call the address book app by another name. Regardless, it's the app you use to see information about the people you know.

- The phone's address book is accessible also from the Phone or Dialer app. Touch the Contacts tab or choose the Contacts item from a list or pop-up menu.

- Unlike other address books, your phone's address book might already be packed with contacts. That's because your Google account was synchronized when you first set up the phone. And if you've added other accounts and social networking apps, those contacts are present as well.

- If you haven't yet set up a Google account, refer to Chapter 2.

- See Chapter 12 for more information on social networking.

- Adding more contacts is covered later in this chapter, in the section "Make New Friends."

Accessing the address book

To peruse your phone's address book, open the People or Contacts app. You may find a launcher icon on the Home screen, but you'll certainly find the app in the apps drawer.

Figure 8-1 shows the People app on a typical Android phone. The address book on your phone may look subtly different, but most of the items illustrated in the figure should be there.

Scroll the list by swiping your finger on the touchscreen. You can use the index on the side of the screen (refer to Figure 8-1) to quickly scroll the list up and down. Large letters may appear as you scroll to help you find your place.

Figure 8-1: The Contacts list.

To do anything with a contact, you first have to choose it: Touch a contact name, and you see more information, similar to what's shown in Figure 8-2.

The list of activities you can do with the contact depends on the information shown and the apps installed on the phone. Here are some options.

Place a phone call. To call the contact, touch one of the contact's phone entries, such as Home or Mobile. You touch either the entry itself or the Phone icon by the entry.

Phone contact

Return to address book

Favorites

‹ Barack Obama

Action Overflow
(Edit, Delete, and so on)

PHONE

202-456-1111
HOME

Send text message

EMAIL

potus@whitehouse.gov
WORK

E-mail contact

ADDRESS

1600 Pennsylvania Ave
Washington , D.C. 20006
HOME

View location

SPECIAL DATES

Figure 8-2: More details about a contact.

Send a text message. Touch the Text Message icon (refer to Figure 8-2) to open the Text Messaging app and send the contact a message. See Chapter 9 for information about text messaging.

Send e-mail: Touch the contact's e-mail address to compose an e-mail message using the Gmail or Email app. When the contact has more than one e-mail address, you can choose to which one you want to send the message. Chapter 10 covers using e-mail on your phone.

Locate your contact on a map. When the contact has a home or business address, you can touch the contact's address, shown in Figure 8-2, to summon the Maps app. Refer to Chapter 14 to see all the fun stuff you can do with Maps.

View social networking info. Visit the contact's Facebook, Twitter, or other social networking account by touching the appropriate item. See Chapter 12 for additional information about social networking on your Android phone.

Some tidbits of information that show up for a contact don't have an associated action. For example, the phone won't sing *Happy Birthday* when you touch a contact's birthday information.

- ✔ Touch the Back icon to view the main address book list after you've viewed a contact's information.

- ✔ Not every contact has a picture, and the picture can come from a number of sources (Gmail or Facebook, for example). See the section "Adding a contact picture" for more information.

- ✔ Many Android phones feature an account named Me. That's your own information as known by the phone. The Me account may be in addition to your other accounts shown in the address book.

- ✔ Some cellular providers add accounts to your phone's address book. You may see entries such as BAL, MIN, or Warranty Center. Those aren't real people; they're shortcuts to various services. For example, the BAL contact is used on Verizon phones to get a text message listing your current account balance.

- ✔ When a contact is referred to as a *joined contact,* the information you see comes from multiple sources, such as Gmail or Facebook. See the section "Joining identical contacts" for information on joining contacts, as well as the section "Separating contacts" for information on splitting improperly joined contacts.

Sorting the address book

The phone's address book displays contacts in a certain order, such as alphabetically by first name first. You can change the order to whatever you like by following these steps:

1. **Open the phone's address book app.**

   It's named either People or Contacts.

2. **Touch the Action Overflow icon and choose Settings.**

   On some phones, touch the Menu icon instead of the Action Overflow icon.

3. **Choose Sort List By to specify how contacts are sorted: by First Name or Last Name.**

   If you don't see the Sort List By command, choose the Display Options command first. The Sort List By command might also be titled List By.

 4. **Choose View Contact Names to specify how the contacts appear in the list: First Name First or Last Name First.**

   This option might be named Display Contacts By on some phones. Also, some phones may use Given Name and Family Name instead of First Name and Last Name.

The address book is updated, displayed per your preferences.

> ✔ You can't mess up the address book sorting or display options. Whatever works for you is great. For example, I prefer my phone's address book sorted by last name and listed first name first.

> ✔ The way the name is displayed doesn't affect the sort order. So if you choose First Name First (as I do) as well as Last Name for the sort order (as I do), you still see the list sorted by last name.

Searching contacts

Rather than scroll your phone's address book with angst-riddled desperation, touch the Search icon. The Search Contacts text box appears. Type a few letters of the contact's name, and you see the list of contacts narrowed to the few who match the letters you type. Touch a name from the search list to view the contact's information.

> ✔ You may find a Search text box always available in some People or Contacts apps, in which case there's no need to first find and touch the Search icon.

> ✔ To clear a search, touch the X, found in the Search text box.

> ✔ No, there's no correlation between the number of contacts you have and how popular you are in real life.

Make New Friends

Having friends is great. Having more friends is better. You'll find myriad ways to add new friends and place new contacts into your phone. This section lists a few of the more popular and useful methods.

Adding a contact from the call log

One of the quickest ways to build up your phone's address book is to add people as they phone you. After someone calls, visit the call log to add that person. Obey these steps:

 1. **Open the Phone or Dialer app.**

 2. **Display the call log.**

Touch the Call Log icon or the History icon, or choose the Call Log or Recent tab at the top of the screen.

3. **Choose the phone number from the list of recent calls.**

   The phone number is shown by itself, minus any contact picture or other information.

4. **Choose Add to Contacts or Create Contact.**

   The phone wants to know whether you're creating a contact or adding the phone number to an existing contact. In this case, I'm assuming that you're creating a contact; otherwise you'd choose an existing contact from the address book list.

5. **If you chose Add to Contacts in Step 4, choose Create a New Contact.**

   The Add to Contacts prompt appears only on some phones, specifically those that don't show a Create Contact option in Step 4.

6. **Choose an account in which to store the contact and, if prompted, touch the OK button.**

   All entries in the phone's address book are associated with a specific account, such as your Gmail account. I recommend choosing your Google (Gmail) account to store the new contact. In that way, you ensure that the contact's information is duplicated from your phone to your Google account on the Internet.

   Other options may also present themselves for storing contact information. For example, if you use Yahoo! Mail more than Google (and Yahoo! Mail is available as a choice), you can choose that option instead.

   You can, optionally, place a green check mark by the Remember This Choice setting so that you're not prompted again to choose an account.

7. **Fill in the contact's information.**

   Fill in the blanks, as many as you know about the caller: name, e-mail, address, and so on. If you don't know any additional information, that's fine; just filling in the name helps clue you in to who is calling the next time that person calls (using the same number).

   Touch the Next button on the onscreen keyboard to hop between the various text fields.

   I recommend that you add the area code prefix to the phone number, if it's not automatically added for you.

8. **Touch the Done or Save button to add the new contact.**

You can also follow these steps to add a new phone number to an existing contact. In Step 4, choose the existing contact from your phone's address book. The new phone number is added to that contact's information.

✔ On some Android phones, you create a new account by long-pressing a recent entry in the call log and choosing the Save to People command.

✔ One account option (Step 6) available on some phones is the Phone or Local account. That choice saves the contact's information only on your phone, not in any other location. I do not recommend that you choose this option because the contact won't be shared with other Android devices or your Internet accounts.

✔ You can create new contacts also from an e-mail message similar to the way you create contacts by using the call log: Touch the picture icon on an incoming message and choose the Create Contact action. Proceed with Steps 6–8 as described in this section. Refer to Chapter 10 for information on using your phone to read e-mail.

Creating a new contact from scratch

Sometimes it's necessary to create a contact when you meet another human being in the real world. In that case, you have more information to input, and it starts like this:

1. **Open the People or Contacts app.**

2. **Touch the Add icon to start creating the new contact.**

   An example of what the Add icon looks like is shown in the margin, though it could also simply be a plus (+) icon. If you can't find it, touch the Action Overflow or Menu icon and choose the New Contact command.

3. **If prompted, choose an account as the place to store the contact.**

   I recommend choosing Google, unless you use another account, such as Yahoo!, listed as your main Internet mail account.

4. **Fill in the information on the add contact screen.**

   Fill in the text fields with the information you know. The more information you provide, the better.

   Use the Action Bar icon (shown in the margin) to expand a field. You may see a pop-up window with specific controls, commands, or options. Use the pop-up to help fill in the field or provide specific information, such as whether a phone number is a mobile, work, or home number.

   Some items may have a large plus sign icon next to them, or you may see the text Add New. Touch that icon or text to add another phone number, e-mail address, or other item. If you see a minus sign icon or Cancel text, you can touch it to remove multiple items.

At the bottom of the new contact screen, you'll find the Add Another Field button. Use that button when you want to add more details for the contact, such as a birthday or website.

5. **Touch the Done or Save button to complete editing and add the new contact.**

The new contact is created. As a bonus, it's also automatically synced with your Google account, or whichever account you chose in Step 3.

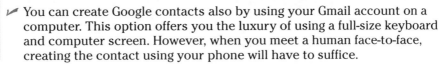

✔ Information from social networking sites is automatically stirred into the contacts list, although sometimes the process creates duplicate entries. See the "Joining identical contacts" section to remedy such a situation.

✔ You can create Google contacts also by using your Gmail account on a computer. This option offers you the luxury of using a full-size keyboard and computer screen. However, when you meet a human face-to-face, creating the contact using your phone will have to suffice.

Importing contacts from your computer

Your computer's e-mail program is doubtless a useful repository of contacts you've built up over the years. You can export these contacts from your computer's e-mail program and then import them into your Android phone. The process isn't the simplest thing to do, but it is a quick way to build up your phone's address book.

The key is to save or export your computer e-mail program's records in the *vCard* (.vcf) file format. These records can then be imported into the phone and read by the address book app. The method for exporting contacts varies depending on the e-mail program:

✔ **In the Windows Live Mail program,** choose Go⇨Contacts, and then choose File⇨Export⇨Business Card (.VCF) to export the contacts.

✔ **In Windows Mail,** choose File⇨Export⇨Windows Contacts, and then choose vCards (Folder of .VCF Files) from the Export Windows Contacts dialog box. Click the Export button.

✔ **On the Mac,** open the Address Book program, and choose File⇨ Export⇨Export vCard.

After the vCard files are created, connect the phone to your computer and transfer the vCard files from your computer to the phone. Directions for making this type of transfer are found in Chapter 20.

After the vCard files have been copied to the phone, you import them into the phone's address book. The method varies from phone to phone.

For most Android phones importing contacts works something like this:

1. **In the People or Contacts app, touch the Action Overflow icon.**

   On some Android phones, touch the Menu icon.

2. **Choose Import/Export.**

3. **Choose the Import from Storage command.**

   This command may be titled Import from SD Card.

4. **Choose to save the contacts to your Google account.**

5. **If prompted, choose the option Import All vCard Files.**

6. **Touch the OK button.**

   Work any additional steps, such as choosing an account type or touching the OK button if prompted.

The imported contacts are also synchronized to your Gmail account, or whichever account you choose (Step 4), which instantly creates a backup copy.

 If you're using Microsoft Outlook and have Exchange Server, add your Outlook contacts by adding your Exchange Server account to the list of accounts available on the phone. All your Outlook contacts, as well as scheduling and other information, are automatically synchronized with your Android phone. See Chapter 2 for information on adding accounts.

Bringing in social networking contacts

You can pour your whole gang of friends and followers into your Android phone from your social networking sites. The operation is automatic: Simply add the social networking site's app to the phone's app inventory as described in Chapter 12. At that time, either you'll be prompted to sync the contacts or they're added instantly to the phone's address book.

Building a new contact from a location

When you use the Maps application to locate a restaurant, a cobbler, or an apothecary, you can quickly create a contact for that business based on its location. Here's how:

1. **After searching for your location by using the Maps app, touch the location's card that appears on the screen.**

   Refer to Chapter 14 for information on how to search for locations.

2. **Touch the Phone icon as if you were calling the place.**

   But you're not calling the place: By touching the Phone icon you start the Phone or Dialer app, where the location's number is displayed.

When a location lacks a Phone icon, you cannot use the Maps app to create a contact.

3. **Choose the Add to Contacts or Add As a Contact command.**

   The command appears when you are about to call a number that isn't in the phone's address book.

4. **Choose the Create New Contact command.**

5. **Fill in information about the business.**

   A long time ago in a galaxy far, far away, the Android operating system actually filled this information in for you by using the Maps app search results. If that's true on your phone, great! Otherwise, you need to manually type in the business name.

6. **Touch the Done or Save button.**

   The new contact is created.

The preferred technique for saving a business in the Maps app is to flag that location as a favorite. See Chapter 14 for details.

Address Book Management

Sure, some folks just can't leave well enough alone. For example, some of your friends may change their phone numbers. They may move. They may finally get rid of their 20-year-old AOL e-mail addresses. When such things occur, you must undertake the task of address book management.

Making basic changes

To make minor touch-ups on any contact, start by locating and displaying the contact's information in the address book app. Touch the Edit icon and start making changes. If the Edit icon isn't visible, touch the Action Overflow or Menu icon and choose the Edit command.

Change or add information by touching a field and typing on the onscreen keyboard. You can edit information as well: Touch a field to change whatever you want.

Some information cannot be edited. For example, fields pulled in from social networking sites can be edited only by that account holder on the social networking site.

When you're done editing, touch the Save button.

Adding a contact picture

To add a picture to a contact, you can snap a picture and save it, grab a picture from the Internet, or use any image already stored in the phone's Gallery app. The image doesn't even have to be a picture of the contact — any image will do.

After the contact's photo or any other suitable image is stored on the phone, follow these steps to update the contact's information:

1. **Locate and display the contact's information.**

2. **Edit the contact's information.**

   Touch the Edit icon or, if it's unavailable, touch the Action Overflow or Menu icon and choose the Edit or Edit Contact command.

3. **Touch the icon where the contact's picture would go, or touch the existing picture assigned to the contact.**

   When no picture is assigned, the icon shows a generic human image.

4. **Touch the Choose Photo from Gallery command.**

   The option could be titled Select Photo from Gallery or just Gallery.

   If you have another image management app on your phone, you can instead choose the app's command from the list.

5. **Browse the Gallery to look for a suitable image.**

   See Chapter 15 for more information on using the Gallery app.

6. **Touch the image you want to use for the contact.**

7. **Optionally, crop the image.**

   You can use Figure 8-3 as a guide, though the cropping tool on your phone may look different from the one shown in the figure.

8. **Touch the Save button to set the cropped image.**

   At this point, the image is cropped and set in the contact's information, but that information hasn't yet been saved.

9. **If necessary, touch the Done or Save button to finish editing the contact.**

   The image is assigned, and it appears whenever the contact is referenced on your phone.

Drag corners to resize

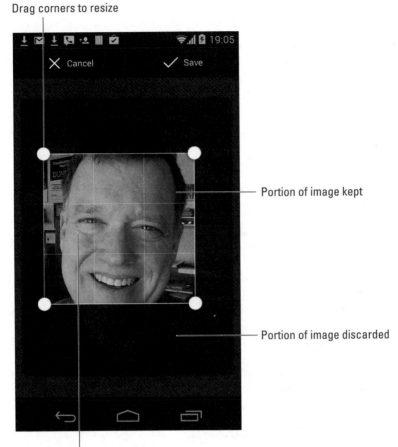

Portion of image kept

Portion of image discarded

Drag crop rectangle

Figure 8-3: Cropping a contact's image.

The contact's image appears when the person calls, in the text messaging app, as well as other instances when the contact is referenced in your phone.

✔ When the contact has no image, a generic image or icon appears.

✔ If you would rather use the phone to take a picture of the contact, choose the Take Photo or Take New Photo command in Step 4. Use the phone's Camera app to take a picture; see Chapter 15 for details on using the Camera app. After you've taken the picture, touch OK or the check mark icon, and then proceed with Step 7.

✔ Pictures can also be added by your Gmail friends and contacts when they add their own images to their accounts.

✔ You may also see pictures assigned to your contacts based on pictures supplied on Facebook or other social networking sites.

✔ Some images in the Gallery may not work for contact icons. For example, images synchronized with your online photo albums may be unavailable.

✔ To remove or change a contact's picture, follow Steps 1–3 in the preceding list. Choose the Remove Photo command to get rid of the existing image.

Making a favorite

A *favorite* contact is someone you stay in touch with most often. The person doesn't have to be someone you like — just someone you (perhaps unfortunately) phone often, such as your bookie.

To create a favorite, display a contact's information and touch the Star icon. When the star is highlighted, the contact is flagged as one of your favorites.

Favorite contacts appear in their own tab on the People or Contacts app, as well as in the Phone or Dialer app (refer to Figure 8-1). To quickly access a favorite, choose the person from the tab.

✔ To remove a favorite, touch the contact's star again. Removing a favorite doesn't delete the contact.

✔ A contact has no idea whether he's one of your favorites, so don't believe that you're hurting his feelings by not making him a favorite.

Joining identical contacts

Your Android phone can pull in contacts from multiple sources (such as Facebook, Gmail, and Twitter). Because of this, you may discover duplicate contact entries in the phone's address book. Rather than fuss over which contact to use, you can join them. Here's how:

1. **Wildly scroll the address book until you locate a duplicate.**

   Well, maybe not *wildly* scroll, but locate a duplicated entry. Because the address book is sorted, the duplicates appear close together (though that may not always be the case).

2. **Select one of the duplicate contacts.**

3. **Touch the Action Overflow or Menu icon and choose the Join command.**

   You may have to first edit the contact, and then touch the Action Overflow or Menu icon to find the Join command. That command might also be titled Join Contact or Link Contact.

After choosing the command, you see a list of contacts that the phone guesses could be identical. It also shows the entire list of contacts in case the guess is incorrect. Your job is to find the duplicate contact.

4. **Choose the duplicate contact from the list.**

The contacts are merged, appearing as a single entry in the address book.

Joined contacts aren't flagged as such in the address book, but you can easily identify them: When looking at the contact's information, a joined contact looks like a single long entry often showing two sources or accounts from which the contact's information is pulled.

Separating contacts

The topic of separating contacts has little to do with parenting, although separating bickering children is the first step to avoiding a fight. Contacts in the address book might not be bickering, but occasionally the phone may automatically join two contacts that aren't really the same person. When that happens, you can split them by following these steps:

1. **Display the improperly joined contact.**

As an example, I'm Facebook friends with other humans named Dan Gookin. My phone accidentally joined my address book entry with another Dan Gookin.

2. **Touch the Action Overflow or Menu icon and choose the Separate command.**

The command might not be available, in which case you need to edit the contact, as described earlier in this chapter. You would then touch the Action Overflow or Menu icon to choose the Separate command.

The Separate command might also be called Separate Contacts.

3. **Touch the OK button to confirm that you're splitting the contacts.**

You don't need to actively look for improperly joined contacts — you'll just stumble across them. When you do, feel free to separate them, especially if you detect any bickering.

Removing a contact

Every so often, consider reviewing your phone's contacts. Purge the folks whom you no longer recognize or you've forgotten. It's simple: View the forlorn contact and touch the Trash icon, shown in the margin. Touch the OK button to confirm. Poof! They're gone.

On some phones, you may have to touch the Action Overflow or Menu icon, and then choose a Delete command. Touch the OK button to remove the contact.

- ✔ Because the phone's address book is synchronized with your Google account, the contact is also removed there.

- ✔ You may not be able to delete contacts associated with specific accounts, such as your social networking friends. To remove those contacts, you need to go to the source, such as Facebook or Twitter.

- ✔ Removing a contact doesn't kill the person in real life.

9

Text Messaging Mania

*T*exting is the popular name for using your Android smartphone to send short, typed messages to another cell phone. Doing so basically turns your sophisticated, twenty-first century mobile communications device into something roughly the equivalent of a nineteenth-century telegraph. Still, texting has its place; teenagers find texting preferable for their communications needs. It's useful, and often best, to send a short burst of text to someone rather than to hold a phone call. In fact, I often text a friend to say "Are you available?" before I call, just to ensure that they have time to talk. And I'm definitely not a teenager.

...iah Gookin
Aug 11, 14:35

How 'bout them Patriots?
Aug 11, 14:35

Awesome
Aug 11, 14:36

Would you like some nuts?
Nov 2, 11:31

Are they in town again?
Nov 2, 11:36

Msg 4U

I can think of several reasons to use your Android phone's texting capabilities. First, texting is short and quick. Second, unlike a phone call, texting is quiet. Third, it's probably the only way you'll get your children or grandchildren to communicate with you.

✔ If you're over 25, you might want to know that the translation of this section's title is "Message for You."

✔ Don't text while you're driving.

✔ Don't text in a movie theater.

✔ Don't text in any situation where it's distracting.

✔ Your cellular service plan may charge for each text message you send. Some plans feature a given number of free (included) messages per month. Other plans, favored by teenagers (and their parents), feature unlimited texting.

✔ The nerdy term for text messaging is *SMS,* which stands for Short Message Service.

Choosing a texting app

Traditionally, Android phones come with one texting app. It's usually called Texting, although Messages, Messaging, and Text Messaging are also popular. The Google Hangouts app can also handle text messages, and it might be your phone's only texting app.

However things work out, you can set the official texting app for your phone by following these steps:

1. **Start the Settings app.**

   Choose the Settings app from the apps drawer.

2. **Choose More or More Settings.**

3. **Choose the Default SMS App command.**

4. **Choose the text messaging app from the menu.**

   If the only option available is Hangouts, that's your SMS app.

The app you choose is the one that receives text messages. You can still use any text messaging app on your phone to compose and send messages.

You can also disable the receipt of text messages from the Hangouts app. Use this procedure if the preceding steps don't work:

1. **Start the Hangouts app.**

2. **Touch the Action Overflow or Menu icon.**

3. **Choose the Settings command.**

   If you don't see this command, display the main Hangouts screen: Touch the app icon in the upper-left corner of the screen until the main screen appears.

4. **Add or remove the check mark by the Turn on SMS option.**

   If you choose to remove the check mark, Hangouts no longer catches incoming text messages.

You cannot disable Hangouts from being your phone's main texting app when no other texting app is available.

Whether to send a text message or an e-mail

Sending a text message is similar to sending an e-mail message. Both involve the instant electronic delivery of a message to someone else. And both methods of communication have their advantages and disadvantages.

The primary limitation of a text message is that it can be sent only to another cell phone. If you use Hangouts as your text messaging app, you can also send a text message to someone with a computer or tablet, but that person also has to be using Hangouts.

E-mail is available to anyone who has an e-mail address, whether or not the person uses a mobile communications device.

Text messages are pithy — short and to the point. They're informal, more like quick chats. Indeed, the speed of reply is often what makes text messaging useful. Like sending e-mail, however, sending a text message doesn't guarantee a reply.

An e-mail message can be longer than a text message. You can receive e-mail on just about any Internet-connected device. E-mail message attachments (pictures, documents) are handled better and more consistently than text message (MMS) media.

Finally, e-mail is considered a wee bit more formal than a text message. But if you're after formal, make a phone call or send a letter.

Composing a text message

Text messages are sent primarily to other cell phones. As long as you have a mobile number to send to, or a contact with a mobile phone, you can fire away the text message. Here's how it works:

1. **Open the phone's texting app.**

   You see a list of current conversations (if any), organized by contact name or phone number. If not, press the Back icon to get to that main screen.

2. **If you see the name of the person you want to text, choose it from the list. Otherwise, touch the Add icon.**

   You might see the New Message or Compose Message command instead of the Add icon (shown in the margin).

3. **If you're starting a new conversation, type a contact name or cell phone number.**

   When the number you type matches one or more existing contacts, those contacts are displayed. Choose one to send a message to that person; otherwise, continue typing the phone number.

   You can add multiple recipients, if you like. Just keep adding contacts or phone numbers. Not every text messaging app offers this feature.

4. **If you're using Hangouts, you may be prompted to send an SMS or find the person on Hangouts. Choose the option to send an SMS.**

5. Type your text message.

Figure 9-1 illustrates a typical text message conversation.

6. Touch the Send icon to send the message.

The Send icon may look similar to what's shown in the margin.

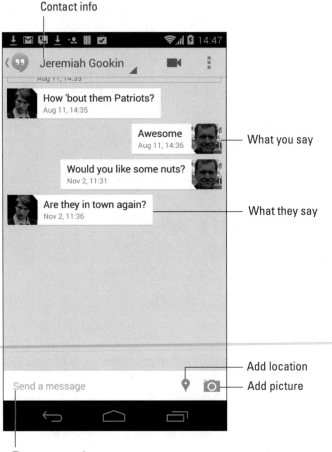

Contact info

Jeremiah Gookin

How 'bout them Patriots?
Aug 11, 14:35

Awesome
Aug 11, 14:36 — What you say

Would you like some nuts?
Nov 2, 11:31

Are they in town again?
Nov 2, 11:36 — What they say

Add location
Add picture

Send a message

Type message here

Figure 9-1: Texting in the Hangouts app.

If you've sent the message to a phone number instead of a contact, consider adding that number to the phone's address book. One way to do that is to long-press the number and choose the command to create a new contact. See Chapter 8 for information on creating contacts.

You can send a text message also from the phone's address book. Display information about a contact and touch the Text Messaging icon (similar to what's shown in the margin) next to the contact's phone number. After you touch that icon, the phone's text messaging app starts and you can compose the message.

- ✔ You can send text messages only to cell phones. Aunt Ida cannot receive text messages on her landline that she's had since the 1960s.

- ✔ You can send a single text message to multiple recipients: Just type additional phone numbers or contact names in the To field when you're composing a new message.

- ✔ When you receive a group message (one that has several recipients), you can choose whether to reply to everyone. Look for a Reply All button when composing your response.

- ✔ Continue a conversation at any time: Open the phone's texting app, peruse the list of existing conversations, and touch one to review what has been said or to pick up the conversation.

- ✔ Do not text and drive. Do not text and drive. Do not text and drive.

Receiving a text message

Whenever a new text message comes in, the message appears briefly at the top of the phone's touchscreen. Then you see the New Text Message notification, similar to the one in the margin.

To view the message, pull down the notifications drawer. Touch the messaging notification, and that conversation window immediately opens.

Forwarding a text message

It's possible to forward a text message, but it's not the same as forwarding e-mail. In fact, when it comes to forwarding information, e-mail has text messaging beat by well over 160 characters.

When forwarding works as an option, your phone lets you forward only the information in a text messaging cartoon bubble, not the entire conversation. Here's how it works:

1. **If necessary, open a conversation in the phone's texting app.**

2. **Long-press the text entry (the cartoon bubble) you want to forward.**

3. **From the menu that appears, choose the Forward or Forward Message command.**

   From this point on, forwarding the message works like sending a new message from scratch.

4. **Type the recipient's name (if the person is a contact), or type a phone number.**

   The text you're forwarding appears, already written, in the text field.

5. **Touch the Send icon to forward the message.**

Common text message abbreviations

Texting isn't about proper English. Indeed, many of the abbreviations and shortcuts used in texting, such as LOL and BRB, are slowly becoming part of the English language.

The weird news is that these acronyms weren't invented by teenagers. Sure, the kids use them, but the acronyms have their roots in the Internet chat rooms of yesteryear. Regardless of a shortcut's source, you might find a shortcut handy for typing messages quickly. Or maybe you can use this reference for deciphering an acronym's meaning. You can type acronyms in either uppercase or lowercase letters.

2	To, also
411	Information
BRB	Be right back
BTW	By the way
CYA	See you
FWIW	For what it's worth
FYI	For your information
GB	Goodbye
GJ	Good job
GR8	Great
GTG	Got to go
HOAS	Hold on a second
IC	I see
IDK	I don't know
IMO	In my opinion
JK	Just kidding
K	Okay
L8R	Later
LMAO	Laughing my [rear] off
LMK	Let me know
LOL	Laugh out loud
NC	No comment
NP	No problem
NRN	No reply needed (necessary)
OMG	Oh my goodness!
PIR	People in room (watching)
POS	Person over shoulder (watching)
QT	Cutie
ROFL	Rolling on the floor, laughing
SOS	Someone over shoulder (watching)
TC	Take care
THX	Thanks
TIA	Thanks in advance
TMI	Too much information
TTFN	Ta-ta for now (goodbye)
TTYL	Talk to you later
TY	Thank you
U2	You too
UR	You're, you are
VM	Voicemail
W8	Wait
XOXO	Hugs and kisses
Y	Why?
YW	You're welcome
ZZZ	Sleeping

Hangouts app doesn't allow you to forward a text message. Instead, long-press the cartoon bubble and choose the Copy command. Paste the text into a new conversation, which is almost the same thing as forwarding the message.

Multimedia Messages

Even though the term *texting* sticks around, a text message can contain media, usually a photo although short videos and audio can also be attached to a text message. Such a message ceases to be a mere *text* message and becomes a *multimedia message*.

- Multimedia messages are handled by the same app you use for text messaging.
- Not every mobile phone can receive multimedia messages. Rather than receive the media item, the recipient may be directed to a web page where the item can be viewed on the Internet.
- The official name for a multimedia text message is Multimedia Messaging Service, which is abbreviated MMS.

Attaching media to a text message

The most consistent way to compose a multimedia message is to attach existing media — something you've already saved on your phone — to the outgoing message. Obey these steps:

1. **Compose a text message as you normally do.**

2. **Touch the Action Overflow or Menu icon, and choose the Insert or Attach command.**

Opt out of text messaging

You don't have to be a part of the text messaging craze. Indeed, you can opt out of text messaging altogether. Simply contact your cellular provider and have them disable text messaging on your phone. They will happily comply, and you'll never again be able to send or receive a text message.

People opt out of text messaging for a number of reasons. A big one is cost: If the kids keep running up the text messaging bill, simply disabling the feature is often easier than continuing to pay all the usage surcharges. Another reason is security: Although cell phone viruses are rare, the scammers love sending malicious text messages. If you opt out, you don't have to worry about any SMS security risks.

You may also see a Paperclip icon on the message composition screen. In Figure 9-1, a Camera icon is used to attach images.

A pop-up menu appears, listing various media items you can attach to a text message. Among the more popular items you may find are

- *Audio:* Attach a song or an audio clip from the music library, or record a new audio clip, such as your voice.

- *Contact:* Attach contact information in the form of a vCard.

- *Location:* Send your location (or any location) to the other phone.

- *Picture:* Take a picture and attach it to the text message, or choose an image stored in the phone's Gallery.

- *Slideshow:* Create a collection of photos to send together.

- *Video:* Shoot a new video to attach, or choose a video you've taken with the phone and stored in the Gallery.

More options may appear on the menu, depending on which apps you have installed on your phone.

3. **Choose a media attachment from the pop-up menu.**

   What happens next depends on the attachment you've selected. You're taken to the appropriate app on your phone, where you can choose an existing media item or create one.

4. **If you like, compose a message to accompany the media attachment.**

5. **Touch the Send icon to send your media text message.**

In just a few, short, cellular moments, the receiving party will enjoy your multimedia text message.

> ✔ Be aware of the size limit on the amount of media you can send; try to keep your video and audio attachments brief.
>
> ✔ An easier way to send a multimedia message is to start with the source, such as a picture or video stored on your phone. Use the Share command or icon (shown in the margin), and choose MMS to share the media item. The various Share commands on your phone are covered throughout this book.
>
> ✔ Some video attachments can be too large for multimedia messages. The messaging app warns you when this happens.

Receiving a multimedia message

A multimedia attachment comes into your phone just like any other text message does. You may see a thumbnail preview of whichever media was sent, such as an image, a still from a video, or the Play icon to listen to audio. To preview the attachment, touch it.

To do more with the multimedia attachment, long-press it and then select an option from the menu that's displayed. For example, to save an image attachment, long-press the image thumbnail and choose the Save Picture command.

You might not be able to save some types of attachments.

Text Message Management

You don't have to manage your messages. I certainly don't. But the potential exists: If you ever want to destroy evidence of a conversation, or even do something as mild as change the text messaging ringtone, it's possible. Heed my advice in this section.

Removing messages

Although I'm a stickler for deleting e-mail after I read it, I don't bother deleting my text message threads. That's probably because I have no pending divorce litigation. Well, even then, I have nothing to hide in my text messaging conversations. If I did, I would follow these steps to delete a conversation:

1. **Open the conversation you want to remove.**

   Choose the conversation from the main screen in your phone's text messaging app.

2. **Touch the Action Overflow or Menu icon and choose the Delete command.**

3. **Touch the Delete icon to confirm.**

   The conversation is gone.

If these steps don't work, an alternative is to open the main screen in the text messaging app and long-press the conversation you want to zap. Choose the Delete command from the pop-up menu, and then touch the OK button to confirm.

Setting the text message ringtone

The sound you hear when a new text message floats in is the text message ringtone. It might be the same sound you hear for all notifications, though on some Android phones it can be changed to something unique. If so, follow these steps to set your Android phone's text message ringtone:

1. **Open the texting app.**

2. **Ensure that you're viewing the main screen, which lists all your conversations.**

   If you're not viewing that screen, touch the app icon in the upper-left corner of the screen until you see the main screen.

3. **Touch the Action Overflow or Menu icon.**

4. **Choose the Settings or Messaging Settings command.**

5. **Choose Select Ringtone.**

    If you're using the Hangouts app, choose your Gmail address (your Google account) from the list, and then choose the Sound command to view ringtone options.

    If you're prompted to choose an app, pick Media Storage, and touch Just This Once. See Chapter 24 for information on dealing with the Always or Just This Once choice.

6. **Pluck a ringtone from the list.**

7. **Touch the OK button.**

If these steps don't seem to work, refer to Chapter 6, which covers setting ringtones for incoming calls.

10

E-Mail This and That

*T*he art of writing a letter is ancient, probably dating back well before the 1940s. No one knows what that first letter said, though I'd venture to guess it probably wasn't a thank-you note. Fast-forward to the dawn of the telegraph: The first message was supposedly, "What hath God wrought?" The first telephone call was supposedly, "Mr. Watson. Come here. I want you." And in the 1960s, the first e-mail message was sent between two computer scientists, one asking the other whether he wanted to buy some cheap Viagra.

Two of the many delightful things your phone can do for you, specifically in the realm of mobile communications, are send and receive e-mail. You can use your phone as a supplement to your computer for your e-mail chores, or your phone can be your only e-mail gizmo.

Ubama

Air Force One

I need to be in Albuquerque Tues can you give me a lift?

2 3 4 5 6 7 8

E-Mail on Your Android Phone

Two apps on your Android phone handle e-mail: Gmail and Email. The Gmail app hooks directly into your Google Gmail account. It's a copy of all the Gmail you send, receive, and archive, just as if you were accessing it on the Internet by using a web browser.

The Email app, which might be called Mail, is used to connect to non-Gmail electronic mail, such as the standard mail service provided by your Internet service provider (ISP) or a web-based e-mail system such as Yahoo! Mail or Windows Live Mail.

Regardless of the app, electronic mail on your phone works just like it does on a computer: You can receive mail, create messages, forward mail, send messages to a group of contacts, work with attachments, and more. As long as your phone has a data connection, e-mail works just peachy.

✔ The stock Android name for the non-Gmail e-mail app is Email. That's how I refer to the app throughout this chapter.

✔ The Gmail app is updated frequently. To review any changes since this book went to press, visit my website at:

  www.wambooli.com/help/android/gmail/

✔ The Email app can be configured to handle multiple e-mail accounts, as discussed later in this section.

✔ Although you can use your phone's web browser to visit the Gmail website, you should use the Gmail app to pick up your Gmail.

✔ If you forget your Gmail password, visit this web address:

  www.google.com/accounts/ForgotPasswd

Setting up an Email account

The Email app is used to access web-based e-mail, or *webmail,* such as Yahoo! Mail, Windows Live Mail, and others. It also lets you read e-mail provided by your Internet service provider, office, or other large, intimidating organization. To get things set up regardless of the service, follow these steps:

1. **Start the Email app.**

   Look for it in the apps drawer, along with all other apps on your phone, though you may find an Email app launcher icon on the Home screen.

   If you haven't yet run the Email app, the first screen you see helps you configure your e-mail account. Continue with Step 2. Otherwise, you're taken to the Email inbox.

   See the next section for information on adding additional e-mail accounts.

2. **Type the e-mail address you use for the account.**

You may find a .com key on the onscreen keyboard, which you can use to more efficiently type your e-mail address. Look for the key in the lower-right corner of the screen.

3. **Type the account's password.**

4. **Touch the Next button on the screen.**

If you're lucky, everything is connected smoothly, and you see the Account Settings or Account Options screen. Move on to Step 5.

If you're unlucky, you have to specify the details, which include the incoming and outgoing server information, often known by the bewildering acronyms POP3 and SMTP. Plod through the fields shown on the screen, filling in the information as provided by your ISP, although you primarily need to specify only the incoming and outgoing server names.

5. **Set account options.**

You might want to reset the Inbox Checking Frequency to something other than 15 minutes. I recommend keeping the other items selected until you become familiar with how your phone handles e-mail.

6. **Touch the Next button.**

7. **Give the account a name and confirm your own name.**

The account is given your e-mail address as a name. If you want to change the name, type something new in that field. For example, I name my ISP's e-mail account *Main* because it's my main account.

The Your Name field lists your name as it's applied to outgoing messages. So if your name is really Lucy Magillicutty and not lmm1950, you can make that change now.

8. **Touch the Done button.**

The button might be titled Next. Either way, you're done.

The next thing you'll see is your e-mail account inbox. The phone proceeds to synchronize any pending e-mail you have in your account, updating the screen as you watch. See the "You've Got E-Mail" section for what to do next.

Adding more e-mail accounts

The Email app can be configured to collect mail from multiple sources. You can add a Yahoo! Mail account, Windows Live Mail account, your corporate e-mail account, or what-have-you. Follow through with these steps:

1. **In the Email app, touch the Action Overflow or Menu icon.**

2. **Choose the Settings command.**

If you don't see the Settings command, you probably aren't at the top level of the Email app. Touch the app icon in the upper-left corner of the screen until you see the Email app's main screen.

3. **Touch the Add Account button atop the screen.**

The Account Setup or Account Options screen appears. From this point, adding the account works as described in the preceding section, starting at Step 2.

You might also be able to add a new Email account by using the Settings app: Scroll down to the Accounts area on the Settings app screen and choose the Add Account item. Select the type of e-mail account you want to add, or choose IMAP for web-based e-mail or POP3 for an ISP e-mail account. A Corporate option is available for organizations with Exchange Server. Then continue following the setup directions as described in the preceding section, starting with Step 2.

- You can repeat the steps in this section to add more e-mail accounts. E-mail from the accounts you configure is accessed by using the Email app.

- I highly recommend getting the necessary information from your organization's friendly IT people if you decide to add a corporate e-mail account.

- For some corporate accounts, you may be prompted to activate the Device Administrator option. That's a fancy term for allowing your corporate IT humans access to your Android phone for the purpose of remotely controlling e-mail. If you're shackled to corporate e-mail, you probably already agreed to such a thing when you signed up to be an employee. Otherwise, keep in mind that you can always get your corporate e-mail at work and you may not even need to use your phone for that purpose.

You've Got Mail

All Android phones work flawlessly with Gmail. In fact, if Gmail is already set up to be your main e-mail address, you'll enjoy having access to your messages all the time from your phone.

Non-Gmail e-mail, handled by the Email program, must be set up before it can be used, as covered earlier in this chapter. After completing the quick and occasionally painless setup, you can receive e-mail on your phone just as you can on a computer.

Getting a new message

You're alerted to the arrival of a new e-mail message in your phone by a notification icon. The icon differs depending on the e-mail's source.

For a new Gmail message, the New Gmail notification, similar to the one shown in the margin, appears at the top of the touchscreen.

 For a new e-mail message, you see the New Email notification.

Specific e-mail apps may sport their own icons, such as a Yahoo! Mail icon. Look for that as well, providing you've added a Yahoo! Mail or similar account.

To review pending e-mail, swipe down the notifications drawer. You see either a single notification representing the most recent message or the total number of pending messages listing the various senders and subjects. Touch the notification to visit either the Gmail or Email app to read the message.

Checking the inbox

To peruse your Gmail, start the Gmail app. Its launcher icon might be found on the Home screen or it can be opened from the apps drawer. A typical Gmail inbox is shown in Figure 10-1.

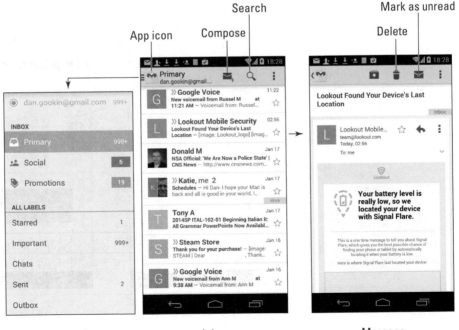

Figure 10-1: The Gmail inbox.

To check your Email inbox, open the Email app. You either see a single account's inbox, or you can choose to view the universal inbox, shown as the Combined Inbox view in Figure 10-2.

Don't bother looking for your Gmail inbox in the Combined Inbox window. (Refer to Figure 10-2.) Gmail is its own app; your Gmail messages don't show up in the universal inbox.

✔ Search your Gmail messages by pressing the Search icon, shown in Figure 10-1.

✔ Gmail is organized using *labels,* not folders. To see your Gmail labels, view the navigation drawer by touching the app icon, as shown in Figure 10-1.

✔ Multiple e-mail accounts gathered in the Email app are color coded. When you view the combined inbox, you see the color codes to the left of each message. The color is shown by each account in the navigation drawer, shown in Figure 10-2.

✔ To view an individual account's inbox, choose the account from the navigation drawer.

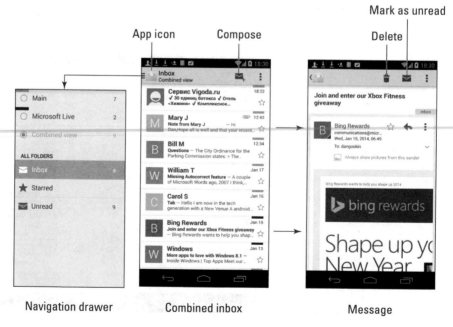

Navigation drawer   Combined inbox   Message

Figure 10-2: Messages in the Email app.

Reading e-mail

As mail comes in, you can read it by choosing a new e-mail notification, as described earlier in this chapter. Reading and working with the message operate much the same whether you're using the Gmail or Email app.

Touch a message in either the Gmail or Email app to read it. Swipe the message up or down by using your finger.

To work with the message, use the icons that appear above the message. These icons, which may not look exactly like those shown in the margin, cover common e-mail actions:

 Reply: Touch this icon to reply to a message. A new message window appears with the To and Subject fields reflecting the original sender(s) and subject.

 Reply All: Touch this icon to respond to everyone who received the original message, including folks on the Cc line. Use this option only when everyone else must get a copy of your reply.

Forward: Touch this icon to send a copy of the message to someone else.

 Delete: Touch this icon to delete a message. This icon is found atop the message.

You may not see the Reply All and Forward icons when the phone is in a vertical orientation, as shown in Figures 10-1 and 10-2. Turn the phone horizontally to see all three icons, along with the Favorites icon.

Additional e-mail commands can be found on the Action Overflow menu. The commands available depend on what you're doing in the Gmail or Email app when you touch the icon.

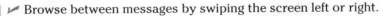

✔ Browse between messages by swiping the screen left or right.

 ✔ Favorite messages can be viewed or searched separately, making them easier to locate later.

✔ If you've properly configured the Email program, you don't need to delete messages you've read. See the "Configuring the server delete option" section, later in this chapter.

✔ I find it easier to delete (and manage) Gmail by using a computer.

Make Your Own E-Mail

Although I use my phone often to check e-mail, I don't often use it to compose messages. That's because most e-mail messages don't demand an
immediate reply. When they do, or when the mood hits me and I feel the
desperation that only an immediate e-mail message can quench, I compose
a new e-mail message on my Android phone using the methods presented in
this section.

Writing a new electronic message

Creating a new e-mail epistle works similarly with both the Gmail and
Email apps. The key is to touch the Compose icon, found atop the screen.
Figure 10-3 shows the layout of the e-mail composition screen, which should
be familiar to you if you've ever written e-mail on a computer.

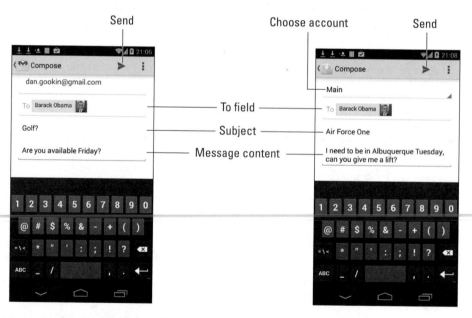

Figure 10-3: Writing a new e-mail message.

Fill in the To, Subject, and message content fields. As you type in the To field,
matching contacts from the phone's address book appear. Choose one from
the list. As with any e-mail message, you can send your message to multiple
recipients.

- Add the Cc and Bcc fields by touching the Action Overflow icon and choosing
the Add Cc/Bcc command.
-

When you have more than one e-mail account configured for the Email app, you can select which account to use for sending the message. Touch the Action Bar icon, shown in Figure 10-3, to choose the sending account. The account being used appears on the screen, such as the Main account shown in the figure.

To send the message, touch the Send icon, shown in the margin.

✔ To cancel a message, touch the Action Overflow icon (or the Menu icon) and choose the Discard command. Touch either the OK or Discard button to confirm.

✔ Copies of the messages you send in the Email app are stored in the Sent mailbox. For Gmail, send messages are saved in your Gmail account.

✔ The Compose icon may look different on your phone. Occasionally, the pencil icon is used, as shown in the margin.

✔ Save a message by choosing the Save Draft command from the Action Overflow menu. Drafts are saved in the Drafts folder. You can open them there for further editing or sending.

✔ Some phones feature a formatting toolbar in the Email app. Use it to change the way the text looks in your message.

Sending e-mail to a contact

A quick and easy way to compose a new message is to find a contact in the phone's address book app. Heed these steps:

1. **Open the phone's address book app.**

   The stock Android app is named People, although the name Contacts is also popular.

2. **Locate the contact to whom you want to send an electronic message.**

3. **Touch the contact's e-mail address.**

4. **Choose Gmail or Email to compose the message.**

   Other options may be available for composing the message. For example, a custom e-mail app you've downloaded may show up there as well.

At this point, creating the message works as described in the preceding sections.

You may be prompted to use the Complete Action Using menu before Step 4. I recommend choosing the Just Once option until you become more familiar with the e-mail apps. Refer to Chapter 24 for more information on the Complete Action Using prompt.

Message Attachments

The key to understanding e-mail attachments on your phone is to look for the paperclip icon. When you find that icon, you can either deal with an attachment for incoming e-mail or add an attachment to outgoing e-mail.

Dealing with an attachment

The only difference between attachments in the Gmail and Email apps is the way they look. The stock Android method of displaying a message attachment is shown in Figure 10-4. That's how Gmail displays attachments, and it might also be the way the Email app displays them, though your phone may highlight the attachment differently.

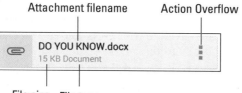

Figure 10-4: Attachment methods and madness.

To deal with the attachment, touch it. In most cases, the attachment opens using a given app on your phone. The app used depends on the type of attachment. For example, a PDF attachment might be opened by the QuickOffice app.

Touching the Action Overflow icon (refer to Figure 10-4) displays commands related to the attachment. Here's a smattering of what you may see:

✔ **Preview:** Open the attachment for viewing.

✔ **Save:** Save the attachment to the phone's storage.

✔ **Download Again:** Fetch the attachment from the mail server.

As with e-mail attachments received on a computer, the only problem you may have is that the phone lacks the app required to deal with the attachment. When an app can't be found, you'll either have to suffer through not viewing the attachment, or simply reply to the message and direct the person to resend the attachment in a common file format.

✔ Common file formats include PNG and JPEG for pictures, and HTML or RTF for documents. PDF and DOCX for Adobe Acrobat and Microsoft Word documents are also common.

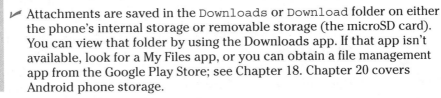

✔ You may see a prompt displayed when several apps can deal with the attachment. Choose one and touch the Just This Once button to view the attachment. Also see Chapter 24 for information on the Always/Just This Once prompt.

✔ Attachments are saved in the `Downloads` or `Download` folder on either the phone's internal storage or removable storage (the microSD card). You can view that folder by using the Downloads app. If that app isn't available, look for a My Files app, or you can obtain a file management app from the Google Play Store; see Chapter 18. Chapter 20 covers Android phone storage.

Sending an attachment

The best way to e-mail an attachment is to use the Share icon, shown in the margin. That's the Android way to send files via e-mail. Here's the general procedure:

1. **Visit the app that created the attachment.**

   For example, to send a photo, open the Gallery or Pictures app.

2. **View the specific item you want to attach.**

   In the Gallery app, view an image full-screen. In the Maps app, view the information card about a location.

3. **Touch the Share icon.**

   A list of apps appears.

4. **Choose Email or Gmail.**

   You may be prompted with an Always/Just This Once prompt. Choose Just This Once until you're comfortable with specific apps on your phone.

5. **Compose the message.**

   The item is attached to the message, so at this point writing the e-mail works just as described earlier in this chapter.

The computer way of attaching a file to a message is to first use the Gmail or Email apps and write the message. Touch the Action Overflow icon and choose the command Attach File. Use the screen that appears to choose an app, or browse through the files stored on the phone to pick one as an attachment.

When you send the message, the attachment rides along with it. In mere Internet moments, the message and attachment are made available to the recipient(s).

✔ Some Email apps may feature the paperclip icon, which you touch to attach a file to the message.

 ✔ It's possible to attach multiple items to a single e-mail message. Just keep touching the attachment icon for the message to add additional goodies.

 ✔ The variety of items you can attach depends on which apps are installed on the phone.

 ✔ Attachments you receive are easily located by using the Downloads app. Open that app to look for items you can share with others by reattaching them to outgoing e-mail.

 ✔ The Gmail and Email apps sometimes accept different types of attachments. So if you cannot attach something by using the Gmail app, try using the Email app instead.

E-Mail Configuration

You can have oodles of fun and waste oceans of time confirming and customizing the e-mail experience on your Android phone. Two of the more interesting things you can do are to modify or create an e-mail signature and specify whether messages retrieved by the Email app can be made available later for pickup by a computer.

Creating a signature

I highly recommend that you create a custom e-mail signature for sending messages from your phone. Here's my signature:

```
DAN

This was sent from my Android phone.
Typos, no matter how hilarious, are unintentional.
```

To create a signature in Gmail, obey these directions:

1. **At the main screen, touch the Action Overflow icon.**

   On some phones, touch the Menu icon to see the actions or commands.

2. **Choose your Gmail account from the list.**

   Touch your e-mail address.

3. **Choose Signature.**

4. **Type or dictate your signature.**

5. **Touch OK.**

You can obey these same steps to change your signature; the existing signature shows up after Step 4.

To set a signature for the Email app, heed these steps:

1. **Touch the Action Overflow icon on the Email app's inbox screen.**

   If the Action Overflow icon isn't available, touch the Menu icon.

2. **Choose the Settings or Email Settings command.**

   You may have to first choose the More command to find the Settings command. Or you may be lucky and find the Signature command.

3. **If prompted, choose an e-mail account from the list.**

   You create a separate signature for each e-mail account, so when you have multiple accounts, you'll need to repeat these steps for each one.

4. **Choose Signature.**

5. **Type or dictate a signature, or edit the existing signature.**

   The preset signature was probably set by your cellular provider, something like "Sent from my Verizon Wireless phone because Verizon has the fastest network available in the most places and you should switch to Verizon right now no matter which phone you have or, if you already have a Verizon phone, buy a second one on the Family plan."

   Feel free to edit the preset signature at your whim.

6. **Touch the OK, Save, or Done button.**

When you have multiple accounts in the Email app, repeat these steps to configure a signature for each one.

Configuring the server delete option

Non-Gmail e-mail that you fetch on your phone typically remains on the e-mail server. That's because, unlike a computer's e-mail program, the phone's Email app doesn't delete messages after it picks them up. The advantage is that you can retrieve the same messages later using a computer. The disadvantage is that you can end up retrieving mail you've already read and replied to.

You can control whether the Email app removes messages after they're picked up. Follow these steps:

1. **Open the Email app and visit the inbox.**

2. **Touch the Action Overflow icon and choose the Settings command.**

   On some phones, touch the Menu icon to see the Settings command.

3. **Choose an e-mail account.**

4. **Choose the Incoming Settings item.**

   If you can't find an Incoming Settings command, you're dealing with a web-based e-mail account, in which case there is no need to worry about the server delete option.

5. **Below the item Delete Email from Server, choose the option When I Delete from Inbox.**

   The only other option besides When I Delete from Inbox is Never. If you see the Never option, choose the other one.

6. **Touch the Done button.**

After making or confirming this setting, messages you delete in the Email app are also deleted from the mail server. The message won't be picked up again, not by the phone, another mobile device, or any computer that fetches e-mail from that same account.

✔ Mail you retrieve using a computer's mail program is deleted from the mail server after it's picked up. That behavior is normal. Your phone cannot pick up mail from the server if a computer has already deleted it.

✔ Deleting mail on the server isn't a problem for Gmail. No matter how you access your Gmail account, from your phone or from a computer, the inbox lists the same messages.

11

Out on the Web

I'm certain that when Tim Berners-Lee developed the World Wide Web back in 1990, he had no idea that people would one day use it on their cell phones. Nope, the web was designed to be viewed on a computer, specifically one with a nice, roomy, high-resolution monitor and a full-size keyboard. Cell phones? They had teensy LED screens. Browsing the web on a cell phone would have been like viewing the *Mona Lisa* through a keyhole.

Well, okay; viewing the web on your cell phone *is* kind of like viewing the *Mona Lisa* through a keyhole. The amazing thing is that you can do it in the first place. For some web pages, it's workable. For others, you have my handy advice in this chapter for making the web useful — nay, enjoyable — on your Android phone.

✔ Browsing the web by using the high-speed mobile data connection can quickly consume your monthly download quota and incur data surcharges. If possible, activate the phone's Wi-Fi connection before you venture out on the web. See Chapter 19 for more information on Wi-Fi.

✔ Many places you visit on the web can instead be accessed directly and more effectively by using specific apps. Facebook, Gmail, Twitter, YouTube, and potentially other popular web destinations each have apps that are preinstalled or can be downloaded free from the Google Play Store. Use those individual apps instead of visiting their associated web pages.

Behold the Web

Rare is the person these days who has had no experience with the World Wide Web. More common is someone who has used the web on a computer but has yet to taste the Internet waters on a mobile device. If that's you, consider this section your quick mobile web orientation.

Using the web browser app

Your phone features a web-browsing app. The stock Android app is Google's own Chrome web browser. Your phone may use another web browser app. Common names for that app include Web, Browser, and Internet. The good news is that all web apps work in a similar way and offer comparable features.

For consistency's sake, this chapter uses the Chrome app as an example. It's also shown in the Figures. If your phone doesn't have the Chrome app, you can obtain a free copy at the Google Play Store. See Chapter 18.

✔ Like all apps, you can find a copy of the phone's web browser in the apps drawer. A launcher icon might also be found on the Home screen.

✔ Chrome is also the name of Google's computer web browser. An advantage of using Chrome is that your bookmarks, web history, and other features are shared between all copies of Chrome that you use.

✔ The first time you fire up the web browser app on some Samsung phones, you may see a registration page. Register your device to receive sundry Samsung bonus stuff — or not. Registration is optional.

Surfing the web on your phone

When you first open the web browser app, you're taken to the home page. That could be your cellular provider's home page or a home page you've set. For the Chrome app, you see the last page you viewed on the app, or you may see Google's main page, illustrated in Figure 11-1.

Here are some handy phone web-browsing tips:

✔ Pan the web page by dragging your finger across the touchscreen. You can pan up, down, left, and right.

✔ Double-tap the screen to zoom in or zoom out.

✒ Pinch the screen to zoom out, or spread two fingers to zoom in.

✒ Tilt the phone to its side to read a web page in landscape mode. Then you can spread or double-tap the touchscreen to make teensy text more readable.

Visiting a web page

To visit a web page, type its address in the address box (refer to Figure 11-1). You can also type a search word, if you don't know the exact web page address. Touch the Go button on the onscreen keyboard to search the web or visit a specific web page.

If you don't see the address box, swipe your finger so that you can see the top of the window, where the address box lurks.

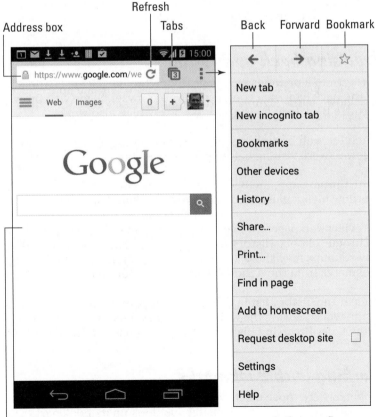

Figure 11-1: The Chrome app beholds the Google home page.

Touch links on a web page to visit the relevant link. If you have trouble touching a specific link, zoom in on the page. On some phones, long-pressing the screen may display a magnification window, which makes it easier to touch links.

- ✓ A Go icon might appear in the address box while you're typing a web page address.

- ✓ To reload a web page, touch the Refresh icon. If you don't see that icon on the screen, touch the Action Overflow or Menu icon to find the Refresh or Reload command. Refreshing updates a website that changes often, and the command can also be used to reload a web page that may not have completely loaded the first time.

- ✓ To stop a web page from loading, touch the Stop (X) icon that appears to the right of the address box.

- ✓ If your phone features a pointing device, such as a trackball, you can use it to hop between links on a web page. Press the trackball to click a link. The same trick applies to arrow keys on the physical keyboard, which can also be used to hop between links.

Browsing back and forth

To return to a previous web page, touch the Back icon. It works just like clicking the Back icon on a computer's web browser. Some web browsers may feature a Back icon by the address box, which also works.

Touch the web browser app's Forward icon to go forward or to return to a page you were visiting before you touched the Back icon.

In the Chrome app, the Back and Forward icons are found atop the Action Overflow menu, illustrated in Figure 11-1.

To review web pages you've visited, visit the web browser's history page. In Chrome, choose History from the Action Overflow menu. Other web browser apps may show web page history on the Bookmarks page: Choose Bookmarks from the Action Overflow menu and touch the History tab.

To clear the history list in the Chrome app, touch the Clear Browsing Data button while viewing the web page history. Ensure that there's a check mark by the Clear Browsing History item, and then touch the Clear button.

Working with bookmarks

Bookmarks are those electronic breadcrumbs you can drop as you wander the web. Need to revisit a website? Just look up its bookmark. This advice assumes, of course, that you bother to create (I prefer *drop*) a bookmark when you first visit the site.

The cinchy way to bookmark a page is to touch the Star icon when viewing the page. The Star icon may be found atop the screen, or you may find it on the Action Overflow menu (refer to Figure 11-1). After touching that icon, you see the add bookmark screen, similar to what's shown on the left in Figure 11-2.

I often edit the Name (or Title) field to something shorter and more descriptive, especially if the web page's title is long. Shorter names look better on the Bookmarks window. Touch the Save or OK button to add the bookmark.

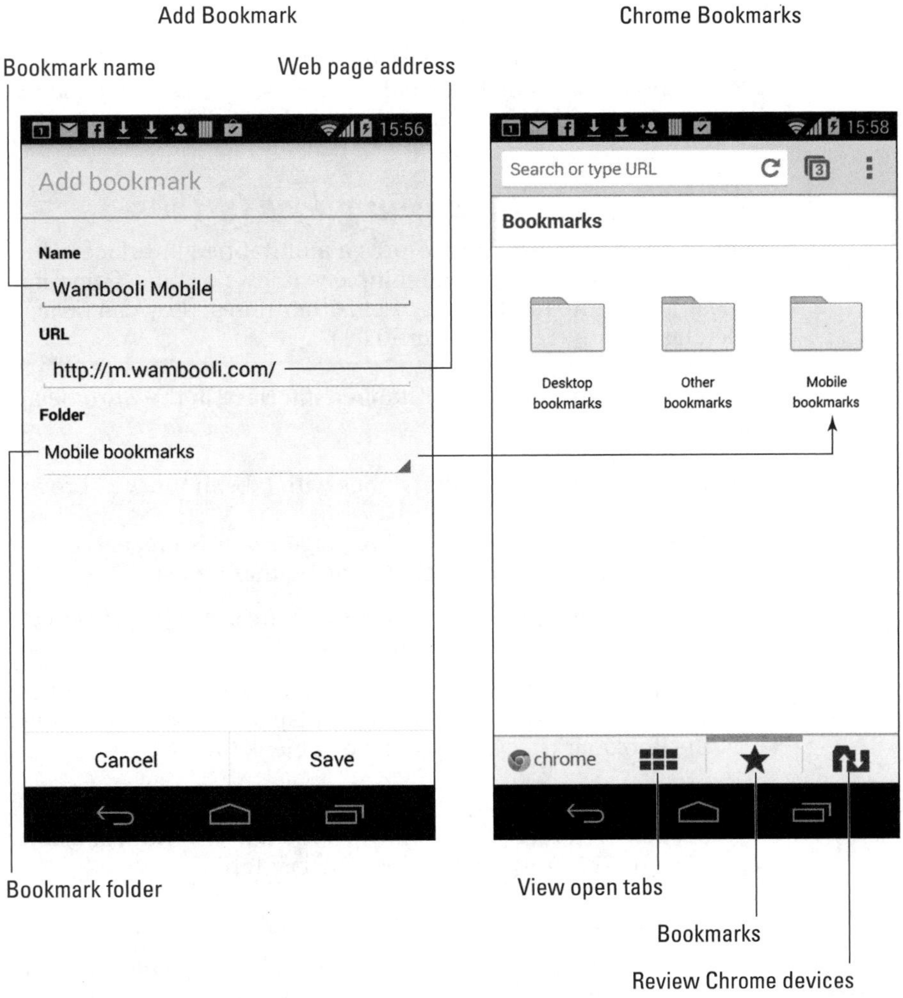

Add Bookmark   Chrome Bookmarks

Bookmark name   Web page address

Figure 11-2: Adding a bookmark.

View bookmarks in Chrome by choosing the Bookmarks command from the Action Overflow menu. Bookmarks are organized by folder, as illustrated in Figure 11-2, right. In other web browser apps, look for the command on the Action Overflow menu or for a Bookmarks icon on the app's main screen, similar to the icon shown in the margin.

Touch a bookmark to visit that page.

- ✔ Remove a bookmark by long-pressing its entry in the Bookmarks list. Choose the Delete or Delete Bookmark command. Touch the OK button to confirm. The bookmark is gone.

- ✔ Bookmarked websites can also be placed on the Home screen: Long-press the bookmark thumbnail and choose the Add Shortcut command. You can add bookmarks to the Home screen also by using a widget. See Chapter 22.

Managing multiple web pages in tabs

Your phone's web browser features a multitabbed interface, where you can browse several web pages in multiple windows or tabs. Sometimes the tabs appear across the top of the screen; other times, they can be accessed by touching an icon (refer to Figure 11-1).

Figure 11-3 illustrates the multitabbed interface in the Chrome app. Touch a tab to switch to that web page.

You can do various interesting things with tabs in the web browser app:

- ✔ **To open a link in another tab,** long-press the link and choose the Open in New Tab command from the menu that appears.

- ✔ **To open a bookmark in a new tab,** long-press the bookmark and choose the Open in New Tab command.

- ✔ **To open a blank tab,** touch the Action Overflow icon and choose New Tab. The New Tab command may display the browser's home screen or the Bookmarks screen instead of a blank tab.

Close a tab by touching its X (Close) button, which either appears on the browser screen directly or is shown in the tab overview, similar to what you see in Figure 11-3. You cannot close the last tab.

- ✔ Some browser apps may refer to the tabs as *windows*.

- ✔ For secure browsing, you can open an *incognito tab:* Touch the Action Overflow icon and choose the New Incognito Tab command. When you go incognito, the web browser app won't track your history, leave cookies, or provide other evidence of which web pages you've visited in the incognito tab. A short description appears on the incognito tab page describing how it works.

Add a new tab   Close tab

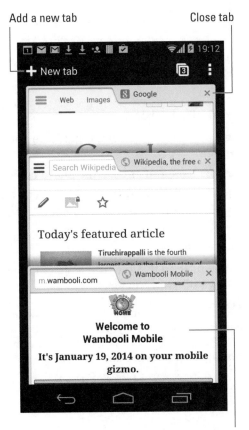

Touch to switch tabs

Figure 11-3: The Chrome app's tabbed interface.

Searching the web

The handiest way to find things on the web is to use the Google Search widget, often found floating on the Home screen. You can also use Google Now, which is covered in Chapter 17. And, of course, you can visit Google's main search page by using the web browser app.

Or, what-the-hey: Be different and use Bing: www.bing.com.

Finding text on a web page

To locate text on a web page, touch the Action Overflow icon and choose the Find in Page command. Type the search text into the Find on Page box. As you type, found text is highlighted on the screen. Use the up or down chevrons to the right of the search box to page through the document. Touch the Back icon to dismiss the Find in Page contextual action bar after you've finished searching.

Sharing a web page

There it is! That web page that you just *have* to talk about to everyone you know. The gauche way to share the page is to copy and paste it. Because you're reading this book, though, you know the better way to share a web page. Heed these steps:

1. **Go to the web page you desire to share.**

   Actually, you're sharing a *link* to the page, but don't let my obsession with specificity deter you.

2. **Touch the Action Overflow icon and choose the Share command.**

   The command might also be called Share Page or Share Via. Either way, a long list of apps is displayed. The variety and number of apps depends on what's installed on your phone.

3. **Choose a method to share the page.**

   For example, choose Email to send the link by e-mail, or choose Facebook to share the link with your friends.

4. **Do whatever happens next.**

   Whatever happens next depends on how you're sharing the link: Compose the e-mail, write a comment in Facebook, or whatever. Refer to various chapters in this book for specific directions.

You cannot share a page you're viewing through an incognito tab.

The Perils and Joys of Downloading

Downloading is an easy concept to grasp, providing you accept how most people misuse the term. Officially, a *download* is a transfer of information over a network from another source to your phone. For the web browser app, the network is the Internet, and the other source is a web page.

- ✔ Most people use the term *download* when they really mean *transfer* or *copy.* Those people must be shunned.

- ✔ New apps are installed on your phone by using the Play Store app, covered in Chapter 18. That's a type of downloading, but it's not the same as the downloading described in this section.

- ✔ While the phone is downloading information, you see the Downloading notification. It's an animated icon, though the icon shown in the margin isn't animated in this edition of the book. Completed downloads feature the Download Complete icon, which is not animated, exactly like the image shown in the margin.

- ✔ The opposite of downloading is *uploading.* That's the process of sending information from your gizmo to another location on a network.

Grabbing an image from a web page

The simplest thing to download is an image from a web page. It's cinchy: Long-press the image. You see a pop-up menu, from which you choose the Save Image command.

- ✓ The image is copied and stored on your phone. You can view the image by using the Gallery app; refer to Chapter 15 for information on the Gallery.

- ✓ Technically, the image is stored on the phone's internal storage. It can be found in the download folder. You can read about file storage in Chapter 20.

Downloading a file

When a link opens a document on a web page, such as a Microsoft Word document or an Adobe Acrobat (PDF) file, you can download that file to your phone. Touch the file link to download. If that doesn't work, long-press the file link and choose the Save Link command.

- ✓ The phone is smart and it does attempt to open or display links you touch.

- ✓ Use the Downloads app to review the items you snag from the Internet. See the next section.

Reviewing your downloads

To review items downloaded from the Internet, or otherwise obtained via the download process on your phone, open the Downloads app. You'll find it eagerly awaiting your attention in the apps drawer.

The Downloads app lists downloaded items organized by date. To view a download, touch an item in the list. The phone then starts the appropriate app to view the item so that you can see it displayed on the touchscreen.

Well, of course, some of the things you can download you cannot view. When this happens, you see an appropriately rude error message.

- ✓ You can quickly review any download by choosing the Download notification.

- ✓ Manage the download list by long-pressing any entry. When you do, a contextual action bar appears atop the screen. Use the icons on the action bar to Delete or Share the downloaded item. As long as the action bar is visible, you can touch items in the list to select them.

Web Controls and Settings

More options and settings and controls exist for the web browser app than just about any other app I've used on any Android phone. It's complex. Rather than bore you with every dangdoodle detail, I thought I'd present just a few of the options worthy of your attention.

Setting a home page

The *home page* is the first page you see when you start the web browser app, and it's the first page that's loaded when you fire up a new tab. To set your home page, heed these directions while using the web browser app:

1. **Browse to the page you want to set as the home page.**

2. **Touch the Action Overflow icon.**

   On some phones, you touch the Menu icon instead.

3. **Choose the command Set Home Page.**

   You may have to choose the More command first, or perhaps a Settings command. You may even have to choose a second Set Home Page command from that menu.

   Some web browsers, such as Chrome, don't have an option for setting a home page.

4. **Touch the Use Current Page button or choose the Current Page item.**

   Because you obeyed Step 1, you don't need to type the web page's address.

5. **Touch OK.**

   The home page is set.

If you want your home page to be blank (not set to any particular web page), set the name of the home page (in Step 4) to about:blank. That's the word *about,* a colon, and then the word *blank,* with no period at the end and no spaces in the middle. I prefer a blank home page because it's the fastest web page to load. It's also the web page with the most accurate information.

Changing the way the web looks

You can do a few things to improve the way the web looks on your phone. The key is to find the command that adjusts text size or the zoom. Heed these steps:

1. **Touch the Action Overflow icon and choose the Settings command.**

   On some phones you'll need to choose More and then Settings.

2. **Choose Text Size or the Screen and Text command.**

   The command might be also titled Default Zoom.

In Chrome, choose the Accessibility command.

3. **Select a better size from the menu.**

    For example, try Large or Huge. Or adjust the slider to select a text size based on a text preview window.

I don't make any age-related comments about text size at this time, and especially at this point in my life.

- ✔ You can spread your fingers to zoom in on any web page.

- ✔ You can also turn the phone sideways to view a web page larger in a horizontal orientation.

Setting privacy and security options

As far as your phone's web browser app settings go, most of the security options are already enabled, including the blocking of pop-up windows (which normally spew ads).

If information retained on the phone concerns you, you can clear it when you use the web browser app: Touch the Action Overflow icon and choose the Settings command. Then choose either the Privacy or Privacy and Security category. Review the items presented to see which information the app is keeping and which it's not.

Choose the Clear Browsing Data command to remove any memorized information you may have typed on a web page. Choose items from the list presented, which can be cleared from the phone's internal storage. Touch the Clear button to remove that information, such as browsing history, cookies, saved passwords, and data from online forms you've filled in.

Remove the check mark from Remember Form Data. These two settings prevent any characters you've input in a text field from being summoned automatically by someone who may steal your phone.

You might be concerned about various warnings regarding location data. What the warnings refer to is the phone's capability to track your location on Planet Earth. That capability comes from the phone's GPS, or global satellite positioning system. It's a handy feature, but one some people find overly intrusive. Resetting that information is handled by the Settings app: Choose the Location or Location Services item. Touch the Master Control icon to turn the services off if you prefer to wander stealthily.

Do be aware that disabling the phone's location services renders a few apps useless, particularly the Maps app.

With regard to general online security, my advice is always to be smart and think before doing anything questionable on the web. Use common sense. One of the most effective ways that the Bad Guys win is by using *human engineering* to try to trick you into doing something you normally wouldn't do, such as click a link to see a cute animation or a racy picture of a celebrity or politician. As long as you use your noggin, you should be safe.

Your Digital Social Life

*S*ocial networking is that twenty-first century phenomenon that proves many odd beliefs about people. For example, it's possible to have hundreds of friends and never leave your house. You can jealously guard your privacy against the wicked intrusions of the government and Big Brother, all while letting everyone on the Internet know that you've just "checked in" to Starbucks and are having an iced mocha frappuccino. And you can share your most intimate moments with humanity, many of whom will "like" the fact that you've just broken up or that your cat was run over by the garbage collection service.

One of your Android phone's key duties is to keep you connected with your social networking universe. You can use specific apps for popular services such as Facebook and Twitter, or your phone may come with a general app that handles all your social networking duties in one spot.

In Your Facebook

Of all the social networking sites, Facebook is the king. It's the online place to go to catch up with friends, send messages, express your thoughts, share pictures and video, play games, and waste more time than you ever thought you had.

- ✓ You can access Facebook on the web by using the phone's web-browsing app, but I highly recommend that you use the Facebook app described in this section.

- ✓ You can access updates to your contacts' Facebook statuses from the phone's address book. See Chapter 8.

- ✓ The Facebook app is frequently updated. Review any new information by visiting my website:

    www.wambooli.com/help/android/facebook/

Setting up your Facebook account

The best way to use Facebook is to have a Facebook account, and the best way to do that is to sign up at www.facebook.com by using your computer. Register for a new account by setting up your username and password.

Don't forget your Facebook username and password!

Eventually, the Facebook robots send you a confirmation e-mail. You reply to that message, and the online social networking community braces itself for your long-awaited arrival.

Now you're ready to access Facebook on your Android phone. To get the most from Facebook, however, you need the Facebook app. Keep reading in the next section.

Getting the Facebook app

Your Android phone may or may not come with the Facebook app. If so, great! If not, you can obtain the Facebook app free from the Google Play Store. That app is your red carpet to the Facebook social networking kingdom.

To get the Facebook app, go to the Google Play Store and search for the Facebook for Android app. Download that app. If you need specific directions, see Chapter 18, which covers using the Play Store app.

- ✓ After you install the Facebook app, you may see a Facebook notification icon. Choose that icon and complete the steps required to complete installation.

- ✓ Some phones may come with a social networking app. The app provides a central location for all your social networking accounts, including Facebook. You can use that app instead of or in addition to the Facebook app.

Running Facebook on your phone

The first time you behold the Facebook app, you'll probably be asked to sign in. Do so: Type the e-mail address you used to sign up for Facebook and then type your Facebook password. Touch the Log In button.

If you're asked to sync your contacts, do so. I recommend choosing the option to synchronize all your contacts, which adds all your Facebook friends to the phone's address book. Touch the Sync button in the upper-right corner of the screen to begin using Facebook.

Eventually, you see the Facebook News Feed, similar to what's shown in Figure 12-1.

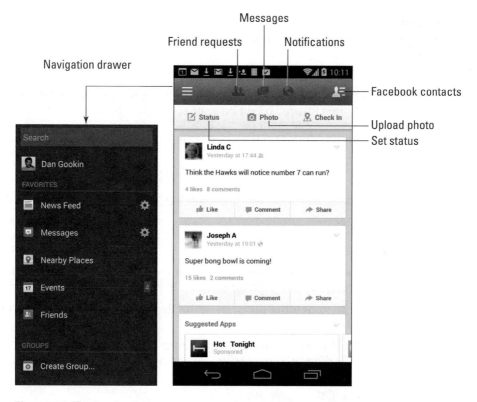

Figure 12-1: The Facebook app.

When you need a respite from Facebook, touch the Home icon to return to the Home screen.

The Facebook app continues to run until you either sign out or turn off the phone. It may also timeout after a period of inactivity. To sign out of Facebook, choose the Log Out command found at the bottom of the navigation drawer. Touch the Confirm button.

- ✔ Show the navigation drawer by touching the Facebook app icon. To hide the drawer, touch that icon again.

- ✔ Refer to Chapter 22 for information on placing a Facebook launcher or Facebook widget on the Home screen.

- ✔ Use the Like, Comment, or Share buttons below a News Feed item to like, comment on, or share something. You can see the comments only when you choose the Comment item.

- ✔ The News Feed is updated when you swipe down on the screen.

- ✔ Notifications for Facebook appear in the notifications area on the screen. They look similar to what's shown in the margin.

Setting your status

The primary thing you live for on Facebook, besides having more friends than anyone else, is to update your status. It's the best way to share your thoughts with the universe, far cheaper than skywriting and far less offensive than a robocall.

To set your status, follow these steps in the Facebook app:

1. **Touch the Status button at the top of the screen.**

   Refer to Figure 12-1 for the Status button's location. If you don't see it, ensure that you're viewing the News Feed and swipe all the way up to the top of the feed.

   The Write Post screen appears. It's where you type your Facebook musing, similar to what's shown in Figure 12-2.

2. **Type something pithy, newsworthy, or typical of the stuff you read on Facebook.**

   When you can't think of anything to post, take off your shoes, sit down, and take a picture of your feet against something else in the background. That seems to be really popular.

3. **Touch the Post button.**

You can also set your status by using the Facebook widget on the Home page, if it's been installed: Touch the What's on Your Mind text box, type your important news tidbit, and touch the Share button.

Status update text   Share status

Choose sharing audience

What you're doing

Upload photo

Share your location

Choose friends

Figure 12-2: Updating your Facebook status.

Uploading a picture to Facebook

One of the many things your Android phone can do is take pictures. Combine that feature with the Facebook app, and you have an all-in-one gizmo designed for sharing the various intimate and private moments of your life with the ogling Internet throngs.

The picture-posting process starts by touching a Photo icon in the Facebook app. Refer to Figures 12-1 and 12-2 for popular Photo icon locations on the main screen and the Write Post screen. After touching the Photo icon, the photo selection screen appears. You have two choices:

- First, you can select an image from pictures shown on the screen. Those images are ones found on the phone. Touch an image, or touch several images to select a bunch, and then proceed with the steps listed later in this section.

- Second, you can take a picture by using the phone's camera.

If you elect to use the phone's camera to take a picture, touch the Camera icon on the photo selection screen. (It's in the lower-left corner.) You then find yourself thrust into Facebook's camera app, shown in Figure 12-3. This is not the same app as the Camera app, covered in Chapter 15.

Switch cameras (front/back)

Flash control

Record video   Take picture   Gallery

Figure 12-3: Snapping a pic for Facebook.

Use the onscreen controls to take your picture. Or you can shoot a quick video. When you're done, touch the Gallery icon. Refer to Figure 12-3 for the location of the Gallery icon, as well as other onscreen controls.

To proceed with uploading your image, follow these steps:

1. **Touch an image in the Gallery to select it.**

2. **Optionally, tap the image to add a tag.**

   You can touch someone's face in the picture and then type the person's name. Or choose from a list of your Facebook friends to apply a name tag to the image.

3. **Use the Rotate icon to reorient the image, if necessary.**

   The icon is shown in the margin. Please don't try to annoy me on Facebook by posting improperly oriented images.

4. **Touch the Compose icon.**

   The Compose icon is shown in the margin.

5. **Add a message to the image.**

   At this point, posting the image works just like adding a status update, similar to what's shown in Figure 12-2.

6. **Touch the Post button.**

   The image is posted as soon as it's transferred over the Internet and digested by Facebook.

The image can be found as part of your status update or News Feed, but it's saved also to Facebook's Mobile Uploads album.

Facebook appears also on the various Share menus you find in other apps on the phone. Choose the Share command to send to Facebook whatever it is you're looking at. (Other chapters in this book give you more information about the various Share menus and where they appear.)

Configuring the Facebook app

The commands that control Facebook are stored on the settings screen. To see that screen, choose the App Settings command in the navigation drawer. You'll behold a host of Facebook app settings. Two commands worthy of your attention are Refresh Interval and Notification Ringtone.

Choose Refresh Interval to specify how frequently the app checks for new Facebook activities. If you find the one-hour value to be too long for your frantic Facebook social life, choose something quicker. Or, to disable Facebook notifications, choose Never.

The Notification Ringtone item sets the sound that plays when Facebook has a new update. Choose the Silent option when you don't want the app to make noise upon encountering a Facebook update.

Touch the Back icon to leave the settings screen and return to the main Facebook screen.

You can manually refresh the Facebook app by swiping down the screen.

Tweet Suite

Twitter is a social networking site, similar to Facebook but with increased brevity. On Twitter, you write short spurts of text that express your thoughts or observations, or you share links. Or, you can just use Twitter to follow the thoughts and twitterings, or *tweets,* of other people.

- ✔ A message posted on Twitter is a *tweet.*
- ✔ A tweet can be no more than 140 characters long. That number includes spaces and punctuation.
- ✔ You can post messages on Twitter and follow others who post messages. It's a good way to get updates and information quickly, not only from individuals but also from news outlets and other organizations.

Setting up Twitter

The best way to use Twitter on your Android phone is to already have a Twitter account. Start by going to http://twitter.com on a computer and follow the directions there for creating a new account.

After you've established a Twitter account, you can use the Twitter app on your phone. Not all Android phones come with Twitter preinstalled. If you don't find the app in the apps drawer, you can obtain the Twitter app from the Google Play Store. Refer to Chapter 18 for information on downloading apps to your phone. Search for the Twitter app from Twitter, Inc.

When you start the Twitter app for the first time, touch the Sign In button. Type your Twitter username or e-mail address and then type your Twitter password. After that, you can use Twitter without having to log in again — until you turn off the phone or exit the Twitter app.

Figure 12-4 shows the Twitter app's main screen, which shows the current tweet feed. The main screen may look subtly different on your phone, depending on the Twitter app version.

See the next section for information on *tweeting,* or updating your status using the Twitter app.

Create new tweet

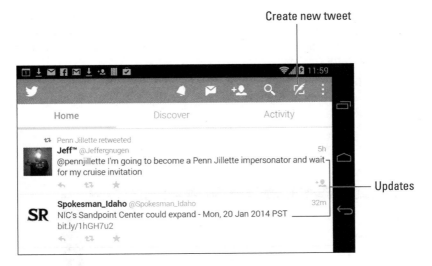

Updates

Figure 12-4: The Twitter app.

 The Twitter app comes with companion widgets you can affix to the Home screen. Use the widgets to peruse recent tweets or compose a new tweet. Refer to Chapter 22 for information on affixing widgets to the Home screen.

Tweeting

The Twitter app provides an excellent interface to the many wonderful and interesting things that Twitter does. Of course, the two most basic tasks are reading and writing tweets.

To read tweets, choose the Home category, which is shown in Figure 12-4. Recent tweets are displayed in a list, with the most recent information at the top. Scroll the list by swiping it with your finger.

To tweet, touch the Create New Tweet icon, shown in Figure 12-4. The new tweet screen appears, as shown in Figure 12-5, so you can compose your tweet.

Touch the Tweet button to share your thoughts with the Twitterverse.

 ✔ You have only 140 characters for creating your tweet. That count includes spaces.

 ✔ The character counter in the Twitter app lets you know how close you're getting to the 140-character limit.

✔ Twitter itself doesn't display pictures, other than your account picture. When you send a picture to Twitter, you use an image-hosting service and then share the link, or URL, to the image. All that complexity is handled by the Twitter app.

✔ The Twitter app appears on various Share menus in other apps. You use those Share menus to send to Twitter whatever you're looking at.

Figure 12-5: Creating a tweet.

Even More Social Networking

The Internet is nuts over social networking. Facebook may be the king, but you'll find lots of landed gentry out for that crown. It almost seems as though a new social networking site pops up every week. Beyond Facebook and Twitter, other social networking sites include, but are not limited to

✔ Google+

✔ LinkedIn

✔ Meebo

✔ Myspace

I recommend first setting up the social networking account on a computer, similar to the way I describe it earlier in this chapter for Facebook and Twitter. After that, obtain an app for the social networking site using the

Google Play Store. Set up and configure that app on your Android phone to connect with your existing account.

- ✔ See Chapter 18 for more information on the Google Play Store.

- ✔ Google+ is Google's social networking app, which is related to the Hangouts app. See Chapter 12 for information on using Hangouts.

- ✔ The HootSuite app can be used to share your thoughts on a multitude of social networking platforms. It can be obtained from the Play Store, as described in Chapter 18.

- ✔ As with Facebook and Twitter, you may find your social networking apps appearing on Share menus in various apps. That way, you can easily share your pictures and other types of media with your online social networking pals.

Text, Voice, and Video Chat

*J*ulius Caesar is quoted as saying, "*Veni. Vidi. Vinci.*" That translates to, "I came. I saw. I conquered." Had Caesar an Android phone, he might have said, "*Veni. Vidi. Dixi,*" where *dixi* is Latin for "I said." That fits more into the theme of what a modern smartphone can do, although I'm sure at least one Android phone owner somewhere dreams of conquering Gaul.

The holy grail of telecommunications is video chat, something that everyone took for granted would happen in the future. As long as your cell phone features a front-facing camera and has the proper app installed — and the app is permitted by your cellular provider to offer you the service — you can video-chat on your Android phone. The future is here.

Let's Hang Out

To sate your video chat desires, your phone comes with an app called Hangouts. It's a communications app, designed by Google to let you connect with one or more of your friends for text and video chat.

✔ The Hangouts app might also serve as your phone's text messaging app. See Chapter 9.

✔ The Hangouts app is a reincarnation of the old Google Talk app.

Using Hangouts

The Hangouts app might appear as a launcher icon on the Home screen; otherwise, you can dig it up in the apps drawer. If you don't see it directly in the list of apps, look for it inside a Google folder. And if you still can't find it, you can obtain the app free from the Google Play Store; see Chapter 18.

Hangouts hooks into your Google account. If you have any previous conversations, they're listed on the main part of the screen, shown in Figure 13-1. On the right side of the screen you see a specific conversation, although it just peeks in when the phone is held vertically.

The Hangouts app listens for incoming conversation requests, or you can start your own. You're alerted via notification of an impending Hangout request. The notification icon is shown in the margin.

- ✔ Conversations are archived in the Hangouts app. To peruse a previous text chat, choose it from the list, as shown in Figure 13-1. Part of the previous chat shows up on the right side of the screen.

- ✔ Text messages appear in the archive with the SMS flag (see Figure 13-1).

- ✔ Video calls aren't archived, but you can review when the call took place and with whom by choosing a video chat item.

- ✔ To remove a previous conversation, long-press it. Touch the Trash icon that appears on the contextual action bar atop the screen. You can also swipe a conversation left or right to remove it.

- ✔ To use Hangouts, your friends must have a Google account. They can be using a computer or mobile device; it doesn't matter which. But they must have a camera available to enable video chat.

Typing at your friends

Text chatting is one of the oldest forms of communication on the Internet. People type text back and forth at each other, which can be tedious, but it remains popular. To text chat in the Hangouts app, obey these steps:

1. **Choose a contact listed on the screen, or fetch one by touching the Add icon.**

   When you touch the Add icon, you're starting a new hangout. Choosing a contact already on the screen continues a hangout. Even a prior video hangout can become a text hangout.

   When you choose a hangout with multiple people, they all receive a copy of the message.

Previous video call

Text message

Add friends/
view contacts

Previous conversation

Group video call

Text hangout

Figure 13-1: Google Hangouts.

2. Touch the action bar by the contact's name and choose Hangouts.

The action bar lets you choose between starting a new hangout or sending a text message (SMS). For this exercise, you're starting a hangout.

A clue that you're starting a hangout is the video icon. When a phone icon appears, you're sending a text message.

3. **Type your message, as shown in Figure 13-2.**

4. **Touch the Send icon to send your comment.**

The Send icon replaces the Location and Photo icons when you start to type.

You type, your friend types, and so on until you grow tired or the battery dies.

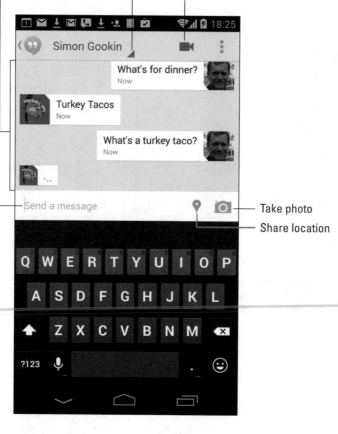

Figure 13-2: Text-chatting.

Adding more people to the hangout is always possible: Touch the Action Overflow icon and choose New Group Hangout. Choose a friend from those listed to invite him into the hangout.

 You can leave the conversation at any time to do other things with your phone. To return to any ongoing hangout, choose the Hangouts notification, as shown in the margin.

Talking and video chat

Take the hangout up a notch by touching the Video icon. (Refer to Figure 13-2.) When you do, your friend receives a pop-up invite, as shown in Figure 13-3. Touch the Accept icon to begin talking.

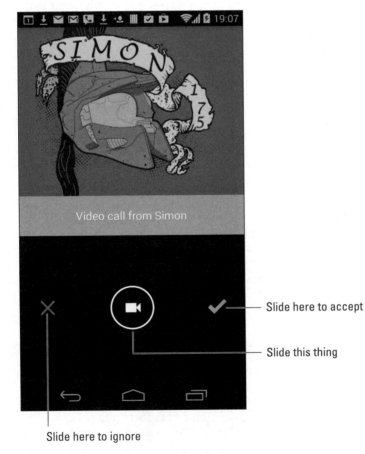

Slide here to accept

Slide this thing

Slide here to ignore

Figure 13-3: Someone wants to video chat!

Figure 13-4 shows what an ongoing video chat might look like. The person you're talking with appears in the big window; you're in the smaller window. Other video chat participants appear at the bottom of the screen as well, as shown in the figure.

The onscreen controls (shown in Figure 13-4) may vanish after a second; touch the screen to see the controls again.

To end the conversation, touch the Exit icon. Well, say "Goodbye" first, and then touch the icon.

- When you're nude, or just ugly, decline the video chat invite. Then choose that contact and reply with a text message or a voice chat instead.

- Use the Speaker icon to choose how to listen when you video-chat. You can choose to use the phone's speaker, headphones, and so on.

- When video-chatting with multiple contacts, choose a contact from the bottom of the screen to see the person in a larger format in the center of the screen.

- If you want to make eye contact, look directly into the phone's front-facing camera. It's right above the touchscreen, either centrally located or to the left or right.

Skype the World

The popular Skype app is used the world over as a free way to make Internet phone calls and to video-chat. Plus, if you're willing to pony up some money, you can make inexpensive calls to phones around the world. So although the Hangouts app might be enough of a topic for this chapter, far more people are using Skype. Skype may end up being a better choice for text, video, and voice chat on your Android phone.

Getting Skype

The typical Android phone doesn't come with the Skype app preinstalled. To get Skype, visit the Google Play Store and obtain the Skype app. In case you find multiple apps, get the one that's from the Skype company itself.

To use Skype, you need a Skype account. You can sign up while using the app, or you can visit www.skype.com on a computer and complete the process by using a nice, full-sized keyboard and widescreen monitor.

Exit video chat

Switch to text chat

Person you're calling

You

Switch cameras

Turn off video

Show speaker options

Mute the microphone

Others in the hangout

Figure 13-4: Video chat in the Hangouts app.

When you start the Skype app for the first time, work through the initial setup screens. You can even take the tour. Be sure to have Skype scour the phone's address book for contacts you can Skype. This process may take a while, but if you're just starting out, it's a great help.

- ✐ Skype is free. Text chat is free. Voice and video chat with one other Skype user is also free. When you want to call a real phone or video chat with a group, you need to boost your account with Skype Credit.

- ✐ It's doesn't cost extra to conduct a gang video chat in the Hangouts app.

- ✐ Don't worry about getting a Skype Number, which costs extra. That's used mostly for incoming calls and, well, that's why you have a phone.

- ✐ Also see Chapter 21, which covers making inexpensive international phone calls by using the Skype app.

Chatting with another Skype user

Text chat with Skype works similarly to texting. The only difference is that the other person must be a Skype user. So in that respect, Skype text chat works a lot like Hangouts chat, covered earlier in this chapter.

To chat, follow these steps:

1. **Start the Skype app and sign in.**

   You don't need to sign in when you've previously run the Skype app. Like most apps on your phone, Skype continues to run until you sign out or turn off the phone.

2. **At the main Skype screen, touch the People tab and choose a contact.**

   Or you can choose one of the contact icons shown on the main screen.

3. **Type your text in the text box.**

   The box is at the bottom of the screen. It says Type a Message Here.

4. **Touch the Blue arrow icon to send the message.**

   As long as your Skype friend is online and eager, you'll be chatting in no time.

At the far right end of the text box, you find a Smiley icon. Use this icon to insert a cute graphic in your text.

- ✔ The Skype Chat notification, shown in the margin, appears whenever someone wants to chat with you. It's handy to see, especially when you may have switched away from the Skype app to work in some other app. Choose that notification to get into the conversation.

- ✔ To stop chatting, touch the Back icon. The conversation is kept in the Skype app, even after the other person has disconnected.

- ✔ For the chat to work, the other user must be logged in on Skype and available to chat.

Seeing on Skype (video call)

Placing a video call with Skype is easy: Start a text chat as described in the preceding section. After the conversation starts, touch the Video Call icon. The call rings through to the contact, and if they want to video chat, they pick up in no time and you're talking and looking at each other.

When someone calls you on Skype, you see the Skype incoming call screen, similar to the one shown in Figure 13-5. Touch the Audio (handset) icon to answer as a voice-only call; touch the Video icon (if it's available) to answer using video. Touch the Decline icon to dismiss the call, especially when it's someone who annoys you.

The incoming call screen (see Figure 13-6) appears even when the phone is sleeping; the incoming call wakes up the phone, just as a real call would.

When you're in a Skype video conversation, the screen looks like Figure 13-6. Touch the screen to see the onscreen controls should they disappear. Touch the red Disconnect icon to end the call.

- ✔ Voice and video chat on Skype over the Internet are free. When you use a Wi-Fi connection, you can chat without consuming your cellular plan's data minutes.

- ✔ You can chat with any user in your Skype contacts list by using a mobile device, a computer, or any other gizmo on which Skype is installed.

- ✔ Video chat is available only on a handful of cell phones that have front-facing cameras and also are allowed to video chat. Not every Android phone with a front-facing camera has video chat available. (Blame the cellular provider.)

Skype contact info

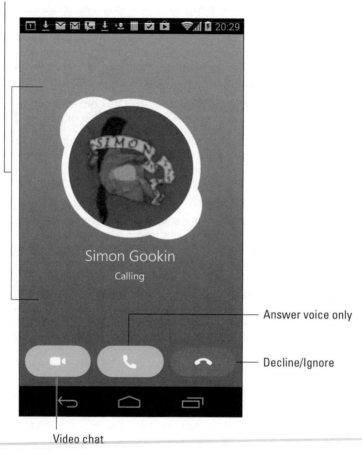

Answer voice only

Decline/Ignore

Video chat

Figure 13-5: An incoming Skype voice call.

✔ Video chat may be available only over Wi-Fi or 4G connections.

✔ If you plan to use Skype a lot, get a good headset.

✔ It's impossible to tell whether someone has dismissed a Skype call or simply hasn't answered. And Skype has no voicemail, so you can't leave a message.

The other human

You

Mute

Switch to text chat

End video chat

Video settings

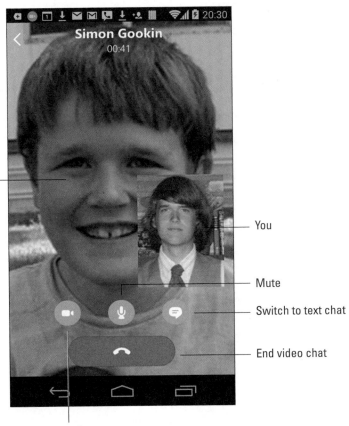

Figure 13-6: A Skype video call.

Part IV
Amazing Phone Feats

Learn how to work the panorama and photo sphere features of the phone's Camera app by visiting www.dummies.com/extras/androidphones.

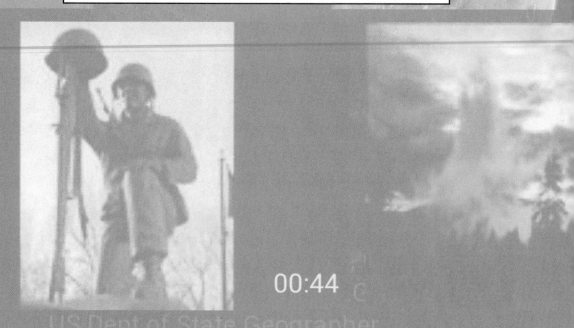

In this part . . .

- ✔ Understand how to use the Maps app.
- ✔ Work with the phone's camera.
- ✔ Explore music on an Android phone.
- ✔ Discover interesting apps.
- ✔ Drool over getting even more apps.

There's a Map for That

*W*here are you? More importantly, where is the nearest Mexican restaurant? Normally, these questions can be best answered when you're somewhere familiar or with someone who knows the territory or while standing at a brightly lit intersection and the restaurant nearby is wafting the aroma of chili peppers and tequila and the sign says *Roberto's*.

The answer to the questions "Where are you?" and "What's nearby?" are readily provided by the Maps app. This app uses your phone's global positioning system (GPS) capabilities to gather information about your location. It also uses Google's vast database to locate interesting places nearby and even get you to those locations. The Maps app is truly amazing and useful — after you understand how it all works.

Basic Map

Perhaps the best thing about using the Maps app is that there's no risk of improperly folding anything. Even better, the Maps app charts everything you need to find your way: freeways, highways, roads, streets, avenues, drives, bike paths, addresses, businesses, and points of interest.

Using the Maps app

Start the Maps app by choosing Maps from the apps drawer, or you may find a Maps app launcher lurking on the Home screen. If you're starting the app for the first time or it has recently been updated, you must agree to the terms and conditions. Do so as directed on the touchscreen.

Your Android phone communicates with GPS satellites to hone in on your current location. (See the later sidebar "Activate your location!") That location appears on the map, similar to Figure 14-1. The position is accurate to within a given range, as shown by a blue circle around your location. If the circle doesn't appear, your location is either pretty darn accurate or you need to zoom in.

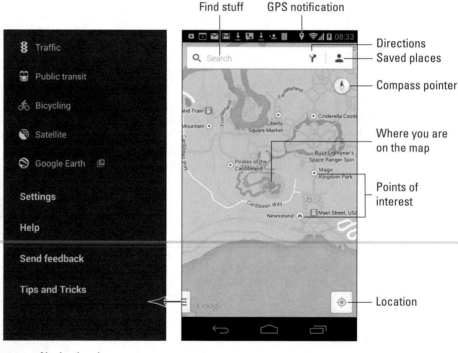

Figure 14-1: Your location on the map.

Here are some fun things you can do when viewing the basic street map:

Zoom in: To make the map larger (to move it closer), double-tap the screen. You can also spread your fingers on the touchscreen to zoom in.

Zoom out: To make the map smaller (to see more), pinch your fingers on the touchscreen.

Pan and scroll: To see what's to the left or right or at the top or bottom of the map, swipe your finger on the touchscreen. The map scrolls in the direction you swipe.

Rotate: Using two fingers, rotate the map clockwise or counterclockwise. Touch the Compass Pointer icon (refer to Figure 14-1) to reorient the map with north at the top of the screen.

Perspective: Touch the screen with two fingers and swipe up or down to view the map in perspective. You can also tap the Location icon to switch to perspective view, although that trick works only for your current location. To return to flat-map view, touch the Compass Pointer icon.

The closer you zoom in to the map, the more detail you see, such as street names, address block numbers, and businesses and other sites — but no tiny people.

- ✔ The blue triangle (refer to Figure 14-1) shows in which general direction the phone is pointing.

- ✔ When the phone's direction is unavailable, you see a blue dot as your location on the map.

- ✔ To view the navigation drawer, touch the icon as shown in Figure 14-1. Swipe the navigation drawer to the left to return to the Maps app.

- ✔ When all you want is a virtual compass, similar to the one you lost as a kid, get the Compass app from the Google Play Store. See Chapter 18 for more information about the Google Play Store.

Activate your location!

The Maps app works best when all the phone's location technologies are activated. The operation is simple: From the apps drawer, open the Settings icon. Choose the Location or Location Services item.

A Master Control icon is found atop the screen. Use it to turn on the phone's location services; ensure that the button reads On. If not, touch the Master Control icon or slide the Off button to the right so that it says, On.

You may find additional settings on the location screen. I recommend that you ensure that each one is activated by placing a check mark next to the service name.

Apps listed on the location screen use location information. You can choose an app icon to examine the app further, but in some cases you won't find any specific controls to disable the app's location requests.

Location information is enhanced when the phone's Wi-Fi is activated. See Chapter 19 for information.

Adding layers

You add details to the map by applying layers: A *layer* can enhance the map's visual appearance, provide more information, or add other fun features to the basic street map, such as the Satellite layer, shown in Figure 14-2.

The key to accessing layers is to touch the Navigation Drawer icon in the lower-left corner of the screen. The navigation drawer displays several layers you can add, such as the Satellite layer shown in Figure 14-2. Another popular layer is Traffic, which lists updated travel conditions.

To remove a layer, choose it again from the navigation drawer; any active layer appears highlighted. When a layer isn't applied, the street view appears.

Your approximate location and direction

Navigation drawer

Figure 14-2: The Satellite layer.

It Knows Where You Are

Many war movies have this cliché scene: Some soldiers are looking at a map. They wonder where they are, when one of them says, "We're not even on the map!" Such things never happen on your phone's Maps app. That's because it always knows where you are.

Well, unless you're on the planet Venus. I've heard that the Maps app won't work there.

Finding out where you are

The Maps app shows your location as a blue dot on the screen. But *where* is that? I mean, if you need to phone a tow truck, you can't just say, "I'm the blue dot on the orange slab by the green thing."

Well, you *can* say that, but it probably won't do any good.

To find your current street address, or any street address, long-press a location on the Maps screen. Up pops a card, similar to the one shown in Figure 14-3. The card gives your approximate address.

If you touch the card, you see a screen with more details and additional information, shown in Figure 14-3, right.

✔ This trick works only when your phone has Internet access. When Internet access isn't available, the Maps app is unable to communicate with the Google map servers.

✔ To make the card go away, touch anywhere else on the map.

Route

✔ The time under the Travel icon (the car in Figure 14-3) indicates how far away the address is from your current location. If the address is too far away, you'll see the Route icon, as shown in the margin.

✔ When you have *way* too much time on your hands, play with the Street View command. Choosing this option displays the location from a 360-degree perspective. In street view, you can browse a locale, pan and tilt, or zoom in on details to familiarize yourself with an area, for example, when you're planning a burglary.

Helping others find your location

You can use your Android phone to send your current location to a friend. If your pal has a phone with smarts similar to those of your Android phone, he can use the coordinates to get directions to your location. Maybe he'll even bring tacos!

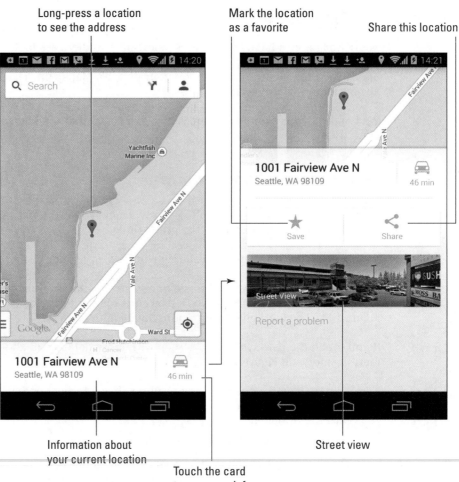

Long-press a location to see the address

Mark the location as a favorite

Share this location

Information about your current location

Touch the card to see more info

Street view

Figure 14-3: Finding an address.

To send your current location to someone else, obey these steps:

1. **Long-press your current location on the map.**

   To see your current location, touch the Location icon in the lower-right corner of the Maps app screen.

   After long-pressing your location (or any location), you see a card displayed showing the approximate address.

2. **Touch the card.**

3. **Touch the Share icon.**

   Refer to Figure 14-3 for this icon's location.

4. **Choose the app to share the message, such as the text messaging app, Gmail, Email, or whichever useful app is listed.**

5. **Continue using the selected app to choose a recipient and otherwise complete the process of sending your location to that person.**

As an example, you can send your location by using the phone's text messaging app. The recipient can touch the link in the text message to open your location in his phone's Maps app. When the location appears, the recipient can follow my advice in the later section "Getting directions" to reach your location. Don't loan him this book either — have him buy his own copy. And bring tacos. Thanks.

Find Things

The Maps app can help you find places in the real world, just as the phone's web browser app helps you find places on the Internet. Both operations work basically the same way: Open the Maps app and type something to find into the Search text box (refer to Figure 14-1). You can type a variety of terms in the Search box, as explained in this section.

Looking for a specific address

To locate an address, type it in the Search box; for example:

```
1600 Pennsylvania Ave., Washington, D.C. 20006
```

Touch the Search button on the keyboard, and that location is shown on the map. The next step is getting directions, which you can read about in the later section "Getting directions."

- ✔ You don't need to type the entire address. Oftentimes, all you need is the street number and street name and then either the city name or zip code.

- ✔ If you omit the city name or zip code, the Maps app looks for the closest matching address near your current location.

- ✔ Touch the X button in the Search box to clear the previous search.

Finding a business, restaurant, or point of interest

You may not know an address, but you know when you crave sushi or perhaps the exotic flavors of Manitoba. Maybe you need a hotel or a gas station, or you have to find a place that fixes dentures. To find a business entity or a point of interest, type its name in the Search box; for example:

```
movie theater
```

This command flags movie theaters on the current Maps screen or nearby.

Have the Maps app jump to your current location, as described earlier in this chapter, to find locations near you. Otherwise, the Maps app looks for places near the area shown on the screen.

Or you can be specific and look for businesses near a certain location by specifying the city name, district, or zip code, such as

```
sushi 98109
```

After typing this command and touching the Search button, you see a smattering of sushi bars found near downtown Seattle, similar to those shown on the left side of side of Figure 14-4.

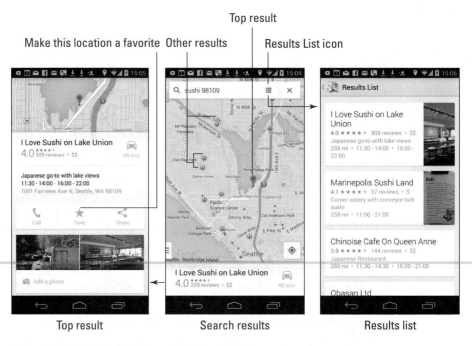

Make this location a favorite · Other results · Top result · Results List icon

Top result · Search results · Results list

Figure 14-4: Search results for sushi in Seattle.

To see more information about a result, touch its card, such as the one for I Love Sushi on Lake Union in Figure 14-4. Or touch the Results List icon to see a whole swath of cards. After touching a card, you can view more details.

Route You can touch the Route icon on the restaurant's (or any location's) details screen to get directions; see the later section "Getting directions." The Route icon also shows up as a car (or other mode of transportation), as shown in Figure 14-4.

✔ Every letter or dot on the screen represents a search result (refer to Figure 14-4).

- Spread your fingers on the touchscreen to zoom in to the map.

- If you *really* like the location, touch the Star icon. That directs the Maps app to keep the location as one of your favorite places. The location is flagged with a Star icon on the Maps app screen. See the next section.

Searching for favorite or recent places

Just as you can bookmark favorite websites on the Internet, you can mark favorite places in the real world by using the Maps app. The feature is called Saved Places.

To visit your favorite places or browse your recent map searches, touch the Saved Places icon at the top of the Maps app screen. If you don't see the icon, touch the X button in the Search box.

The Saved Places window sports various categories of places you've starred (marked as favorites), locations you've recently searched for, or places you've been.

- Mark a location as a favorite by touching the Star icon when you view the location's details.

- The Recently Accessed Places list allows you to peruse items you've located or searched for recently.

- Touch the app icon to return to the Maps app when you've finished looking at saved places.

Locating a contact

You can hone in on where your contacts are located by using the map. This trick works when you've specified an address for the contact — either home or work or another location. If so, your phone can easily help you find that location or even give you directions.

The secret to finding a contact's location is to touch the contact's address as it appears in the phone's address book app, People or Contacts. Sometimes the Place icon is used to help display a location on the Maps app. The Place icon looks like the one shown in the margin.

Your Phone Is Your Copilot

Finding a location is only half the job. The other half is getting there. Thanks to its various direction and navigation features, the Maps app stands at the ready, waiting to be your copilot. It's just like having a backseat driver, but one who knows where he's going and — *bonus* — has a Mute option.

Getting directions

Route

One command associated with locations found in the Maps app is getting directions. The command is called Route, and it shows the Route icon (see the margin) or a mode of transportation, such as a car, bike, or bus. Here's how it works:

1. **Touch the Route icon in a location's card.**

2. **Choose a method of transportation.**

   The available options vary, depending on your location.

3. **Set a starting point.**

   You can type a location or choose from one of the locations shown on the screen, such as your current location, your home location, or any location you've previously searched. Touch the Starting Location item to choose another location.

4. **Ensure that the starting location and destination are what you want.**

   If they're backward, touch the Swap icon, which is labeled in Figure 14-5.

5. **Choose a route card.**

   One or more routes are listed on the screen, as shown in Figure 14-5. Touch one of the cards to see the details, which are shown to the right in the figure.

6. **Peruse the results.**

The map shows your route, highlighted as a blue line on the screen.

To see a list of directions, touch the results card, shown at the bottom of the screen. You'll see a scrolling list of turns, distances, and directions. Touch the Preview icon to get a bird's-eye view of your route.

- ✔ The Maps app alerts you to any toll roads on the specified route. As you travel, you can choose alternative, non-toll routes if available. You're prompted to switch routes during navigation; see the next section.

- ✔ You may not get perfect directions from the Maps app, but it's a useful tool for places you've never visited.

Navigating to your destination

Maps and lists of directions are so twentieth century. I don't know why anyone would bother, especially when your Android phone features a digital copilot, in the form of voice navigation.

To use navigation, obey these steps:

1. **Choose a location on the map.**

   It must be some spot other than your current location. You can search for a spot, type a location, or long-press any part of the map.

Starting location

Mode of transportation   Swap   Route

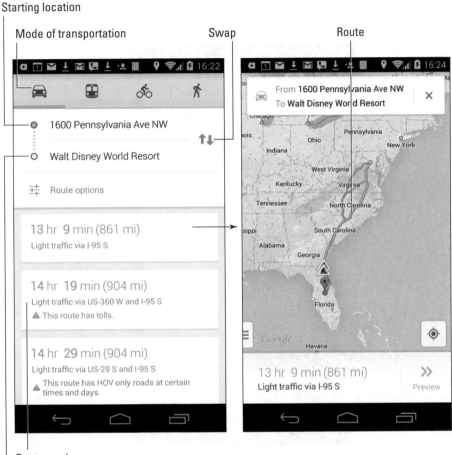

Route card

Destination

Figure 14-5: Planning a trip.

2. **Choose a card from the search results.**

   This process works identically to finding any location; see the earlier section "Find Things."

Route

3. **Touch the Route icon.**

   The Route icon can look like the icon shown in the margin, but most often it looks like a car.

4. **Ensure that My Location is chosen on the next screen, similar to what's shown in Figure 14-6.**

   If you don't see My Location, touch the top entry (where My Location should be), and then choose the My Location item from the next screen.

Your starting point or
current location

Destination

Route

Start navigation

Current location

Figure 14-6: Plotting your course.

5. Choose a card representing the route you want to take.

Sometimes only one card is available, but others may appear. The variety depends on traffic conditions, toll roads, zombie attacks, and similar things you might want to avoid.

6. Touch the Start icon.

And you're on your way.

While navigating, the phone displays an interactive map that shows your current location and turn-by-turn directions for reaching your destination. A digital voice tells you how far to go and when to turn, for example, and gives you other nagging advice, such as to sit up, be nice to other drivers, and call your mother once in a while.

To exit navigation, touch the Close icon at the bottom of the screen.

- ✔ The neat thing about Navigation is that whenever you screw up, a new course is immediately calculated.

- ✔ When you tire of hearing the navigation voice, touch the Action Overflow icon and choose the Mute Voice Guidance command.

- ✔ I refer to the navigation voice as "Gertrude."

- ✔ The phone stays in navigation mode until you exit. A navigation notification can be seen atop the touchscreen while you're in navigation mode.

- ✔ You can touch the Action Overflow icon while navigating and choose Step by Step List to review your journey. The Route Preview command lets you see the big picture.

- ✔ In navigation mode, your phone consumes a *ton* of battery power. I highly recommend that you plug the phone into your car's power adapter (the "cigarette lighter") for the duration of the trip.

The Whole Google Earth

The Earth app is similar to the Maps app, but with one huge difference: It covers the entire planet. And while you can get around and explore your locale or destination using the Maps app, Earth is more of a look-and-see, interactive world atlas.

Your phone may or may not have come with the Earth app. If you don't find the Earth app in the apps drawer, visit the Google Play Store and download a free copy.

If you're familiar with the Google Earth program on a computer, the Earth app should be familiar to you. Its interface is shown in Figure 14-7. It has similar features to the Maps app, but it's customized for viewing the globe.

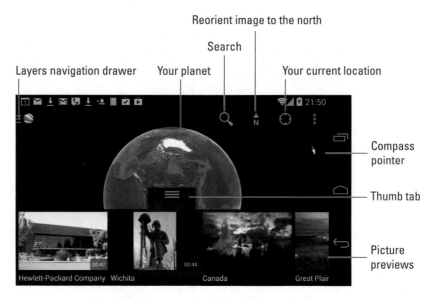

Figure 14-7: Earth, most likely your home planet.

The best advice for using the Earth app is to explore: Drag your finger around the screen to pan and tilt the globe; pinch and spread your fingers to zoom out and zoom in, respectively.

✔ Items in the Layers navigation drawer are used to show or hide map details.

✔ Use the thumb tab to slide the picture previews up or down.

✔ If you enjoy looking up as much as you enjoy looking down, consider getting the Sky Map app. Search the Google Play Store for the Sky Map app from Sky Map Devs. (It was once known as Google Sky Map.)

Pics and Vids

The second thing that Alexander Graham Bell thought of, right after the busy signal, was the camera phone. Sadly, it proved somewhat impractical because cameras and phones of the 1890s weren't really portable. And it was difficult to talk on the phone and hold still for 60 seconds to get the best exposure.

Not until the end of the twentieth century did the marriage of the cell phone and digital camera become successful. It may seem like an odd combination, yet it's quite handy to have the phone act as a camera because most people keep their phones with them. That way, should you chance upon Bigfoot or a UFO, you can always take a picture or video — even when there's no cell signal, which is often the case when I try to photograph Bigfoot.

The Phone's Camera

A camera snob will tell you that no true camera has a ringtone. You know what? He's correct: Phones don't make the best cameras. Regardless, your phone has a camera. It can capture both still and moving images. That task is carried out by using the Camera app.

- The Camera app is typically found on the Home screen, often in the favorites tray. Like every other app, a copy also dwells in the apps drawer.

- When you use the Camera app, the navigation icons (Back, Home, Recent) turn into tiny dots. The icons are still there, and they still work, but you may find them difficult to see.

- When you first start the Camera app, it asks about location settings. I recommend accepting the settings as presented. You can change them afterwards, if you like. See the section "Setting and finding a picture's location" elsewhere in this chapter.

Snapping a picture

After it's started, the Camera app takes over the phone, turning the touch-screen into a viewfinder. The stock Android version of the Camera app is shown in Figure 15-1. Your phone may use a customized version of the Camera app that presents the onscreen controls in a different manner. Even so, all variations of the Camera app sport similar features.

To take a still image, follow these steps:

1. **Start the Camera app.**

2. **Ensure that the camera mode is set to single shot.**

   The Camera app shoots both still images and video. To snap a picture, you must choose single-shot mode. In Figure 15-1, the Single Shot icon is shown. If another icon appeared in that spot, you'd touch that icon and choose Single Shot as the camera mode.

3. **Point the camera at the subject.**

4. **Touch the Shutter icon.**

The phone makes a noise when the picture is snapped.

After the image is snapped, it appears on the screen as a thumbnail. Touch that thumbnail to review the image. If the thumbnail disappears, swipe the screen to the left to review previous images. You can also review any photos taken by the phone by using the Gallery app, as described in the "Your Digital Photo Album" section.

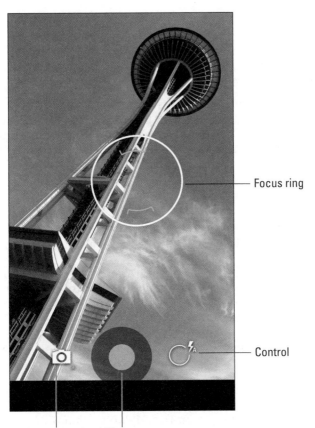

Focus ring

Control

Camera mode   Shutter

Figure 15-1: The stock Android Camera app.

- ✔ The camera focuses automatically. Drag the focus ring around the touch-screen to adjust the focus on a specific object. (Refer to Figure 15-1).

- ✔ When the markers in the focus ring turn green, the camera is focused. If they turn red, the camera is unable to focus on the object.

- ✔ Your phone can take pictures in either landscape or portrait orientation. No matter how you take the picture, the image is stored upright. Even so, you can reorient images later; see the "Rotating pictures" section.

- ✔ You can take as many pictures as you like, as long as you don't run out of space for them in the phone's storage. See Chapter 20 for storage information.

- ✔ If your pictures appear blurry, ensure that the camera lens on the back of the phone isn't dirty.

- Zooming in or out is done either by using onscreen controls or by touching the Volume key. Some phones feature a slider to zoom in or out; others may have you pinch or spread your fingers on the screen.

- Be careful using the Volume key to zoom! Some phones may use the Volume key as an alternative Shutter icon.

- The phone stores pictures in the DCIM/Camera folder. They are stored in the JPEG or PNG file format, with the jpg or png filename extension, respectively. Phones with removable storage feature a settings option in the Camera app to control whether images are saved on internal or removable storage.

Recording video

To capture moving pictures, or video, switch the camera mode to video recording. The same icon is used to switch between still and moving images.

When video mode is active, the Camera app's screen changes subtly: The Shutter icon becomes a Record icon. Touch that icon to start recording video.

While video is being recorded, the Record icon changes to either a Pause or Stop icon. A timer appears on the touchscreen, indicating how long you've been recording video. Touch the Pause or Stop icon to pause or stop recording, respectively.

- As with taking a still image, video recorded by the Camera app is kept on the phone's internal storage. You can peruse videos by using the Gallery app. See the later section, "Your Digital Photo Album."

- The focus ring (labeled in Figure 15-1) may not appear while you're capturing video.

- Video recording uses the same zoom techniques as recording still images. Refer to the preceding section.

- Some versions of the Camera app may allow you to grab a still image while the phone is recording. Simply touch the screen, and the image is snapped and saved.

- Hold steady! The camera still works when you whip the tablet around, but wild gyrations render the video unwatchable.

- Video is saved in the MPEG-4 video file format and feature the mp4 filename extension. The files are found in the DCIM/Camera folder on the phone's internal storage.

Deleting immediately after you shoot

Sometimes, you just can't wait to banish an image to bit hell. Either an annoyed person is standing next to you, begging that the photo be deleted, or you're just not happy and you feel the urge to smash into digital shards the picture you just took. Hastily follow these steps:

1. **Touch the image thumbnail that appears on the screen or swipe the screen to the left.**

   Either technique displays the image you just snapped. If you don't see the thumbnail, tap the screen. If you still don't see it, swipe the screen to the left.

2. **Touch the Delete icon.**

   If you don't see the icon, touch the screen so that the icon shows up.

You might be prompted to remove the image or it might be deleted immediately. If prompted, touch the OK button to confirm.

Also see the later section, "Your Digital Photo Album," for information on managing the phone's images.

Setting the flash

The Camera app features three flash settings. The current setting is shown on the Control icon (refer to Figure 15-1, where the setting is Auto flash). To change the flash setting, follow these steps in the Camera app:

1. **Touch the Control icon.**

   Not every Camera app features a Control icon. If your phone's Camera app lacks such an icon, look for an icon representing the flash setting, similar to the one shown in Figure 15-2. Touch that icon to set the flash. On other phones, touch the Menu icon to look for a flash setting command.

2. **Choose the flash setting.**

   After touching the Control or Flash Setting icon, shown in Figure 15-2, the flash mode is displayed. Three options are available: flash off, auto flash, and flash on.

3. **Select a flash mode.**

   In the stock Android Camera app, the flash mode you choose is reflected on the Control icon.

While the methods for setting the flash may vary, the icons shown in the middle of Figure 15-2 are common for the standard flash settings: off, auto, and on.

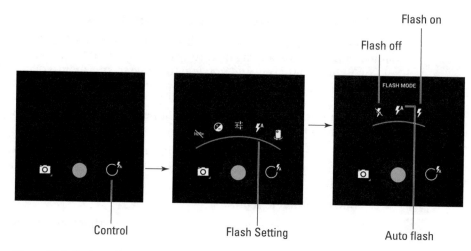

Figure 15-2: Flash settings.

TIP

✔ The auto flash mode turns on the phone's flash in low-light situations, not when it's bright.

✔ When the flash mode is set on, the flash always activates.

✔ When the flash mode is off, the flash never activates, not even in low-light situations.

✔ A good time to turn on the flash is when taking pictures of people or objects in front of something bright, such as Aunt Betty holding her prized peach cobbler in front of an exploding volcano.

✔ A so-called flash setting is available also for shooting video in low-light situations. In that case, the flash LED is on the entire time the video is being shot. This setting is made similarly to setting the flash, although the options are only on and off. It must be set before you shoot video and, yes, it uses a lot of battery power.

Setting the resolution

You don't always have to set the highest resolution for your images, especially when you're shooting for the web or uploading pictures to Facebook, where you really won't want the subjects to be completely recognizable. Such low-resolution images have saved many a political career.

As with other features, not every version of the Camera app follows the same set of directions for setting image resolution. You might find an icon directly on the touchscreen or on a menu displayed by touching the Control icon, the Action Overflow icon, or a Menu icon.

In the stock Android Camera app, you use the Control icon to set single-shot resolution. Follow these steps:

1. **Touch the Control icon.**

   An arch of additional icons appears, as shown in Figure 15-3, left.

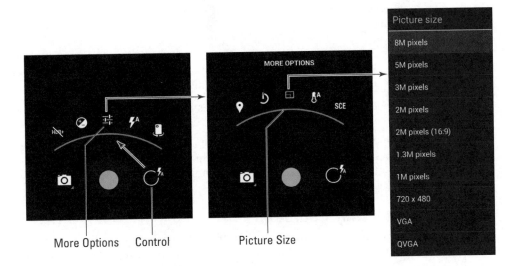

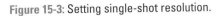

Figure 15-3: Setting single-shot resolution.

2. **Choosing the More Options icon.**

   It's the middle icon. Touch it to see a new set of icons, as shown in Figure 15-3, middle.

3. **Touch the Picture Size icon.**

   The icons disappear and the Picture Size menu appears.

4. **Choose an available resolution.**

   Of the resolutions shown in Figure 15-3, QVGA is the lowest, and VGA is the second lowest. The highest resolution is 8M pixels, or 8 megapixels.

Video recording uses image quality settings, not resolution. To set the image quality for videos, switch the Camera app to video mode as described earlier in this chapter. Then follow the same initial steps you used for setting single-shot resolution. In the stock Android Camera app, you take these steps: Touch the Control icon, touch the Settings icon, and then choose the Video Quality command. Select an item from the onscreen menu.

As with setting single-shot resolution, the highest video quality isn't always required. For example, if you're shooting a video that you plan on uploading to the Internet, select one of the lower if not the lowest quality.

Resolution and video quality for the front-facing camera are set by switching to the front camera (see the next section) and then following the same steps outlined in this section. The resolution and quality choices are more limited, however, because the front-facing camera is not as sophisticated as the rear camera.

✔ Set the resolution or video quality *before* you shoot! Especially when you know where the video will end up (on the Internet, on a TV, or in an e-mail), it helps to set the quality first.

✔ A picture's *resolution* describes how many pixels, or dots, are in the image. The more dots, the better the image looks and prints.

✔ *Megapixel* is a measurement of the amount of information stored in an image. A megapixel is approximately 1 million pixels, or individual dots that compose an image. It's often abbreviated MP.

Shooting yourself

Providing that your phone features a front-facing camera, you can direct the Camera app to use that camera to shoot still images and videos of yourself. The vernacular term is *selfie* for self-shot. Get ready with your duck face!

To take your own mug shot, start the Camera app and switch to the front camera. On the stock Android Camera app, touch the Control icon and then touch the Front Camera icon, shown in the margin. Other variations of the Camera app have a similar control, appearing as an icon on the Camera app screen or found on a menu.

When you see yourself in the Camera app's viewfinder, you've completed the task successfully. Smile. Click.

Touch the same icon again to switch back to the rear camera. The icon may change its appearance, but you should find it in the same location in the Camera app.

Your Digital Photo Album

The pictures and videos you take with your phone don't simply disappear after you touch the Camera app's Shutter icon. Although you can generally preview a previously shot picture or video, the place you go to look at the gamut of visual media is the app named Gallery.

✔ Your Android phone may call the Gallery app by some other name.

✔ Google features an app called Photos. It's tied into both Google's Picasa Web albums as well as Google+ social networking. You do not have to use the Photos app, although it's a better choice than the Gallery app if you use Google.

Visiting the Gallery app

Start the Gallery app by locating its icon. It might be on the Home screen directly or in a folder. And it can always be found in the apps drawer. How the Gallery looks varies from phone to phone, but generally the images are organized by albums. The albums relate to the image's source and how photos are synchronized between photo-sharing services and your phone. Figure 15-4 shows a typical Gallery app with images organized into albums, or piles.

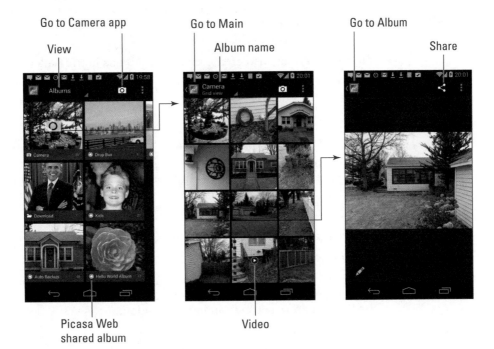

Figure 15-4: The Gallery app.

Touch an album in the Gallery app to display that album's contents; the pictures appear in a grid of thumbnail previews (see Figure 15-4, middle). Swipe the screen left and right to peruse them all.

Touch an individual thumbnail in the album to view that item full size on the screen, as shown in Figure 15-4, right. You can rotate the phone horizontally (or vertically) to see the image in another orientation.

Videos stored in an album appear with a Play icon on the screen. Touch that icon to play the video. As the video is playing, touch the screen again to see the controls to pause the video.

 You back up from an image or a video to an album by touching the Back icon or the app icon in the upper-left corner of the screen.

- The Camera album contains pictures you've shot using the phone's camera.

- The Download album contains images downloaded from the Internet.

- Albums labeled with the Picasa icon have been synchronized between your phone and Picasa Web on the Internet. As a Google Account holder, you have a Picasa Web account, which can be used to share images with your cohorts on the Internet.

- Various apps may also create their own albums in the Gallery app.

- If you synchronize pictures between your phone and a computer, the program that does the synchronizing also creates its own albums.

Setting and finding a picture's location

Your phone's camera not only takes pictures but also keeps track of where you stood on Planet Earth when you touched the Shutter icon. The feature is called Geo-Tag and people either love it or hate it. If you hate it, you can disable the feature by heeding these directions:

1. **Ensure that the Camera app is in single-shot mode.**

2. **Touch the Control icon.**

   Your phone's Camera app may instead feature a command button, a Settings icon, or perhaps a Menu or Action Overflow icon that contains the Camera app's settings and configuration.

3. **Choose Settings.**

   The Settings icon is shown in the margin.

4. **Choose Location.**

   The Location icon is shown in the margin.

The Geo-Tag feature has been disabled.

 When the Geo-Tag feature has been disabled, the Control icon in the stock Android Camera app changes as shown in the margin.

To reenable the Geo-Tag feature, repeat these steps.

When the Geo-Tag feature is enabled, you can coordinate between the phone's Gallery and Maps apps to see exactly where a picture was taken. To do so, view the image in the Gallery app. With the image displayed on the screen, touch the Action Overflow icon (or the Menu icon) and choose the Show on Map command. The Maps app starts, displaying the spot where the image was taken.

Sharing from the Gallery

The key to getting images out of the phone and into the world is to look for the Share icon, as shown in the margin. Touch that icon while viewing an image (refer to Figure 15-4, right), and peruse the apps shown on the list to choose a sharing method. Here are some of your choices:

Bluetooth: Send the picture or video to another device via the Bluetooth connection. That other device could be a printer, for example, in which case you can print the picture. See Chapter 19 for details on sharing with Bluetooth.

Gmail and Email: Attach the image to a new message you compose using the Gmail or Email app.

Facebook: Share the photo on the Facebook app.

Drive: Save the photo on your Google Drive. Likewise, if you have the Dropbox app installed, an Add to Dropbox option appears for saving the image on that cloud storage site as well.

To review all the options, you may have to choose the See All command. The total number of apps available for sharing images depends on the variety of apps installed on your phone.

For sharing videos, choose the YouTube option, found by choosing See All from the menu. Fill in the information on the screen and touch the Upload button to publish your video.

Image Management

The Gallery app is more than just a photo album. It also sports features that let you perform some minor image surgery. This section discusses a few of the more interesting options.

Cropping an image

One of the few, true image-editing commands available in the Gallery app is Crop. You can use Crop tool to slice out portions of an image, such as when removing ex-spouses and convicts from a family portrait. To crop an image, obey these directions while using the Gallery app:

1. **Summon the image you want to crop.**

   You must view the image on the screen by itself.

2. **Touch the Action Overflow icon.**

   On some phones, touch the Menu icon to view the list of commands.

3. **Choose Crop.**

   Sometimes you must choose an Edit command before you can find the Crop command.

   If the Crop command is unavailable, you have to choose another image. (Not every album lets you modify images.)

4. **Work the crop-thing.**

   You can drag the rectangle around to choose which part of the image to crop. Drag an edge of the rectangle to resize the left and right or top and bottom sides. Or drag a corner of the rectangle to change the rectangle's size proportionally. Use Figure 15-5 as your guide.

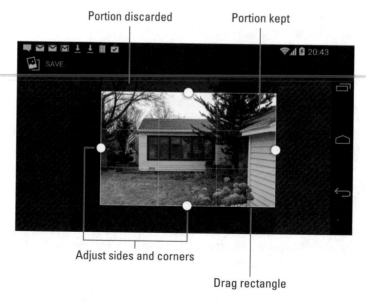

Figure 15-5: Working the crop thing.

5. **Touch the Done or Save button when you've finished cropping.**

   Only the portion of the image within the rectangle is saved; the rest is discarded.

Most versions of the Gallery app do not let you undo a crop action. I have seen a couple that actually created a duplicate, cropped image and left the original untouched. Experiment on a throwaway picture to see which way your phone's Gallery app behaves.

Rotating pictures

Showing someone else an image on your phone can be frustrating, especially when the image is a vertical picture that refuses to fill the screen when the phone is in a vertical orientation. You can fix that issue by rotating the picture.

To rotate, view the image in the Gallery app. Touch the Action Overflow icon and choose either the Rotate Left or the Rotate Right command. Repeat a command if you need to reorient the image more than 90 degrees.

- ✓ On some phones you may have to choose an Edit command first, and then locate the Rotate commands.
- ✓ Instead of commands, you might find Rotate icons.
- ✓ To undo an image rotation, simply rotate the image again but in the opposite direction.

Deleting photos and videos

It's entirely possible, and often desirable, to remove unwanted, embarrassing, or questionably legal images and videos from the Gallery. The limitation is that you can remove only those images copied to or created by the phone's camera. That category includes all the images in the Camera album, the Download album, and any albums you've synchronized from your desktop computer.

 To delete an image, view it in the Gallery app. Touch the Delete icon and then touch the OK button to confirm. Poof! It's gone.

- ✓ If the Delete icon doesn't show up, touch the screen. If the icon still doesn't show up, look for it on the Action Overflow menu.
- ✓ You can perform mass execution of images when viewing an album: Touch the Action Overflow icon and choose the Select Item command. Touch images to select them, and then touch the Delete icon to rid yourself of the lot. Touch the OK button to confirm.
- ✓ You can't undelete an image you've deleted. There's no way to recover such an image using available tools on the phone.
- ✓ You cannot edit some images, such as images brought in from social networking sites or from online photo-sharing services.

O Sweet Music!

In This Chapter

- Keeping music on your phone
- Listening to a song
- Copying music from your computer
- Purchasing music
- Organizing your music into playlists
- Listening to streaming music

*P*ush-button phones and tone dialing were introduced in the 1970s. People realized that the tones generated by dialing certain numbers sounded like popular tunes. My parents' home number sounded like *Yankee Doodle*. On your Android phone, however, listening to music is much more than enjoying dialing tones.

Just like those popular mobile-music gizmos that rhyme with "pie rod," your Android phone can play music. You can listen to songs you buy online, synchronize them from a computer, or find music on the Internet. Some phones can even listen to FM radio. So wherever you go with your phone, which should be everywhere, you also carry your music library.

The Hits Just Keep On Comin'

Your Android phone is ready to entertain you with music whenever you want to hear it. Simply plug in the headphones, summon the music-playing app, and choose tunes to match your mood. It's truly blissful — well, until someone calls you and the phone ceases being a musical instrument and returns to being the ball-and-chain of the digital era.

- ✔ To handle music-playing duties, your phone comes with a music-playing app. The stock Android app is Google's own Play Music app. That's the app covered in this chapter.

✔ In addition to the Play Music app, your phone may feature another music-playing app. I've seen names such as Music and My Music. These apps behave similarly to the Play Music app, albeit with subtle differences.

✔ Be wary of music subscription services offered through your phone's manufacturer or cellular provider. I've subscribed to such services only to find them canceled for various reasons. To avoid that disappointment, stick with the services described in this chapter until you feel comfortable enough to buy into another service.

Browsing the music library

After you start the Play Music app, you see a screen similar to Figure 16-1. If you're displeased with the quantity of available music, refer to the later section "More Music for Your Phone."

To view your music library, choose My Library from the navigation drawer, as shown in Figure 16-1. Your music library appears on the main Play Music screen. Touch a tab to view your music by categories such as Artists, Albums, or Songs.

You can choose the Listen Now category from the navigation drawer to see songs you frequently listen to or tunes the phone guesses you will like. The more you use the Play Music app, the more you'll appreciate the results displayed.

✔ Music is stored on your phone's internal storage as well as on the microSD card.

✔ Use the View action bar, shown in Figure 16-1, to choose which music to view: The All Music item shows all music available on the phone as well as with your Play Music account on the Internet. The On Device item directs the Play Music app to show only the music stored directly on the phone.

✔ The size of the phone's storage limits the total amount of music you can keep on your phone. Also consider that pictures and videos stored on your phone horn in on some of the space that could be used for music.

✔ See the later section "More Music for Your Phone" for information on getting music into your phone.

✔ Album artwork generally appears on imported music as well as on music you purchase online. If an album has no artwork, it cannot be manually added or updated (at least, not by using the Play Music app).

✔ When your phone is unable to recognize an artist, it uses the title Unknown Artist. This happens with music you copy manually to the phone. Music that you purchase, import, or synchronize with a computer generally retains the artist and album information. (Well, the information is retained as long as it was supplied by the original source.)

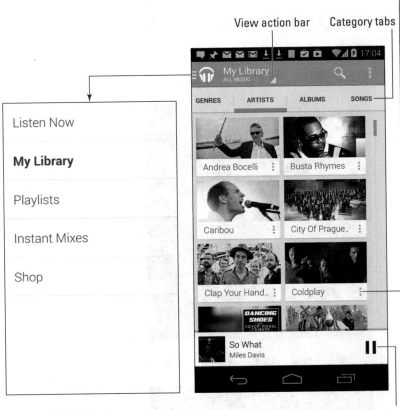

Artist Action Overflow

View action bar   Category tabs

Listen Now

My Library

Playlists

Instant Mixes

Shop

Navigation drawer

Song currently playing

Figure 16-1: The Play Music app.

Playing a tune

To listen to music on your phone, you first find a song in your music library, as described in the preceding section. After you find the song, you touch its title. The song plays on another screen, similar to what's shown in Figure 16-2.

While the song is playing, you're free to do anything else with the phone. In fact, the song continues to play even when the phone is locked; a shortcut to the song, along with control icons, appears right on the lock screen along with information about the song.

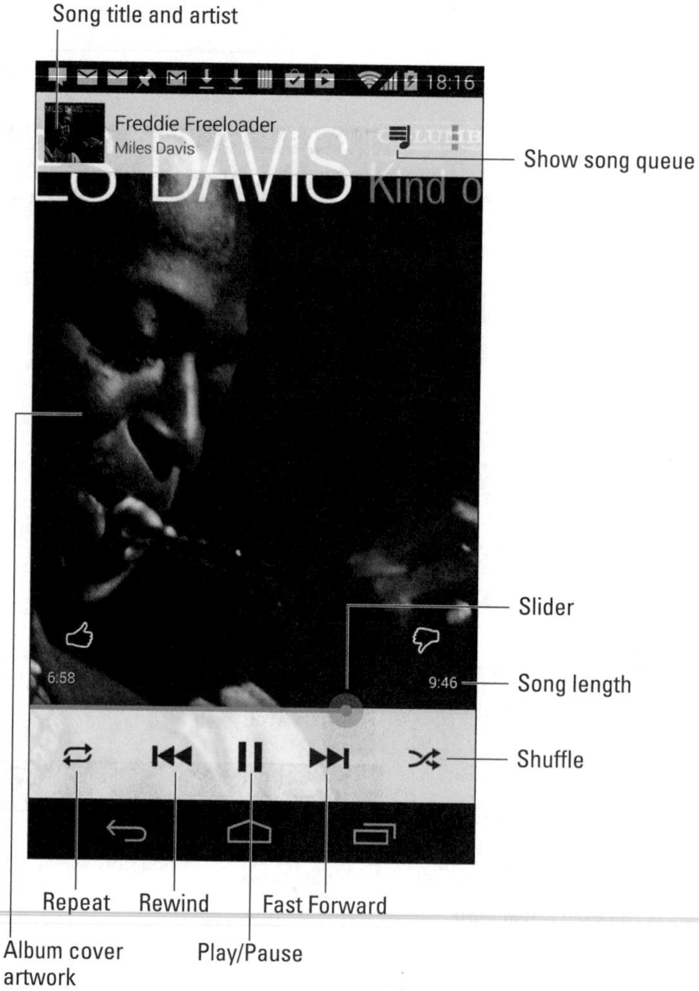
Song title and artist
18:16
Freddie Freeloader
Miles Davis
Show song queue
Slider
6:58
9:46
Song length
Shuffle
Repeat
Rewind
Fast Forward
Album cover artwork
Play/Pause

Figure 16-2: A song is playing.

After the song has finished playing, the next song in the list plays.

The next song doesn't play if you have the Shuffle icon activated (refer to Figure 16-2). In that case, the Play Music app randomly chooses another song from the same list. Who knows which one is next?

The next song might not play also when you have the Repeat option on: The three repeat settings are illustrated in Table 16-1, along with the Shuffle settings. To change settings, simply touch either the Shuffle or the Repeat icon.

Table 16-1	Shuffle and Repeat Icons	
Icon	*Setting*	*What Happens When You Touch the Icon*
⤭	Shuffle is off	Songs play one after the other
⤭	Shuffle is on	Songs play in random order
⮂	Repeat is off	Songs don't repeat
⮂①	Repeat current song	The same song plays over and over
⮂	Repeat all songs	All songs in the list play over and over

To stop the song from playing, touch the Pause icon (labeled in Figure 16-2).

When music plays on the phone, a notification icon appears, similar to the one shown in the margin. Use this notification to quickly summon the Play Music app and pause the song or see which song is playing.

- The volume is set by using the Volume key on the side of the phone: Up is louder, down is quieter.

- While browsing the music library, you see the currently playing song displayed at the bottom of the screen.

- Determining which song plays next depends on how you chose the song that's playing. If you chose a song by artist, all songs from that artist play, one after the other. When you choose a song by album, that album plays. Choosing a song from the entire song list causes all songs in the phone to play.

- To choose which songs play after each other, create a playlist. See the "Organize Your Tunes" section, later in this chapter.

- After the last song in the list plays, the phone stops playing songs — unless you have the Repeat option on, in which case the song or list plays again.

Pinning your music

Most of the music you have in your Google Play Music library, especially music obtained from the Play Store, is actually stored on the Internet, not on the phone. As long as you have an Internet connection, your phone can play the music. But when you don't have an Internet connection . . . silence.

To make your music available off-line, you need to pin it to the phone's storage. That sounds weird, but it's a virtual pin so there's no blood. Here's how it works:

1. **Display the Play Music app's navigation drawer.**

2. **Choose My Library.**

   Behold your music library.

3. **Locate the song, artist, or album you want to keep stored on the phone.**

4. **Touch the Action Overflow icon by the song, artist, or album.**

5. **Choose the Keep on Device command.**

The music is downloaded to the phone and made available to play all the time.

- ✔ Pinned music (stored on the phone) features a Pin icon, similar to what's shown in the margin. That icon can be used also when viewing an album; touch it to keep the entire album on the device.

- ✔ When you copy music to the phone from a computer, the music is always kept on the device. See the later section "Borrowing music from your computer."

- ✔ To review the music already on the phone, go to the main Play Music app screen. Touch the View action bar and choose the On Device command.

Being the life of the party

You need to do four things to make your Android phone the soul of your next shindig or soirée:

- ✔ Connect it to external speakers.
- ✔ Use the Shuffle command.
- ✔ Set the Repeat command.
- ✔ Provide plenty of drinks and snacks.

The external speakers can be provided by anything from a custom media dock, a stereo, or the sound system on the Times Square Jumbotron. As long as the device has a standard line input, you're good.

"What's this song?"

You might consider getting a handy, music-oriented widget called Sound Search for Google Play. You can obtain it from the Google Play Store and then add it to the Home screen, as described in Chapter 22. From the Home screen, you can use the widget to identify music playing within earshot of your phone.

To use the widget, touch it on the Home screen. The widget immediately starts listening to your surroundings, as shown in the middle of the sidebar figure. After a few seconds, the song is recognized and displayed. You can choose to either buy the song at the Google Play Store or touch the Cancel button and start over.

The Sound Search widget works best (exclusively, I would argue) with recorded music. Try as you might, you cannot sing into the thing and have it recognize a song. Humming doesn't work, either. I've tried playing the guitar and piano and — nope — that didn't work either. But for listening to ambient music, it's a good tool for discovering what you're listening to.

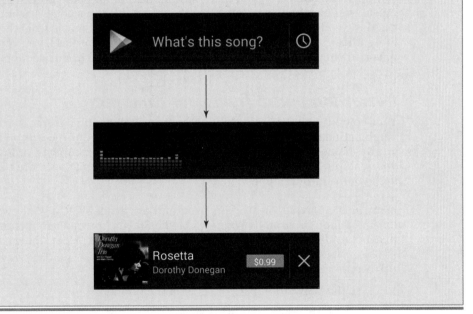

Oh, and you need an audio cable. Get one with a mini-headphone connector for the phone's headphone jack and an audio jack that matches the output device. Look for such a cable at Radio Shack or any store where the employees wear name tags.

After you connect your phone to the speakers, start the Play Music app. Choose the party playlist you've created, per directions elsewhere in this chapter. If you want the songs to play in random order, touch the Shuffle icon.

You might also consider choosing the List Repeat command (see Table 16-1) so that all songs in the list repeat.

> ✔ To play all songs saved on your phone, choose the Songs category and touch the first song in the list.
>
> ✔ See the later section "Organize your Tunes" for information on creating playlists. Build one playlist for your book club and another one for your theater friends.
>
> ✔ Enjoy your party, and please drink responsibly.

More Music for Your Phone

Although the odds are good that your phone did not come preinstalled with music, you may find some tunes available — typically a generic sampling of the Google Play Music library. Or if you've purchased music from the Play Store, those songs and albums appear in the list. Regardless, you can add music to your phone in a number of ways, as covered in this section.

Borrowing music from your computer

Your computer is the equivalent of the twentieth-century stereo system — a combination tuner, amplifier, and turntable, plus all your records and CDs. If you've already copied your music collection to your computer, or if you use your computer as your main music-storage system, you can share that music with your Android phone.

Many music-playing, or jukebox, programs are available. On Windows, the most common program is Windows Media Player. You can use this program to synchronize music between your phone and the PC. Here's how it works:

1. **Connect the phone to the PC.**

   Use the USB cable that comes with the phone.

   Over on the PC, an AutoPlay dialog box appears in Windows, prompting you to choose how best to mount the phone into the Windows storage system.

   Ensure that your phone is connected as a media player or uses something called MTP. See Chapter 20 if you have difficulty making the connection.

2. **On the PC, choose Windows Media Player from the AutoPlay dialog box.**

   If an AutoPlay dialog box doesn't appear, start the Windows Media Player program.

3. **On the PC, ensure that the Sync list appears, as shown in Figure 16-3.**

   Click the Sync tab or Sync toolbar button to view the Sync list. Your phone should appear in the list, similar to what's shown in the figure.

4. **Drag to the Sync area the music you want to transfer to your phone.**

   Figure 16-3 shows a list of songs in the Sync list. To add more, drag an album or an individual song to the Sync list. Dragging an album sets up all its songs for transfer.

5. **Click the Start Sync button to transfer the music from the PC to your Android phone.**

   The Start Sync button may be located atop the list, as shown in Figure 16-3, or it might be found at the bottom of the list.

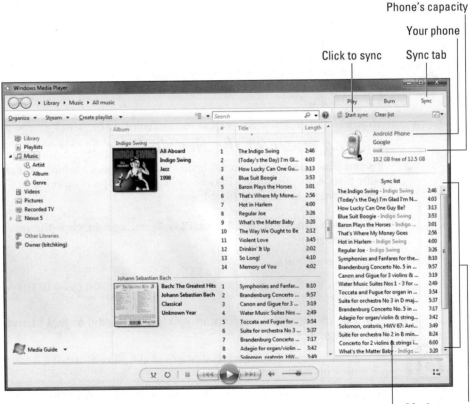

Figure 16-3: Adding music to your phone.

6. **Close the Windows Media Player when the transfer is complete.**

   Or keep it open — whatever.

7. **Unplug the phone from the USB cable.**

   You can unplug the USB cable from the computer as well. If you need more information about the phone-to-computer connection, see Chapter 20.

The steps for synchronizing music with other media jukebox programs work similarly to those just outlined.

✔ You cannot use iTunes to synchronize music with Android phones.

✔ On some phones you can copy music from a computer to your phone but then can't find the music. That's because a handful of phones don't allow copied music to be played. In that case, only music you buy online can be played on the device.

✔ The phone can store only so much music! Don't be overzealous when copying over your tunes. In Windows Media Player (refer to Figure 16-3), a capacity-thermometer thing shows you how much storage space is used and how much is available on your phone. Pay heed to the indicator!

Buying music at the Google Play Store

It's possible to get your music from the same source where you get apps for your phone — the Google Play Store. Getting apps is covered in Chapter 18. Getting music is covered right here:

1. **Touch the Apps icon in the Play Music app to view the navigation drawer.**

2. **Choose Shop.**

   The Play Store app starts, immediately whisking you to the Music part of the store.

3. **Use the Search icon to help you locate music, or just browse the categories.**

   Keep an eye out for special offers at the Play Store. It's a great way to pick up some free tunes.

   Eventually you'll see a page showing details about the song or album. Choose a song from the list to hear a preview. The button next to the song or album indicates the purchase price or says FREE for free music.

4. **Touch the FREE button to get a free song, touch the BUY or price button to purchase a song or an album.**

   Don't worry — you're not buying anything yet.

5. **To buy music, choose your credit card or payment source.**

   If a credit card or payment source doesn't appear, choose the Add Card option to add a payment method. Sign up with Google Checkout and submit your credit card or other payment information.

   You may be prompted to type your Google password.

6. **Touch the Buy or Confirm button.**

   The song or album is added to the music library.

The music you buy at the Play Store isn't downloaded to your phone. It shows up, but it plays over the Internet. That means you can hear it only when the phone has an Internet connection. To ensure that the music is always available, see the earlier section, "Pinning your music."

✐ You'll eventually receive a Gmail message listing a summary of your purchase.

✐ All music sales are final. Don't blame me; I'm just writing down Google's current policy for music purchases.

✐ If you plan on downloading an album or multiple songs, connect to a Wi-Fi network. That way, you won't run the risk of a data surcharge on your cellular plan. See Chapter 19 for information on activating Wi-Fi.

✐ Music you purchase from the Google Play Music store is available on any mobile Android device with the Play Music app installed, provided you use the same Google account on that device. You can also listen to your tunes by visiting the `music.google.com` site on any computer connected to the Internet.

Organize Your Tunes

The Play Music app categorizes your music by album, artist, song, and so forth, but unless you have only one album and enjoy all the songs on it, that configuration probably won't do. To better organize your music, you can create *playlists*. That way, you can hear the music you want to hear, in the order you want, for whatever mood hits you.

Reviewing your playlists

To view any playlists that you've already created or that have been preset on the phone, display the Play Music app's navigation drawer and choose Playlists. You'll see the playlists on the screen, similar to what's shown in Figure 16-4.

To see which songs are in a playlist, touch the playlist album icon. To play the songs in the playlist, touch the first song in the list.

Playlist name

Playlist Action Overflow

Figure 16-4: Playlists in the Play Music app.

A playlist is a helpful way to organize music when a song's information may not have been completely imported into the phone. For example, if you're like me, you probably have a lot of songs labeled Unknown. A quick way to remedy that situation is to name a playlist after the artist and then add those unknown songs to the playlist. The next section describes how it's done.

Building playlists

The Play Music app features two "auto" playlists, one for the last songs you've added and another for free and purchased songs. Beyond that the playlists you see are those you create. Here's how it works:

1. **Locate music you want to add to a playlist.**

2. **Touch the Action Overflow icon by the album or song.**

3. **Choose the Add to Playlist command.**

   Ensure that you're viewing a song or an album; otherwise the Add to Playlist command doesn't show up.

4. **Choose an existing playlist. Or to create a playlist, choose New Playlist.**

   If you choose to create a playlist, type a name for the playlist and touch the OK button.

The song or album is added to the playlist you selected, or it's placed into a new playlist you created. You can continue to add songs to the playlist by repeating Steps 1–3.

✔ You can have as many playlists as you like on the phone and stick as many songs as you like into them. Adding songs to a playlist doesn't noticeably affect the phone's storage capacity.

✔ To remove a song from a playlist, open the playlist and touch the menu icon by the song. Then choose Remove from Playlist.

✔ Removing a song from a playlist doesn't delete the song from the music library; see the next section.

✔ Songs in a playlist can be rearranged: While viewing the playlist, use the tab on the far left end of a song title to drag that song up or down in the list.

✔ To delete a playlist, touch the Action Overflow icon in the playlist icon's lower-right corner (labeled in Figure 16-4). Choose the Delete command. Touch OK to confirm.

Deleting music

Depending on the source, you have two ways to deal with unwanted music in the Play Music app's library. The different ways depend on whether or not the song is stored directly on the phone.

■ For music stored on the device, locate the song or album and touch the Action Overflow icon. Choose the Delete command. Touch the OK button to remove the song.

If you don't see a Delete command on the menu, the song is available only through Google Play Music. To remove it, visit Google Play on the Internet at music.google.com. View your library to locate the song. Click the Action Overflow icon by a song and choose the Delete command. Click the Delete Song button to confirm.

Your Phone Is a Radio

Although they're not broadcast radio stations, some sources on the Internet — *Internet radio* sites — play music. Lamentably, your Android phone doesn't come with any Internet radio apps, but that doesn't stop you from finding a few good ones at the Google Play Store. Two free services that I can recommend are

✔ TuneIn Radio

✔ Pandora Radio

The TuneIn Radio app gives you access to hundreds of Internet radio stations broadcasting around the world. They're organized by category, so you can find just about whatever you want. Many of the radio stations are also broadcast radio stations, so odds are good that you can find a local station or two, which you can listen to on your phone.

Pandora Radio lets you select music based on your mood and then customizes, according to your feedback, the tunes you listen to. The app works like the Internet site www.pandora.com, in case you're familiar with it. The nifty thing about Pandora is that the more you listen, the better the app gets at finding music you like.

These apps are available at the Google Play Store. They're free, though paid versions might also be available.

✔ Some phones may feature FM radio apps. These apps magically pull radio signals from the air and put them into your ear. The phone's radio hardware requires that a headset be plugged in for the app to work.

✔ It's best to listen to Internet radio when your phone is connected to the Internet via a Wi-Fi connection. Streaming music can use a lot of your cellular data plan's data allotment.

✔ See Chapter 18 for more information about the Google Play Store.

✔ Internet music of the type delivered by the apps mentioned in this section is referred to by the nerds as *streaming music.* That's because the music arrives on your phone as a continuous download from the source. Unlike music you download and save, streaming music is played as it comes in and not stored long-term.

Apps Various and Sundry

*W*hen cell phones started to become sophisticated, manufacturers began installing a few basic apps, or programs. Those early apps were pitiful. In fact, I remember my first cell phone that came with a smattering of apps; I never touched them. Still, it's kind of traditional for a phone to come with an alarm clock, a calculator, a calendar, and perhaps a few games. Your Android phone is no different, and this chapter covers those basic apps, which I believe you'll find less pitiful and more useful than the traditional apps of yore.

The Alarm Clock

Your Android phone keeps constant and accurate track of the time, which is displayed at the top of the Home screen and also when you unlock the phone. When you'd rather have the phone wake you up, you can take advantage of the Clock app, which might also be called Alarm or Alarm & Timer or a similar name.

The Clock app features a basic display, which shows the time and temperature and gives you access to music or perhaps a slideshow. Figure 17-1, left, shows the stock Android Clock app.

Figure 17-1: A typical clock app.

You create alarms by viewing the alarm portion of the Alarm app: Touch the Alarms icon. In some variations of the Clock app, you might have to choose Alarms from a menu or a tab.

An alarm must be set to make it active.

Add a new alarm by touching the Add icon and setting the alarm time, frequency, ringtone, and other information. The alarm you create appears on the Alarms screen, similar to the one shown in Figure 17-1, right.

Alarms must be set, or else they won't trigger. Set an existing alarm by touching its Master Control icon, changing Off to On.

✔ When an alarm is set, an Alarm status icon appears atop the screen, similar to what appears in the margin. The icon is your clue that an alarm is set and ready to trigger.

✔ For a larger time display, you can add the Clock widget to the Home screen. Refer to Chapter 22 for more information about widgets on the Home screen.

✔ Turning off an alarm doesn't delete the alarm.

✔ To delete an alarm, choose the Delete (Trash) icon, shown in Figure 17-1, right. For some Clock apps, you have to long-press the alarm and choose the Delete Alarm command, or touch the red X to remove it.

✔ The alarm doesn't work when you turn off the phone. The alarm goes off, however, when the phone is sleeping. The alarm sounds also when you've silenced the phone.

✔ Consider getting a docking station so that you can use your phone as a nighttime music station and clock.

✔ So tell me: Do alarms go *off,* or do they go *on*?

The Calculator

The Calculator is perhaps the oldest of all traditional cell phone apps. It's probably also the least confusing and frustrating app to use.

Start the Calculator app by choosing its icon from the apps drawer. The Calculator presents itself, along the lines of what's shown in Figure 17-2.

Not every phone's calculator app looks the same, though they all have the same basic mode of operation.

✔ In the stock Android Calculator app, shown in Figure 17-2, you can swipe the screen to the left to see a panel of strange, advanced mathematical operations you'll probably never use.

✔ Long-press the calculator's results to cut or copy the results.

✔ I use the calculator most often to determine my tip at a restaurant. In Figure 17-2, I calculated an 18 percent tip on a tab of $89.56.

Figure 17-2: The Calculator.

The Calendar

Feel free to toss out any datebook you have. You never need to buy another one again because the ideal datebook and appointment calendar is the Calendar app. Combined with the Google Calendar feature on the Internet, you can manage all your scheduling right on your Android phone. It's almost cinchy.

- ✔ Google Calendar works with your Google account to keep track of your schedule and appointments. You can visit Google Calendar on the web at

  ```
  http://calendar.google.com
  ```

- ✔ You automatically have a Google Calendar; it comes with your Google account.

- ✔ I recommend that you use the Calendar app on your phone to access Google Calendar. It's a better way to access your schedule than using the Internet app to reach Google Calendar on the web.

✔ Before you throw away your datebook, copy into the Calendar app some future appointments and info, such as birthdays and anniversaries.

✔ The Calendar app may be called the S Planner app on some Samsung phones. It's the same thing.

✔ You can install the Calendar widget on the Home screen for quick access to looming appointments. See Chapter 22 for details on adding widgets to the Home screen.

Browsing dates and appointments

Figure 17-3 shows the Calendar app's three views: month, week, and day. They look subtly different in horizontal orientation, but it's the same information. Not shown is the agenda view, which displays only upcoming events. Each view is chosen from the View action bar, illustrated in the figure.

✔ Use month view to see an overview of what's going on, and use week or day view to see your appointments.

✔ I check week view at the start of the week to remind me of what's coming up.

✔ To scroll from month to month, swipe the screen up or down. In week view and day view, scroll from left to right.

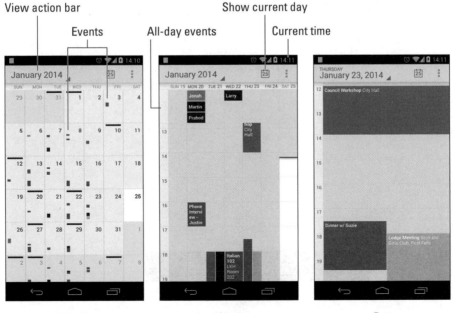

Figure 17-3: The Calendar app.

✔ Touch the Today icon to be instantly whisked back to the current day.

✔ The current day is highlighted in month and week view. A horizontal bar marks the current time (refer to week view in Figure 17-3).

✔ Different colors flag your events. The colors represent a calendar category to which the events are assigned. See the later section, "Creating an event," for information on calendars.

Reviewing appointments

To see more detail about an event, touch it. When you're using month view, touch the event's date to see the week view. Then choose the event again to see its details, similar to the event shown in Figure 17-4.

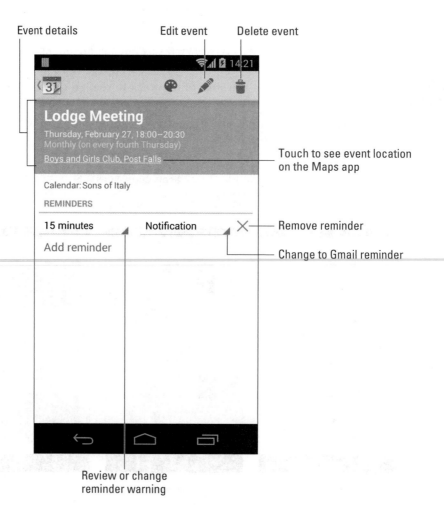

Figure 17-4: Event details.

The details you see depends on how much information was recorded when the event was created. Some events have only a minimum of information; others may have details, such as a location for the event. When the event's location is listed, you can touch that location, and the Maps app pops up to show you where the event is being held.

 Touch the Back icon to dismiss the event's details.

✔ Birthdays and a few other events on the calendar may be pulled from the phone's address book or from some social networking apps. That probably explains why some events are listed twice; they're pulled in from two sources.

✔ The best way to review upcoming appointments is to choose the Agenda item from the View action bar.

✔ To quickly view upcoming events from the Home screen, slap down the Calendar widget. As in agenda view, the widget displays only a list of your upcoming appointments. See Chapter 22 for information on applying widgets to the Home screen.

✔ Google Now also lists any immediate appointments or events. See the later section "Google Now."

Creating an event

The key to making the calendar work is to add events: appointments, things to do, meetings, or full-day events such as birthdays or colonoscopies. To create an event, follow these steps in the Calendar app:

1. **Select the day for the event.**

   Or if you like, you can switch to day view, where you can touch the starting time for the new event.

2. **Touch the New Event icon.**

   The icon is shown in the margin, although it might appear only when the phone is oriented horizontally. If you don't see that icon, or any Add icon, touch the Action Overflow or Menu icon to locate the New Event command.

   The New Event screen appears. Your job now is to fill in the blanks to create the event.

3. **Set information for the event.**

   The quantity and order of the information you can fill in varies between the different versions of the Calendar app. The most important information includes:

   • Event title or name

   • Event date, starting time, and ending time

- Whether the event repeats

- A reminder for the event

- The calendar or event category

The more information you supply, the more detailed the event, and the more you can do with it on your phone as well as on Google Calendar on the Internet.

4. **Touch the Done or Save button to create the event.**

The Done button has a check mark by it, and it's located in the upper-right corner of the New Event screen.

The new event appears on the calendar, reminding you that you need to do something on such-and-such a day.

When an event's day and time arrives, an event reminder notification appears, similar to what's shown in the margin. You might also receive a Gmail notification, depending on how you chose to be reminded when the event was created.

- You can change an event at any time: Simply touch the event to bring up more information and then touch the Edit icon to make modifications. (Refer to Figure 17-4.)

- Calendar categories are handy because they let you organize and color-code your events. They can be confusing because Google calls them "calendars." I think of them more as categories: I have different calendars (categories) for my personal and work schedules, government duties, clubs, and so on.

- Try to avoid using the Phone or Device category for your events. Those events appear on your phone but aren't shared with your Google account.

- My advice is to type location information for an event as though you're typing a search query for the Maps app. When the event is displayed, the location becomes a link; touch the link to see where you need to go on the map.

- When the event lasts all day, such as a birthday or your mother-in-law's visit that was supposed to last for an hour, touch the All Day box to add a check mark.

- When you have events that repeat twice a month — say, on the first and third Mondays — you need to create two separate events, one for the first Monday and another for the third. Then have each event repeat monthly.

- You can set additional reminders by touching the Add Reminder icon.

✔ To remove an event, touch the event to bring up more information and then touch the Delete icon. Touch the OK button to confirm. When deleting repeating events, you'll need to specify whether all events are being removed or only the one.

✔ It's necessary to set an event's time zone only when it takes place in another time zone or when an event spans time zones, such as an airline flight. In that case, the Calendar app automatically adjusts the starting and stopping times for events, depending on where you are.

✔ If you forget to set the time zone and you end up hopping around the world, your events are set according to the time zone in which they were created, not the local time.

The Game Machine

For all its seriousness and technology, one of the best uses of a smartphone is to play games. I'm not talking about silly arcade games (though I admit that they're fun). No, I'm talking about some serious portable gaming.

To whet your appetite, your Android phone may have come with a small taste of what the device can do in regard to gaming; look for preinstalled game apps in the apps drawer. If you don't find any, choose from among the hordes available at the Google Play Store, covered in Chapter 18.

Game apps use phone features such as the touchscreen or the accelerometer to control the action. It takes some getting used to, especially if you regularly play using a game console or PC, but it can be fun — and addicting.

The e-Book Reader

Your Android phone comes with Google's own e-book reader app. It has the clever name Play Books, and it can be found in the apps drawer or perhaps on the phone's Home screen.

Begin your reading experience by opening the Play Books app. If you're prompted to turn on synchronization, touch the Turn On Sync button.

The Play Books app organizes books into a library and displays them for reading, similar to the way they're shown in Figure 17-5. The library lists any titles you've obtained for your Google Books account. Or when you're returning to the Play Books app after a break, you see the current page of the e-book you were last reading. You can choose either mode from the navigation drawer, as shown in the figure.

Scroll through the library by swiping the screen.

View action bar

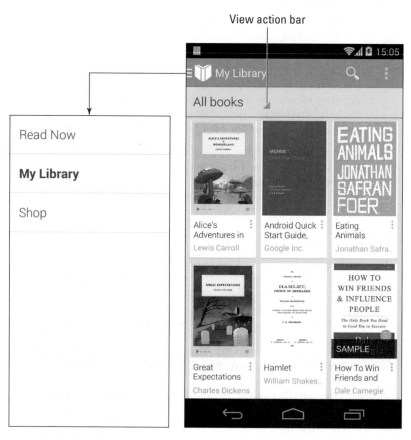

Navigation drawer

Figure 17-5: The Play Books library.

Touch a book in the Play Books app library to open it. If you've opened the book previously, you're returned to the page you last read. Otherwise, the first page you see is the book's first page.

To begin reading, touch a book to open it.

Figure 17-6 illustrates the basic book-reading operation in the Play Books app. You turn pages by swiping left or right, but probably mostly left. You can also turn pages by touching the far left or right side of the screen.

The Play Books app also works in a vertical orientation, which you may find easier for reading although you won't see all the icons shown in Figure 17-6.

Display library   Search the book   Adjust the text display

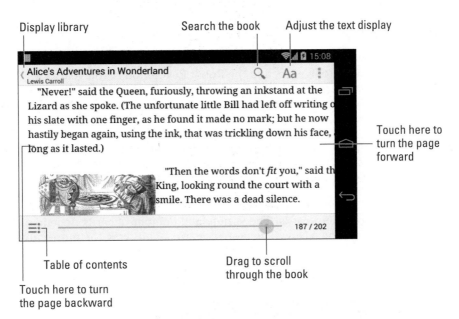

Touch here to turn the page forward

Touch here to turn the page backward

Table of contents

Drag to scroll through the book

Figure 17-6: Reading an e-book in the Play Books app.

- If you don't see a book in the library, touch the Menu icon and choose the Refresh command.

- To ensure that your reading material is always available, touch the Action Overflow icon on a book's cover and choose the Keep on Device command. That way, the phone doesn't need an Internet connection to synchronize and download books to the library. I choose this command before I leave on a trip where an Internet signal may not be available (such as in an airplane).

- To remove a book from the library, touch the Action Overflow icon on the book's cover and choose the Delete from Library command.

- If the onscreen controls (refer to Figure 17-6) disappear, touch the screen to see them again.

- The *Aa* icon is used to adjust the display. Touching this icon displays a menu of options for adjusting the text on the screen and the brightness.

- To return to the library, touch the Play Books app icon in the upper-left corner of the screen or touch the Back icon.

- Synchronization allows you to keep copies of your Google Books on all your Android devices as well as on the `books.google.com` website.

- If you have a Kindle device, you can obtain the Amazon Kindle app for your phone. Use the app to access books you've purchased for the Kindle, or just as a supplement to Google Books.

Google Now

Don't worry about the phone controlling too much of your life: It harbors no insidious intelligence, and the Robot Revolution is still years away. Until then, you can use your phone's listening capabilities to enjoy a feature called Google Now. It's not quite like having your own personal Jeeves, but it's on its way.

Finding the Google Now feature can be fun! On some phones, you drag your finger all the way up the touchscreen to summon it. Other phones may feature the Google Now screen as the far left Home screen. Or you can summon Google Now by touching the Google Search widget on the Home screen.

Figure 17-7 illustrates a typical Google Now screen. Below the search text box, you'll find cards. The variety and number of cards depend on how often you use Google Now. The more it learns about you, the more cards appear.

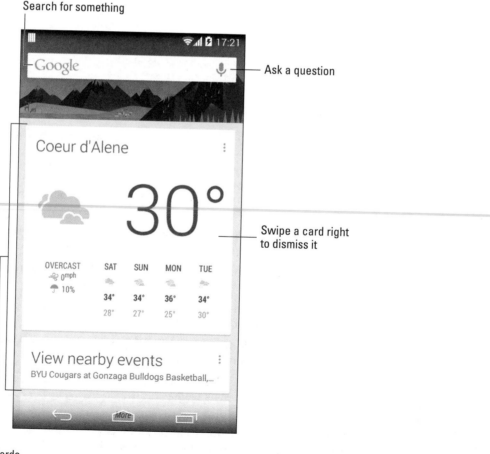

Search for something

Ask a question

Swipe a card right to dismiss it

Cards

Figure 17-7: Google Now is ready for business. Or play.

TIP

Barking orders to Google Now

One way to have a lot of fun is to use the Google Now app verbally. Just say "OK Google." Say it out loud. Any time you see the Google Now app, it's listening to you. Or when the app is being stubborn, touch the Microphone icon.

You can speak simple search terms, such as "Find pictures of Megan Fox." Or you can give more complex orders, among them:

✔ Will it rain tomorrow?

✔ What time is it in Frankfurt, Germany?

✔ How many Euros equal $25?

✔ What is 103 divided by 6?

✔ How can I get to Disneyland?

✔ Where is the nearest Canadian restaurant?

✔ What's the score of the Lakers–Celtics game?

✔ What is the answer to life, the universe, and everything?

When asked such questions, Google Now responds with a card as well as a verbal reply. When a verbal reply isn't available, Google search results are displayed.

You can use Google Now to search the Internet, just as you would use Google's main web page. More interesting than that, you can ask Google Now questions; see the sidebar, "Barking orders to Google Now."

✔ Google Now might also dwell in the apps drawer. It might be named Google Now or just Google. On some phones, you may have to touch a Get Google Now link to obtain the app.

✔ You cannot manually add cards to the Google Now screen. The only way to get more cards to show up is to use Google Now.

The Video Player

It's not possible to watch "real" TV on your phone, but a few apps come close. The YouTube app is handy for watching random, meaningless drivel, which I suppose makes it a lot like TV. Then there's the Play Movies & TV app, which lets you buy and rent real movies and TV shows from the Google Play Store. And when you tire of those apps, you can use the Camera app with the front-facing camera to pretend that you're the star of your own reality TV show.

Watching YouTube

YouTube is the Internet phenomenon that proves that real life is indeed too boring and random for television. Or is that the other way around? Regardless, you can view the latest videos on YouTube — or contribute your own — by using the YouTube app on your Android phone.

Search for videos in the YouTube app by touching the Search icon. Type the video name, a topic, or any search terms to locate videos. Zillions of videos are available.

The YouTube app displays suggestions for any channels to which you're subscribed, which allows you to follow favorite topics or YouTube content providers.

- ✔ Use the YouTube app to view YouTube videos, rather than use the Chrome app to visit the YouTube website.

- ✔ Orient the phone horizontally to view the video in a larger size.

- ✔ Because you have a Google account, you also have a YouTube account. I recommend that you log in to your YouTube account when using the YouTube app: Touch the Action Overflow icon and choose the Sign In command. Log in if you haven't already. Otherwise, you see your account information, your videos, and any video subscriptions.

- ✔ Not all YouTube videos are available for viewing on mobile devices.

Renting movies

You can use the Google Play Store not only to buy apps and books for your phone but also to rent movies. Open the Play Movies & TV app, found in the apps drawer.

Renting or purchasing a movie is done at the Play Store, and it works just like purchasing an app (covered in Chapter 18). Choose a movie or TV show to rent or buy. Touch the price button, and then choose your method of payment.

Movies and shows rented at the Play Store are available for viewing for up to 30 days after you pay the rental fee. After you start the movie, you can pause and watch it again and again during a 24-hour period.

If your phone features an HDMI out port, you can view videos on an HDMI monitor or TV. All you need is an extremely overpriced cable to make it happen.

More Apps

*Y*our Android phone may have come packed with diverse and interesting apps, or it may have only a paltry selection of tepid sample apps. Regardless of the assortment, you're in no way limited to the original collection. That's because hundreds of thousands of different apps are available for your phone: productivity apps, references, tools, games, and more. They're all found at the central shopping place for all Android phones, the place commonly called the Google Play Store.

RADIO
AudioAddict Inc
★★★★★

Lookout Security & Antivirus
Lookout Mobile Security
★★★★★

Google Hindi Input
Google Inc. ◇
★★★★☆

Backgrounds HD Wallpaper
om Media

Welcome to the Play Store

The Google Play Store is one of the things that make owning an Android phone rewarding. You can visit the Play Store not only to obtain more apps for your phone but also to go shopping for music, books, and videos (films and TV shows). Someday, Google might even sell robots at the Play Store. Until then, the selection seems adequate and satisfying.

✔ Officially, the store is the Google Play Store. It may also be referenced as Google Play. The app is named Play Store.

 ✔ The Google Play Store was once known as Android Market, and you may still see it referred to as the Market.

 ✔ This section talks about getting apps for your phone. For information on getting music, see Chapter 16. Chapter 17 mentions renting movies and TV shows. As well as buying books.

 ✔ *App* is short for application. It's a program, or software, you can add to your phone to make it do new, wondrous, or useful things.

 ✔ All apps you download can be found in the apps drawer. Further, apps you download have launcher icons placed on the Home screen. See Chapter 22 for information on moving apps on the Home screen.

 ✔ I highly recommend that you connect your phone to a Wi-Fi network if you plan to obtain apps, books, or movies at the Play Store. Not only does Wi-Fi give you speed, but it also helps avoid data surcharges. See Chapter 19 for details on connecting your phone to a Wi-Fi network.

 ✔ The Play Store app is frequently updated, so its look may change from what you see in this chapter. Updated information on the Google Play Store is available on my website:

    www.wambooli.com/help/android/google-play/

Visiting the Play Store

You access the Google Play Store by opening the Play Store app, found in the apps drawer. You may also find a launcher on the Home screen.

After opening the Play Store app, you see the main screen, similar to the one shown in Figure 18-1. Categories appear that help you browse for apps, games, books, and so on. The rest of the screen highlights popular or recommended items.

Find apps by choosing the Apps category from the main screen, also known as Store Home. The next screen lists popular and featured items plus categories you can browse by swiping the screen right to left. The category tabs appear toward the top of the screen.

When you have an idea of what you want, such as an app's name or even what it does, searching works fastest: Touch the Search icon at the top of the Play Store screen. (Refer to Figure 18-1.) Type all or part of the app's name or perhaps a description.

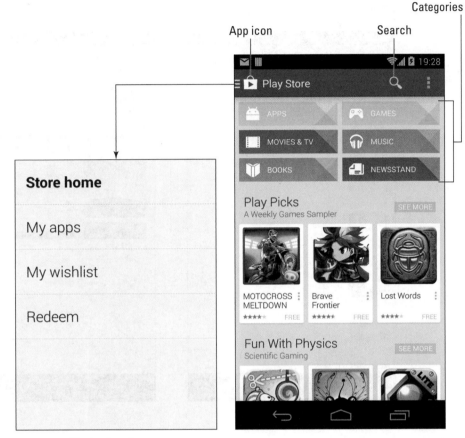

Figure 18-1: The Google Play Store.

To see more information about an item, touch it. Touching something doesn't buy it but instead displays a more detailed description, screen shots, a video preview, comments, plus links to similar items, as shown in Figure 18-2.

Return to the main Google Play Store screen at any time by touching the Google Play app icon in the upper-left corner of the screen.

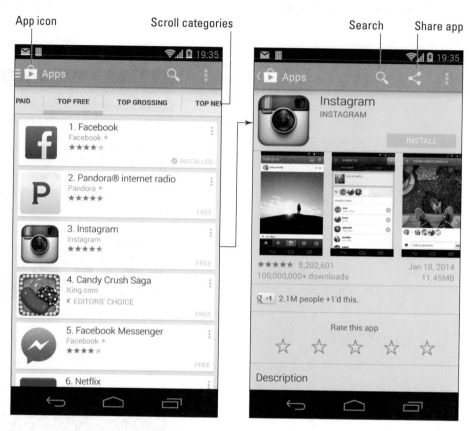

Figure 18-2: Hunting down an app.

- The first time you open the Play Store app, you have to accept the terms of service; touch the Accept or OK button.

- You can be assured that all apps that appear in the Play Store can be used with your phone. There's no way to download or buy something that's incompatible.

- Pay attention to an app's ratings. Ratings are added by people who use the apps — people like you and me. Having more stars is better. You can see additional information, including individual user reviews, by choosing the app.

- Another good indicator of an app's success is how many times it's been downloaded. Some apps have been downloaded tens of millions of times. That's a good sign.

- See Chapter 22 for more information on widgets and live wallpapers.

Obtaining a new app

After you locate an app you want, the next step is to download it from the Google Play Store into your phone. The app is installed automatically, building up your collection of apps and expanding what the phone can do.

Good news: Most apps are free. Better news: Even the apps you pay for don't cost dearly. In fact, it seems odd to sit and stew over whether paying 99 cents for a game is "worth it."

I recommend that you download a free app first, to familiarize yourself with the process. Then try your hand at downloading a paid app.

Free or not, the process of obtaining an app works pretty much the same. Follow these steps:

1. **Open the Play Store app.**

2. **Find the app you want and open its description.**

   The app's description screen looks similar to the one shown in Figure 18-2, right.

   The difference between a free app and a paid app is found on the button used to obtain the app. For a free app, the button says Install. For a paid app, the button shows the price.

   You may find three other buttons by an app: Open, Update, and Uninstall. The Open button opens an app that's already installed on your phone; the Update button updates an already installed app; and the Uninstall button removes an installed app. See the later sections "Updating an app" and "Uninstalling apps" for more information on using the Update and Uninstall buttons, respectively.

3. **Touch the Install button to get a free app; for a paid app, touch the button with the price on it.**

   The next screen describes the app's permissions. The list isn't a warning, and it doesn't mean anything bad. It's just that the Play Store is informing you which phone features the app has access to.

4. **Touch the Accept button.**

   For a paid app, you may have to choose a method of payment, or input a new method if one isn't on file. Choose a credit card, if you have one set up with Google Wallet. If not, you can input credit card information per the directions on the screen.

5. **For a paid app, touch the Buy button.**

   The Downloading notification appears atop the screen as the app is downloaded. You're free to do other things on your phone while the app is downloaded and installed.

6. **Touch the Open button to run the app.**

Or if you were doing something else while the app was downloading and installing, choose the Successfully Installed notification, as shown in the margin. The notification features the app's name with the text Successfully Installed beneath it.

At this point, what happens next depends on the app you've downloaded. For example, you may have to agree to a license agreement. If so, touch the I Agree button. Additional setup may involve setting your location, signing in to an account, or creating a profile, for example.

After you complete the initial app setup, or if no setup is necessary, you can start using the app.

✔ Apps you download are added to the Apps screen, made available like any other app on your phone.

✔ When you dither over getting an app, consider adding it to your wish list. Touch the Wish List icon (shown in the margin) when viewing the app. You can review your wish list by choosing the My Wishlist item from the Play Store app's navigation drawer (refer to Figure 18-1).

✔ Some apps may install launcher icons on the Home screen after they're installed. See Chapter 22 for information on removing the icon from the Home screen, if that is your desire.

✔ For a paid app, you'll receive a Gmail message from the Google Play Store, confirming your purchase. The message contains a link you can click to review the refund policy in case you change your mind about the purchase.

✔ Be quick on that refund: Some apps allow you only 15 minutes to get your money back. You know when the time limit is up because the Refund button on the app's description screen changes its name to Uninstall.

✔ Also see the "Uninstalling apps" section, later in this chapter.

Installing apps from a computer

You don't need to use the Play Store app on your phone to install apps. Using a computer, you can visit the Google Play website, choose an app, and have it installed remotely. It's kind of cool, yet kind of mysterious. Here's how it works:

1. **Use your computer's web browser to visit the Google Play store on the Internet.**

   The address is `https://play.google.com/store`.

   Bookmark this site in the computer's web browser.

2. **If necessary, click the Sign In link to log in to your Google account.**

   Use the same Google account that you used when setting up your phone. You need to have access to that account so that Google can remotely update your various Android gizmos.

3. **Browse for something.**

   You can hunt down apps, books, music — the whole gamut. It works just like browsing the Play Store on your phone.

4. **After clicking the Install or Buy button to obtain the item, choose your Android phone from the Device menu.**

   The menu lists all your Android devices, or at least those compatible with what you're getting.

   Your phone may be listed by its technical name, such as SCH-I605 or other random numbers and letters. If the technical name starts with the phone manufacturer's name, it's probably your phone and not another of your Android devices.

5. **For a free app, click the Install button; for a paid app, click the Continue button.**

   If you're getting a free app, installation proceeds. Otherwise, for a paid app, you choose your payment source, such as a credit card, and then click the Buy button.

Never buy an app twice

Any apps you've already purchased in the Google Play Store, say for another tablet or mobile device, are available for download on your current Android phone. Simply find the app and touch the Install button to install it as described in this chapter.

You can review any already-purchased apps in the Play Store: Choose the My Apps item from the navigation drawer (shown in Figure 18-1). Choose the All tab from the top of the screen. You'll see all the apps you've ever obtained at the Google Play Store, including apps you've previously paid for. Those apps are flagged with the text Purchased. Choose that item to reinstall the paid app.

As if by magic, the app is installed on your phone — even though you used a computer to do it.

Manage Your Apps

The apps you install on your Android phone originate from the Play Store. And that's where you can return to for app management. The task includes reviewing apps you've downloaded, updating apps, and removing apps that you no longer want or severely hate.

Reviewing your apps

To peruse the apps you've downloaded from the Google Play Store, follow these steps:

1. **Start the Play Store app.**

2. **Choose My Apps from the navigation drawer.**

   Touch the Play Store app icon (refer to Figure 18-1) to view the navigation drawer.

3. **Peruse your apps.**

There are two categories for apps: Installed and All, as shown in Figure 18-3. Installed apps are found on your phone; All apps include apps you have downloaded but have not installed.

Touch an app to see details. Touch the Open button to run the app, the Update button to update to the latest version, or the Uninstall button to remove the app. Later sections in this chapter describe the details on updating and uninstalling apps.

- ✔ While viewing an app's details, you can place a check mark by the Allow Automatic Updating option. That setting helps keep your apps current, although not every app features automatic updating.

- ✔ Uninstalled apps remain on the All list because you did, at one time, download the app. To reinstall them (and without paying a second time for paid apps), choose the app from the All list and touch the Install button.

Apps in need
of an update

Update button

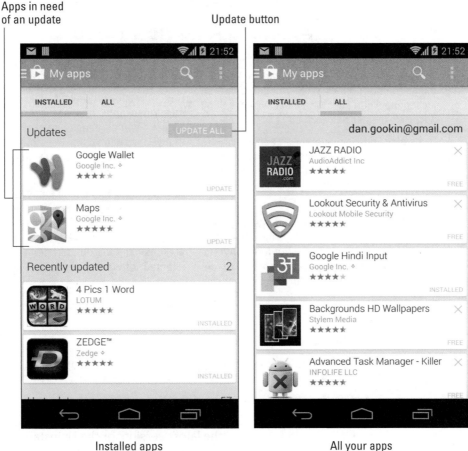

Installed apps

All your apps

Figure 18-3: The My Apps list.

Sharing an app

When you love an app so much that you just can't contain your glee, feel free to share that app with your friends. You can easily share a link to the app in the Play Store by obeying these steps:

1. **In the Play Store, choose the app to share.**

   You can choose any app, but you need to be at the app's details screen, the one with the Free or price button.

2. **Touch the Share icon.**

   A menu appears listing various apps and methods for sharing the app's Play Store link with your pals.

Avoiding Android viruses

How can you tell which apps are legitimate and which might be viruses or evil apps that do odd things to your phone? Well, you can't. In fact, most people can't because most evil apps don't advertise themselves as such.

The key to knowing whether an app is evil is to look at what it does, as described in this chapter. If a simple grocery-list app uses the phone cellular signal and the app doesn't need to access the Internet, it's suspect.

In the history of the Android operating system, only a handful of malicious apps have been distributed, and most of them were found in Asia. Google routinely removes these apps from the Play Store, and a feature of the Android

operating system even lets Google remove apps from your phone. So you're pretty safe.

Generally speaking, avoid "hacker" apps, porn, and those apps that use social engineering to make you do things on your Android phone that you wouldn't otherwise do, such as text an overseas number to see racy pictures of politicians or celebrities.

Also, I highly recommend that you abstain from obtaining apps from anything but the official Google Play Store. The Amazon Market is okay, as is Samsung's app store. Other markets are basically distribution points for illegal or infected software. Avoid them.

3. **Choose a sharing method.**

   For example, choose Gmail to send a link to the app in an e-mail message.

4. **Use the chosen app to send the link.**

   What happens next depends on which sharing method you've chosen.

The end result of these steps is that your friend receives a link. That person can touch the link on a mobile Android device and be whisked instantly to the Google Play Store, where the app can be viewed and installed.

Updating an app

Whenever a new version of an app is available, you see it flagged for updating, as shown in Figure 18-3. Don't worry if it's been a while since you've been to the My Apps screen; apps in need of an update also display an App Update notification, similar to what's shown in the margin.

To update an individual app, view its information screen: Choose the app from the My Apps screen (refer to Figure 18-3). Touch the Update button. Or from the list of installed apps, touch the Update All button to update a slew of apps at once.

The updating process often involves downloading and installing a new version of the app. That's perfectly fine; your settings and options aren't changed by the update process.

Look for the App Update notification to remind yourself that apps are in need of an update. You can choose that notification to be taken instantly to the app's screen, where the Update button eagerly awaits your touch.

Uninstalling apps

I can think of a few reasons to remove an app. It's with eager relish that I remove apps that don't work or annoy me. It's also perfectly okay to remove redundant apps, such as when you have multiple e-book readers that you don't use. And if you're desperate for an excuse, removing apps frees up a modicum of storage.

Whatever the reason, remove an app by following these directions:

1. **Open the Play Store app.**

2. **Choose My Apps from the navigation drawer.**

   Figure 18-1 illustrates the navigation drawer; touch the app icon in the upper-left corner to view it.

3. **In the Installed list, touch the app that offends you.**

4. **Touch the Uninstall button.**

5. **Touch the OK button to confirm.**

   The app is removed.

The app continues to appear on the All list even after it's been removed. That's because you downloaded it once. That doesn't mean that the app is installed.

 ✔ You can always reinstall paid apps that you've uninstalled. You aren't charged twice for doing so.

 ✔ You can't remove apps that are preinstalled on the phone by either the phone's manufacturer or your cellular service provider. I'm sure there's a technical way to uninstall the apps, but seriously: Just don't use the apps if you want to remove them and discover that you can't.

Part V
Nuts and Bolts

Learn how to synchronize photos with Dropbox on the Internet at www.dummies.com/extras/androidphones.

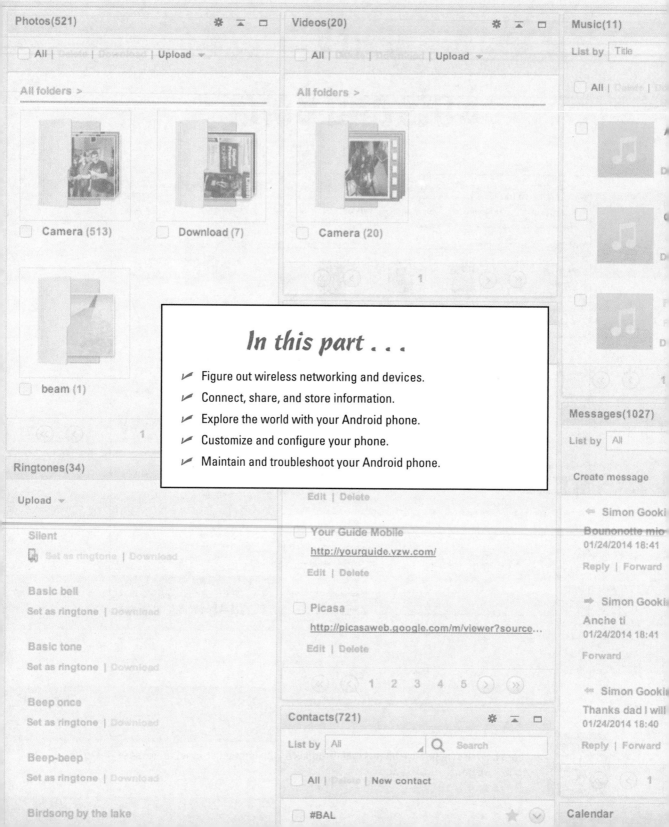

In this part . . .

- ✐ Figure out wireless networking and devices.
- ✐ Connect, share, and store information.
- ✐ Explore the world with your Android phone.
- ✐ Customize and configure your phone.
- ✐ Maintain and troubleshoot your Android phone.

19

No Wires, Ever!

ortable implies that something can be moved, but not how far or how easily. My first TV was a "portable," which meant that it had handholds on the sides; the TV weighed about 25 pounds. *Cordless* implies a degree of freedom beyond portable, but still requires a charging station. Cordless devices typically have a range beyond which they fail to communicate. *Wireless* is at the top of the mobility heap. It implies freedom from wires but is also lightweight and tiny.

Your Android phone is truly wireless. Forget for a second that you need a wire to charge it. That's not really a hindrance. After the battery is charged, you can take your phone anywhere and use it wirelessly. You can access the mobile network, a Wi-Fi network, and even wireless gizmos and peripherals. This chapter describes the degrees to which you can keep your phone wireless.

mperial Wambooli
Connected

CDA COTTAGE
Secured with WPA2 (WPS available)

LuckyDog
Secured with WPA/WPA2 (WPS available)

Eagle
PA/WPA2 (WPS

Android Wireless Networking

You know that wireless networking has hit the big-time when you see people asking Santa Claus for a Wi-Fi router at Christmas. Such a thing would have been unheard of years ago because routers were used primarily for woodworking back then. Today, wireless networking is what keeps gizmos like your Android phone connected to the Internet.

Using the mobile network

You pay your cellular provider a handsome fee every month. The fee comes in two chunks. One chunk (the less expensive of the two) is the telephone service. The second chunk is the data service, which is how your Android phone gets on the Internet. This system is the *cellular data network* or *mobile network*.

Several types of cellular data networks are available. When your phone uses one, a status icon appears atop the touchscreen, cluing you in to which network the phone is accessing. Here's the gamut:

- **4G LTE:** The fourth generation of wide-area data networks is comparable in speed to standard Wi-Fi Internet access. It's fast. It also allows for both data and voice transmission at the same time.

- **3G:** The third generation of wide-area data networks is several times faster than the previous generation of data networks.

- **1X:** Several types of the original, slower cellular data signals are still available. They all fall under the 1X banner. It's slow.

Your phone always uses the best network available. So, when a 4G LTE network is within reach, that network is used for Internet communications. Otherwise, the 3G network is chosen, and then 1X as a form of last-ditch desperation.

- A notification icon for the type of network being used appears in the status area, right next to the Signal Strength icon. The icons representing the network speed vary from phone to phone and between the various cellular providers.

- When a data network isn't available, no icon appears on the status bar. In fact, it's entirely possible for the phone to have no data signal but still be able to make phone calls.

- See Chapter 24 for information on how to monitor mobile data usage and avoid surcharges.

- Your phone uses the Wi-Fi signal when it's available and a connection has been made. Data transferred via a Wi-Fi network doesn't count against your cellular data usage. Therefore I recommend connecting to and using a Wi-Fi network wherever possible. That's because:

- Accessing the mobile data network isn't free. Your phone most likely has some form of subscription plan for a certain quantity of data. When you exceed that quantity, the costs can become prohibitive.

Understanding Wi-Fi

The mobile data connection is nice and is available pretty much all over, but it costs you money. A better option, and one you should seek out when it's available, is *Wi-Fi,* or the same wireless networking standard used by computers for communicating with each other and the Internet.

Making Wi-Fi work on your Android phone requires two steps. First, you must activate Wi-Fi by turning on the phone's wireless radio. The second step, covered in the following section, is connecting to a specific wireless network.

Wi-Fi stands for *wireless fidelity.* It's brought to you by the numbers 802.11 and the letters B, N, and G.

Activating Wi-Fi

Follow these steps to activate Wi-Fi on your Android phone:

1. **At the Home screen, touch the Apps icon.**

2. **Open the Settings app.**

3. **Ensure that the Wi-Fi master control icon is on.**

   If not, slide the master control from Off to On to activate the phone's Wi-Fi radio.

If you've already configured your phone to connect to an available wireless network, it's connected automatically. Otherwise, you have to connect to an available network, which is covered in the next section.

To turn off Wi-Fi, repeat the steps in this section, but in Step 3 slide the master control icon from On to Off. Turning off Wi-Fi disconnects your phone from any wireless networks.

✔ You can quickly peruse your phone's Wi-Fi settings by choosing the Wi-Fi quick action. See Chapter 3 for more information on quick actions.

✔ Some phones may come with a Power Control widget affixed to a Home screen. One of the buttons on that widget is used to turn Wi-Fi on or off.

✔ Using Wi-Fi to connect to the Internet doesn't incur data usage charges.

✔ The Wi-Fi radio places an extra drain on the battery, but it's truly negligible. If you want to save a modicum of juice, especially if you're out and about and don't plan to be near a Wi-Fi access point for any length of time, turn off the Wi-Fi radio.

Connecting to a Wi-Fi network

After activating the Wi-Fi radio on your Android phone, you can connect to an available wireless network. Heed these steps:

1. **Open the Settings app.**

   It's found in the apps drawer, but you'll also find a shortcut in the quick actions drawer.

2. **Choose Wi-Fi or Wireless & Networks.**

   Don't touch the Master Control icon, which turns the Wi-Fi radio on or off; touch the Wi-Fi text on the left side of the Settings app screen.

   You see a list of Wi-Fi networks. In Figure 19-1, I the Imperial Wambooli network is currently connected. That's my office network.

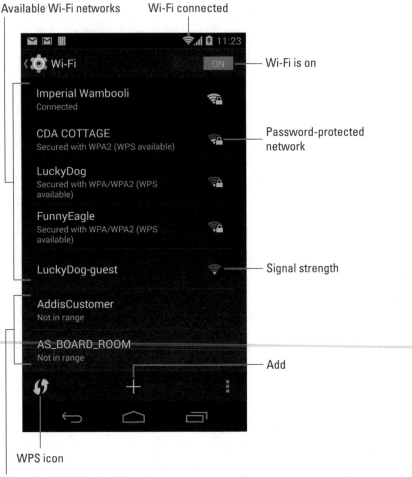

Available Wi-Fi networks   Wi-Fi connected

Wi-Fi is on

Password-protected network

Signal strength

Add

WPS icon

Memorized Wi-Fi networks

Figure 19-1: Hunting down a wireless network.

3. **Choose a wireless network from the list.**

   When no wireless networks are shown, you're sort of out of luck regarding Wi-Fi access from your current location.

4. **If prompted, type the network password.**

   Putting a check mark in the box by the Show Password option makes it easier to type a long, complex network password.

5. **Touch the Connect button.**

   You should be immediately connected to the network. If not, try the password again.

 When the phone is connected, you see the Wi-Fi status icon atop the touchscreen, looking similar to the icon shown in the margin. This icon indicates that the phone's Wi-Fi is on — connected and communicating with a Wi-Fi network.

Some wireless networks don't broadcast their names, which adds security but also makes accessing them more difficult. In these cases, touch the Add icon (refer to Figure 19-1) to manually add the network. The command might be titled Add Network. You need to type the network name, or *SSID,* and specify the type of security. You also need the password, if one is used. You can obtain this information from the girl with the pink hair and pierced lip who sold you coffee or from whoever is in charge of the wireless network at your location.

- ✔ Not every wireless network has a password. They should! I don't avoid connecting to any public network that lacks a password, but I don't use that network for shopping, banking, or any other secure online activity.

- ✔ Some public networks are open to anyone, but you have to use the web browser app to get on the web and find a login page that lets you access the network. Simply browse to any page on the Internet, and the login page shows up.

- ✔ The phone automatically remembers any Wi-Fi network it's connected to as well as its network password. An example is the AS_BOARD_ROOM network, shown in Figure 19-1.

- ✔ To disconnect from a Wi-Fi network, simply turn off Wi-Fi. See the preceding section.

- ✔ Unlike the mobile network, a Wi-Fi network's broadcast signal goes only so far. My advice is to use Wi-Fi when you plan to remain in one location for a while. If you wander too far away, your phone loses the signal and is disconnected.

Connecting via WPS

Many Wi-Fi routers feature WPS, which stands for Wi-Fi Protected Setup. It's a network authorization system that's really simple and quite secure. If the wireless router features WPS, you can use it to quickly connect your phone to the network.

To make the WPS connection, touch the WPS connection button on the router. The button is labeled WPS or sports the WPS icon, shown in the margin. On your phone, visit the Wi-Fi screen in the settings app as described in the preceding section. Touch the WPS icon, shown in Figure 19-1, to connect to the network.

- If the WPS router requires a PIN (Personal Identification Number), touch the
- Action Overflow icon on the Wi-Fi settings screen and choose the WPS Pin
- Entry item.

Share the Connection

You and your Android phone can get on the Internet anywhere you receive a mobile data signal. Pity the poor laptop that sits there, unconnected, seething with jealousy!

Well, laptop, be jealous no more! It's possible to share your phone's mobile signal in one of two ways. The first is to create a mobile *hotspot,* which allows any Wi-Fi–enabled gizmo to access the Internet via your phone. The second is a direct connection between your phone and another device, which is the *tethering* concept.

Sharing the digital cellular connection might not be an option for your phone. Further, sharing the connection may incur data surcharges or usage fees if your cellular contract doesn't allow for these services to be used.

Creating a mobile hotspot

The mobile hotspot feature allows your Android phone to share its cellular data connection by creating a Wi-Fi network. Other Wi-Fi devices — computers, laptops, other mobile devices — can then access that Wi-Fi network and use the phone's cellular data network. The process is referred to as *creating a mobile wireless hotspot,* though no heat or fire is involved.

To set up a mobile hotspot with your phone, heed these steps:

1. **Turn off the Wi-Fi radio.**

   There's no point in creating a Wi-Fi hotspot when one is already available.

2. **Plug the phone into a power source.**

   The mobile hotspot feature can draw a lot of power.

3. **Open the Settings app.**

   It's found on the apps screen. Some phones may feature a Mobile Hotspot or 4G Hotspot app. If so, open it instead.

4. **Touch the More item in the Wireless & Networks section, and then choose Tethering & Portable Hotspot.**

   The Tethering & Mobile Hotspot item might be found on the main settings app screen.

   You may see text describing the process. If so, dismiss the text.

5. **Touch the box to place a check mark by the Portable Wi-Fi Hotspot or Mobile Hotspot item.**

   The hotspot is on, but you may want to confirm some of the settings.

   If the hotspot doesn't come on or the item is disabled, your phone is incapable of creating a Wi-Fi hotspot or that feature is unavailable under your data subscription plan.

6. **Choose the Set Up Wi-Fi Hotspot item to give the hotspot a name, or SSID, and then review, change, or assign a password.**

   Touch the fields on the Set Up Wi-Fi Hotspot screen to assign a name and password. Touch the Save or OK button to set your changes.

 When the mobile hotspot is active, you see the Hotspot Active notification icon, similar to the one shown in the margin. You can then access the hotspot by using any computer or mobile device that has Wi-Fi capabilities.

To turn off the mobile hotspot, remove the check mark as described in Step 5.

 ✔ The range for the mobile hotspot is about 30 feet. Items such as walls and tornados can interfere with the signal, rendering it much shorter.

 ✔ When you use the mobile hotspot, data usage fees apply, and they're on top of the fee your cellular provider may charge for the basic service. These fees can add up quickly.

 ✔ Don't forget to turn off the mobile hotspot when you're done using it.

Tethering the Internet connection

A more intimate way to share the phone's digital cellular connection is to connect the phone directly to a computer and activate the tethering feature. Not every Android phone has this capability.

Yes: I am fully aware that tethering goes against the wireless theme of this chapter. Still, it remains a solid way to provide Internet access to another gizmo, such as a laptop or a desktop computer. Follow these steps to set up Internet tethering:

1. **Connect the phone to a computer or laptop by using the USB cable.**

   I've had the best success with this operation when the computer is a PC running Windows.

2. **Open the Settings app.**

3. **Choose More, and then choose Tethering & Mobile Hotspot.**

4. **Place a check mark by the USB Tethering item.**

Internet tethering is activated.

The other device should instantly recognize the phone as a "modem" with Internet access. Further configuration may be required, which depends on the computer using the tethered connection. For example, you may have to accept the installation of new software when prompted by Windows.

✔ When tethering is active, a Tethering or Hotspot Active notification icon appears, similar to what's shown in the margin. Choose that notification to further configure tethering.

✔ Unlike creating a Wi-Fi hotspot, you don't need to disable the Wi-Fi radio to activate USB tethering.

✔ Sharing the digital network connection incurs data usage charges against your cellular data plan. Be careful with your data usage when you're sharing a connection.

The Bluetooth Connection

Technology nerds have long had the desire to connect high-tech gizmos to one another. The Bluetooth standard was developed to sate this desire in a wireless way. Although Bluetooth is wireless *communication,* it's not the same as wireless networking. It's more about connecting peripheral devices, such as keyboards, printers, headphones, and other gear. It all happens in a wireless way, as described in this section.

Understanding Bluetooth

Bluetooth is a peculiar name for a wireless communications standard. Unlike Wi-Fi networking, with Bluetooth you simply connect two gizmos. One would be your Android phone, and the other would be some type of peripheral, such as a keyboard, printer, or speakers. Here's how the operation works:

1. **Turn on the Bluetooth wireless radio on both gizmos.**

2. **Make the gizmo you're trying to connect to discoverable.**

3. **On your phone, choose the peripheral gizmo from the list of Bluetooth devices.**

4. **Optionally, confirm the connection on the peripheral device.**

For example, you may be asked to input a code or press a button.

5. **Use the device.**

When you're done using the device, you simply turn it off. Because the Bluetooth gizmo is paired with your phone, it's automatically reconnected the next time you turn it on (that is, if you have Bluetooth activated on the phone).

 Bluetooth devices are marked with the Bluetooth logo, shown in the margin. It's your assurance that the gizmo can work with other Bluetooth devices.

Bluetooth was developed as a wireless version of the old RS-232 standard, the serial port on early personal computers. Essentially, Bluetooth is wireless RS-232, and the variety of devices you can connect to and the things you can do with Bluetooth are similar to what you could do with the old serial port standard.

Activating Bluetooth

You must turn on the phone's Bluetooth radio before you can use one of those Borg-earpiece implants and join the ranks of the walking connected. To turn on Bluetooth, open the Settings app and slide the master control next to Bluetooth to the On position.

When Bluetooth is on, the Bluetooth status icon appears. It uses the Bluetooth logo, shown in the margin.

To turn off Bluetooth, repeat the steps in this section, but slide the master control to the Off position.

- You can turn on Bluetooth also by choosing the Bluetooth quick action.

- When the Power Control widget is installed on the Home screen, touch the Bluetooth icon to turn it on. See Chapter 22 for more information on installing Home screen widgets.

- Activating Bluetooth can quickly drain the phone's battery. Be mindful to use Bluetooth only when necessary, and remember to turn it off when you're done.

Pairing with a Bluetooth device

To make the Bluetooth connection between your phone and some other gizmo, such as a Bluetooth headset, follow these steps:

1. **Ensure that Bluetooth is on.**

   Refer to the preceding section.

2. **Turn on the Bluetooth gizmo or ensure that its Bluetooth radio is on.**

   Some Bluetooth devices have separate power and Bluetooth switches.

3. **Open the Settings app.**

4. **Touch the Bluetooth item.**

5. **Touch the Search for Devices button.**

You see a list of available and paired devices, similar to Figure 19-2. Don't fret if the device you want doesn't yet appear in the list.

6. **If the other device has an option to become visible, select it.**

For example, some Bluetooth gizmos have a tiny button to press that makes the device visible to other Bluetooth gizmos.

Likewise, if the other device needs to see the phone, touch the phone's name at the top of the Bluetooth screen, shown in Figure 19-2. That action makes the phone visible to the other device.

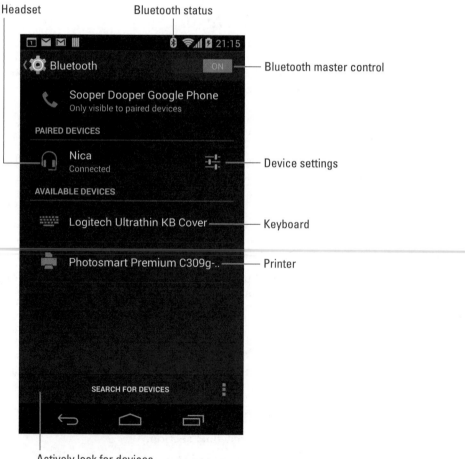

Figure 19-2: Finding Bluetooth gizmos.

7. Choose the device.

The phone and Bluetooth device attempt to pair. You may be required to type the device's passcode or otherwise acknowledge the connection.

After pairing, you can begin using the device.

To break the connection, you can either turn off the gizmo or disable the Bluetooth radio on your phone. Because the devices are paired, when you turn on Bluetooth and reactivate the device, the connection is instantly reestablished.

- How you use the device depends on what it does. For example, you use a Bluetooth headset to talk and listen on the phone. As long as the headset is paired with the phone and powered on, you can use it.

- When a Bluetooth headset is paired, a Bluetooth icon appears on the in-call screen. Use that icon to switch between a Bluetooth headset and the phone's microphone and speaker.

- You can turn the Bluetooth earphone on or off after it has been paired.

- To unpair a device, touch the Settings icon by the device's entry in the Bluetooth screen (refer to Figure 19-2). Choose the Unpair command to break the Bluetooth connection and stop using the device.

- Only unpair devices you don't plan on using again in the future. Otherwise, simply turn off the Bluetooth device.

- Bluetooth can use a lot of power. Especially for battery-powered devices, don't forget to turn them off when you're no longer using them with your phone.

Printing from the Cloud

Another way to print from your phone is to obtain the Google Cloud Printing app from the Play Store. By coordinating between your Google account on a desktop computer, the Chrome web browser, and the phone, you can print on your home or office printer — no Bluetooth required.

For more information on Google Cloud Print, refer to my website here:

www.wambooli.com/blog/?p=4736

Printing to a Bluetooth printer

 One of the common ways to print pictures or even documents with an Android phone is to pair the phone with a Bluetooth printer. The secret is to find and use the Share icon, choose Bluetooth, and then select the printer. As you may suspect, the actual steps for that process can be more complicated. That's why I list them here:

1. **View the document, web page, or image you want to print.**

   You can print from the Chrome app, the Gallery app, or from a number of other apps.

2. **Touch the Share icon.**

   If a Share icon isn't visible in the app, look for a Share command on the Action Overflow icon's menu.

3. **Choose Bluetooth.**

   If the Bluetooth option isn't available, you may not be able to print from the app. Even so, check out the nearby sidebar, "Printing from the Cloud."

4. **Choose your Bluetooth printer from the list of items on the Bluetooth screen.**

5. **If a prompt appears on the printer, confirm that your phone is printing a document.**

   The document is uploaded (sent from the phone to the printer), and then it prints. You can view the upload status by checking the phone's notifications.

Not everything on an Android phone can be printed on a Bluetooth printer. When you can't find the Share icon or the Bluetooth item isn't available on the Share menu, you can't print using Bluetooth.

Android Beam It to Me

Quite a few Android phones feature an NFC radio, where *NFC* stands for Near Field Communications and *radio* is a type of vegetable.

NFC allows the phone to communicate with other NFC devices, which allows for the quick transfer of information. The technology is called Android Beam.

Turning on NFC

You can't play with the Android Beam feature unless the phone's NFC radio has been activated. To confirm that it has been activated, or to activate it, follow these steps:

1. **Open the Settings app.**

2. **Choose the More command, which is found below the Wireless & Networks heading.**

3. **Ensure that a check mark appears by the NFC item.**

   If it doesn't, touch the box to add a check mark.

With NFC activated, you can use your phone to communicate with other NFC devices. These devices include other Android phones, Android tablets, as well as payment systems for various merchants.

To disable NFC, repeat these steps, but in Step 3 remove the check mark.

Using Android Beam

The Android Beam feature works when you touch your phone to another NFC device, such as another Android phone or tablet. As long as the two devices have an NFC radio and the Android Beam feature is active, they can share information. You can beam contacts, map locations, web pages, YouTube videos, and lots of other things. Generally speaking, if the app features the Share icon, you can probably use Android Beam and other content by simply touching the two gizmos.

When two Android Beam devices touch — usually back-to-back — a prompt appears on the screen: Touch to Beam. Touch the screen, and the item you're viewing is immediately sent to the other device. That's pretty much it.

Using Jim Beam

Follow these steps to enjoy a bottle of Kentucky straight bourbon whiskey:

1. **Unscrew cap.**

2. **Pour.**

3. **Enjoy.**

It isn't truly necessary to pour the whiskey into another container for consumption, though many users find a glass, mug, or red Solo cup useful.

Alcohol and social networking do not mix.

20

Connect, Store, Share

In This Chapter

- Getting the phone and a computer to talk
- Mounting the phone as computer storage
- Synchronizing media
- Copying files between the phone and computer
- Understanding phone storage
- Connecting your phone to an HDMI monitor

I don't believe that your computer is jealous of your phone. It might be. My phone is jealous of my laser printer, which I know because they refuse to talk with each other. But the computer? That situation was resolved by using the USB connection. Now the computer and phone are bosom buddies, connecting, chatting, and sharing long into the wee hours. Apparently, your Android phone is incredibly capable of sharing its stuff with a computer, and it's eager to share, providing you know some of the tricks explained in this chapter.

.io   theater   Web Pages   Work

bloggers.p   bookmark.   Chapter   City
df   htm   1.docx   Budget.doc
                                      x

The USB Connection

The most direct way to mate an Android phone with a computer is to use a USB cable. Coincidentally, a USB cable comes with the phone. It's a match made in heaven, but like many matches, it often works less than smoothly. Rather than hire a counselor to put the phone and computer on speaking terms, I offer you some good USB connection advice in this section.

ument.   don't do   dumbcrim.   electronic
'f   this.docx   txt   messages
                                   merged.do
                                   cx

Connecting the phone to a computer

Communication between your computer and your Android phone works fastest when both devices are physically connected. This connection happens by using the USB cable. As with nearly every computer cable in the Third Dimension, the USB cable has two ends:

✔ The A end of the USB cable plugs into the computer.

✔ The other end of the cable plugs into the phone.

The connectors are shaped differently and cannot be plugged in either backward or upside down.

✔ When the USB connection has been made successfully, a USB notification appears, similar to the one shown in the margin. Don't freak if you don't see it; not every phone displays this notification.

✔ The phone-computer connection works best with a powered USB port. If possible, plug the USB cable into the computer itself or into a powered USB hub.

✔ If you don't have a USB cable for your phone, go to any computer- or office-supply store. Get a USB-A-male-to-micro-USB cable.

✔ USB 3.0 cables can also be used to charge Android phones, but only when the phone features a USB 3.0 connector. If so, using a USB 3.0 cable allows for faster data transfer, providing you connect the cable to a USB 3.0 port on the computer. (The ports are colored blue.)

✔ You don't have to use a USB 3.0 cable with an Android phone. The micro-USB cables can still be attached, although data transfer doesn't take place at top speed.

✔ A flurry of activity takes place when you first connect an Android phone to a Windows PC. Notifications pop up about new software that's installed. Don't fret if you see a message about software not being found. That's okay. If you see an AutoPlay dialog box prompting you to install software, do so.

Configuring the USB connection

Upon the successful connection of your Android phone to a computer, you have the option of configuring the USB connection. A menu appears, either automatically or when you choose the USB notification. If not, you can manually configure the USB connection by following these steps:

1. **Open the Settings app.**

2. **Choose Storage.**

3. **Touch the Action Overflow icon and choose the USB Computer Connection command.**

4. **Choose either Media Device (MTP) or Camera (PTP).**

   I recommend that you select Media Device (MTP) if it's not already selected.

MTP stands for *Media Transfer Protocol.* When that setting is chosen, the computer believes the phone to be a portable media player, which it is, kinda. This option is the most common option.

PTP stands for *Picture Transfer Protocol.* In this setting, the computer is misled into thinking that the phone is a digital camera. Select this option only when the MTP option fails to make the connection.

- ✔ If you can't get the USB connection to work, check to see whether the phone features a proprietary synchronization program, such as Samsung's Kies utility. See the later section, "Connecting wirelessly with Kies Air."

- ✔ No matter which USB connection option you've chosen, the phone's battery charges whenever it's connected to a computer's USB port — as long as the computer is turned on, of course.

Connecting your phone to a Mac

You need special software to deal with the Android-phone-to-Macintosh connection. That's because the Mac doesn't natively recognize Android phones. Weird, huh? It's like Apple wants you to buy some other type of phone. I just don't get it.

To deal with the Android-phone–USB connection on a Mac, you need to obtain special software, the Android File Transfer program. On your Mac, download that program from this website:

```
www.android.com/filetransfer
```

Install the software. Run it. From that point on, when you connect your Android phone to the Macintosh, a special window appears, similar to what's shown in Figure 20-1. It lists the phone's folders and files. Use that window for file management, as covered later in this chapter.

You can transfer files easily between your phone and a Macintosh (and a PC) also by using cloud services such as Google Drive and Dropbox. See the later section, "Sharing files with the cloud."

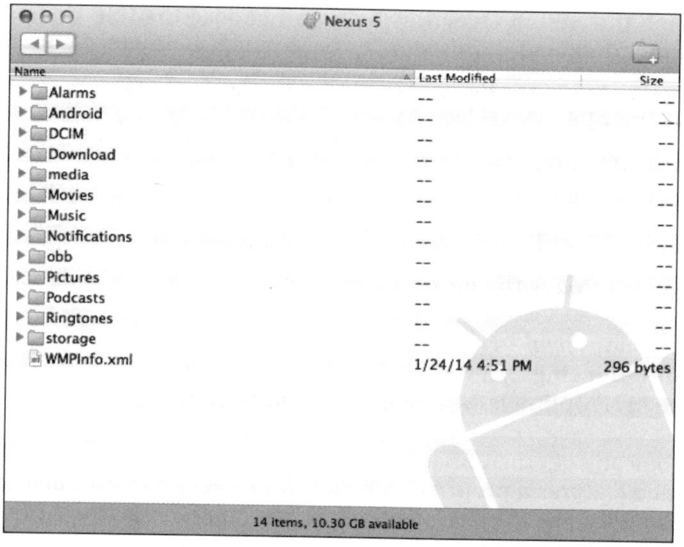

Figure 20-1: The Android File Transfer program.

Disconnecting the phone from the computer

The process of disconnecting your phone from the computer is cinchy: When you've finished transferring files, music, or other media between your PC and the phone, close all programs and folders opened on your computer — specifically, those you've used to work with the phone's storage. Then you can disconnect the USB cable. That's it.

✔ It's a Bad Idea to unplug the phone while you're transferring information or while a folder window is open on your computer. Doing so can damage the phone's storage, rendering unreadable some of the information that's kept there. To be safe, close the programs and folder windows you've opened before disconnecting.

✔ Unlike other external storage on the Macintosh, there's no need to eject the phone's storage when you're done accessing it. Simply disconnect the phone. The Mac doesn't get angry when you do so.

Files from Here, Files to There

The point of making the USB connection between your Android phone and a computer is to exchange files. You can't just wish the files over. Instead, I recommend following the advice in this section.

I recommend that you have a good understanding of basic file operations before you transfer files between a computer and the phone. You need to be familiar with file operations such as copy, move, rename, and delete. Knowing what folders are and how they work also helps. The good news is that you don't need to manually calculate a 64-bit cyclical redundancy check on the data, nor do you need to know what a parity bit is.

Transferring files between the phone and a computer

I can think of plenty of files you would want to copy from a computer to your cell phone: pictures, videos, and audio files. You can also copy vCards exported from your e-mail program, which helps to build the phone's address book. Likewise, you may want to copy files from the phone to the computer. Either way it works the same. Follow these steps:

1. **Connect the phone and the computer by using the USB cable.**

   Specific directions are offered earlier in this chapter.

2. **On a PC, if the AutoPlay dialog box appears, choose the Open Folder/ Device to View Files option.**

   When the AutoPlay dialog box doesn't appear, you can view files manually: Open the Computer window, and then open the phone's icon found at the bottom of that window. Open the storage icon to view files.

   The phone's folder window looks like any other folder in Windows. The difference is that the files and folders in that window are on your cell phone, not on the computer.

   On a Macintosh, the Android File Transfer program should start (refer to Figure 20-1).

3. **Open the source and destination folder windows.**

   Open the folder that contains the files you want to copy. The folder can be found on the computer or on the phone. Then open the folder on the computer or phone where you want the file copied. Have both folder windows, computer and phone, visible on the screen, similar to what's shown in Figure 20-2.

4. **Drag the file icon from one folder window to the other.**

   Dragging the file copies it, either from phone to computer or computer to phone.

   If you want to be specific, drag the file to the phone's download folder or to the root folder, as shown in Figure 20-2. On the PC, drag to the My Documents, My Pictures, or My Videos folder, as appropriate. You can also drag directly to the desktop and decide later where to store the file.

   The same file-dragging technique can be used for transferring files from a Macintosh. You need to drag the icon(s) to the Android File Transfer window, which works just like any folder window in Finder.

Drag files to here to copy to the root

Files on your computer

Specific folders on the Nexus 7
Files on the phone

Figure 20-2: Copying files to an Android phone.

5. Close the folder windows and disconnect the USB cable when you're done.

Refer to specific instructions earlier in this chapter.

Although this manual technique works, the best way to transfer media to the phone is to use a media program, such as the Windows Media Player. See Chapter 16 for information on synchronizing music. You can also synchronize pictures and videos in the same way by using a media program on the computer.

✔ Phones with both internal and removable storage prompt Windows to display two AutoPlay dialog boxes. Each dialog box represents a different storage source, internal storage as well as the microSD card.

✔ Files you've downloaded on the phone are stored in the download folder.

✔ Pictures and videos on the phone are stored in the DCIM/Camera folder.

✔ Music on the phone is stored in the Music folder, organized by artist.

Connecting wirelessly with Kies Air

Samsung phones feature an app called Kies Air, which is used to wirelessly connect your Android phone to a computer. As long as both the phone and the computer are on the same Wi-Fi network, the connection is made and files can be transferred with relatively little pain.

Follow these steps to use Kies Air to share files between your Samsung Android phone and a computer:

1. **Ensure that both the phone and the computer are connected to the same Wi-Fi network.**

2. **Start the Kies Air app on your Samsung phone.**

3. **Touch the Start button.**

   Kies Air should immediately recognize your Wi-Fi network. It now sits and waits for an incoming request from a computer.

4. **On the computer, open the web browser, such as Internet Explorer or something better.**

5. **On the computer, type the URL displayed on the phone's touchscreen.**

   On my phone's screen I see the URL `http://192.168.1.143:8080`, which is what I type into the computer web browser's address box. The text and numbers you see will probably be different.

   After typing the URL into your computer's web browser, you'll see an Access Request prompt on the phone. The prompt should state the network name of the computer requesting access.

6. **In the proper location on the web page shown on the computer, type the PIN listed on the phone touchscreen, and then click the OK button.**

   The phone and computer are now connected via the Wi-Fi network.

A web page appears on the computer in the web browser's window, similar to what's shown in Figure 20-3. That web page is being hosted by your phone. It allows access to the device's resources, as illustrated in the figure.

To download an item, or copy it from the phone to your computer, click to select the item as shown in Figure 20-3. Then click the Download link. The item is transferred to your computer just like any file you download from the Internet, although the download comes from your Samsung phone.

Media card transfer

If your phone features removable storage, you can use it to transfer files. Remove the microSD from the phone and insert it into a computer. From that point, the files on the card can be read by the computer just as they can be read from any media card.

See Chapter 1 for details on how to remove the microSD card from your phone. You can't just yank out the thing! You also need a microSD adapter to insert the card into a media reader on the computer. Or you can get a microSD card thumb drive adapter, in which case you merely need a USB port to access the card's information.

Items you can sync

Select items

Download from phone to computer

Upload from computer to phone

Categories

Figure 20-3: Kies Air web page on a computer.

To send a file to the phone, click one of the Upload links, as illustrated in Figure 20-3. Click the Choose File button and then use the Upload dialog box to find a file. Click to select that file, and then click the OK button to send it from the computer to the phone.

To end the Kies Air connection, touch the Stop button on the phone's touch-screen. You can then close the web browser window on your computer.

 ✔ While the connection is active, you can quickly switch to the Kies Air app on the phone by choosing the Kies Air notification.

✔ Newer Samsung phones may use the Kies 3 program, which requires a direct phone-to-computer connection.

✔ My guess is that Kies is pronounced *kees*. I have no idea what it stands for, or whether it's even an acronym at all.

✔ Don't click the Back button on your computer's web browser screen when using the Kies Air website. Just use the controls on the web page itself to navigate

Sharing files with the cloud

A handy way to share files between a computer and your Android phone is to use cloud storage. That's just fancy talk for storing files on the Internet.

Many choices are available for cloud storage, including Google's own Google Drive and Microsoft's Skydrive. I'm fond of the Dropbox service.

All files saved to cloud storage are synchronized instantly with all devices that access the storage. Change a file on a computer and it's updated on your phone. The files are also available directly on the Internet from a web page. Even so, I recommend that you use a specific cloud storage app on your phone to access the files.

To make the file transfer from the computer to the phone, save a file in the cloud storage folder. On your phone, open the cloud storage app, such as Drive or Dropbox. Browse the folders and touch the file's icon to view that file on your phone.

To transfer a file from your phone to a computer, view the file or media and then touch the Share icon. Choose the Drive or Dropbox icon to share the item via Google Drive or Dropbox, respectively.

Because all devices that share the cloud storage are instantly synchronized, you don't need to worry about specific file transfers. All files saved to cloud storage are available to all devices that can access that storage.

✔ The Google Drive app is named Drive. It's part of the Google suite of apps on just about every Android phone.

✔ You can obtain the Dropbox app from the Play Store, but you also need to get a Dropbox account and probably get the Dropbox program for your computer. Visit `www.dropbox.com` to get started.

✔ These cloud storage services are free for a limited amount of storage. Beyond that you need to pay a monthly fee.

Phone Storage Mysteries

Somewhere deep in your phone's bosom lies a storage device. It's like the hard drive in a computer: The thing can't be removed, but that's not the point. The point is that the storage is used for your apps, music, videos, pictures, and a host of other information. This section describes what you can do to manage that storage.

Reviewing storage stats

To see how much storage space is available on your phone, open the Settings app and choose the Storage category. The Storage screen details information about storage space, similar to what's shown in Figure 20-4.

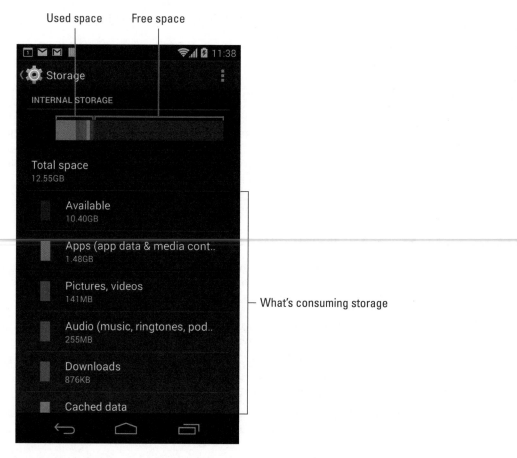

Figure 20-4: Phone storage information.

If your phone has external storage, look for the SD Card category at the bottom of the Storage screen (not shown in Figure 20-4).

Touch a category on the Storage screen to view details on how the storage is used or to launch an associated app. For example, touching Apps (refer to Figure 20-4) displays a list of running apps. Choosing Pictures, Videos lets you view pictures and videos.

✔ Videos, music, and pictures, in that order, consume the most storage space on your phone.

✔ To see how much storage space is not being used, refer to the Available Space item.

✔ Don't bemoan that the Total Space value is far less than the phone's storage capacity. For example, in Figure 20-4, a 16GB phone shows only 10.40 GB available. The missing space is considered overhead, as are several gigabytes taken by the government for tax purposes.

Managing files

You probably didn't get an Android phone because you enjoy managing files on a computer and wanted another gizmo to hone your skills. Even so, you can practice the same type of file manipulation on a phone as you would on a computer. Is there a need to do so? Of course not! But if you want to get dirty with files, you can.

The main tool for managing files on your phone is the Files or My Files app. Not every Android phone comes with such an app, so you can always obtain a file management app at the Play Store. The one that I use is called ASTRO File Manager, but many others are also available.

Where phone files lurk

Files on your phone don't just lazily jostle around like marbles in a paper bag. Nope, like files on a computer, files on your phone are organized into folders. On most Android phones, specific folders are used for file organization. Here are the common locations:

✔ /download: This folder contains files you've downloaded using the phone's web browser app.

✔ /dcim/camera: Pictures and videos are stored in this folder.

✔ /music: Music on your phone is organized in this folder. Subfolders are organized by artist.

These folders can exist on either the internal storage or the microSD card. So when you can't find the file or folder you're looking for on one media, look in the other.

Make the HDMI connection

A popular feature on several Android phones is the capability to connect the phone to an HDMI TV set or monitor. To make that connection, the phone must have an HDMI connector, and you need to buy an HDMI cable. After doing so, you can enjoy viewing your phone's media on a larger-size screen. And I must confess, nothing beats playing *Angry Birds* on an 80-inch plasma TV.

After making the HDMI connection, you see a pop-up menu on the screen or you can choose the HDMI notification. Among the options you'll find for using the larger screen are the following:

- **Gallery:** You can view pictures or a slideshow, according to the directions on the screen.

- **Music:** Choose a playlist, an album, or an artist, and enjoy watching the Music app on the big screen. (The sound should play from the TV's speakers.)

- **Mirror on Display:** The screen output on your Android phone is duplicated on the HDMI TV or monitor. This option is the one you choose when you want to watch a rented movie on the big screen.

HDMI stands for High Definition Multimedia Interface.

On the Road Again

In This Chapter

▶ Understanding roaming

▶ Disabling data-roaming features

▶ Entering airplane mode

▶ Contacting friends abroad

▶ Using Skype for international calls

▶ Going overseas with your phone

*Y*ou're in a land far, far away. The sun shines warmly upon your face. A gentle breeze wafts over crashing waves. You wiggle your toes in the soft, grainy sand. And the number one thought on your mind is, "Can my Android phone get a signal?"

The vernacular term is *bars,* as in the signal bars you see when the phone is actively communicating with a cellular network. That network pretty much covers the globe these days. That means from Cancun to the Gobi Desert, you'll probably be able to use your phone. How that happens and how to make it happen less expensively are the topics for this chapter.

20:43

SAT, DECEMBER 28

Charging, 51%

Where the Android Phone Roams

The word *roam* takes on an entirely new meaning when applied to a cell phone. It means that your phone receives a cell signal whenever you're outside your cell phone carrier's operating area. In that case, your phone is *roaming.*

Roaming sounds handy, but there's a catch: It almost always involves a surcharge for using another cellular service — an *unpleasant* surcharge.

Relax: Your Android phone alerts you whenever it's roaming. A Roaming icon appears at the top of the screen, in the status area, whenever you're outside your cellular provider's signal area. The icon differs from phone to phone, but generally the letter *R* figures in it somewhere, similar to what's shown in the margin.

There's little you can do to avoid incurring roaming surcharges when making or receiving phone calls. Well, yes: You can wait until you're back in an area serviced by your primary cellular provider. You can, however, altogether avoid using the other network's data services while roaming. Follow these steps:

1. **Open the Settings app.**

2. **In the Wireless & Networks section, touch the More item.**

3. **Choose Mobile Networks.**

   On some Android phones, you may have to choose Battery & Data Manager and then Data Delivery.

4. **Remove the check mark by the Data Roaming option.**

   On some phones the option is titled Global Data Roaming Access. Choose it and then choose the Deny Data Roaming Access option.

Your phone can still access the Internet over the Wi-Fi connection when it roams. Setting up a Wi-Fi connection doesn't make you incur extra charges, unless you have to pay to get on the wireless network. See Chapter 19 for more information about Wi-Fi.

Another network service you might want to disable while roaming has to do with multimedia, or *MMS*, text messages. To avoid surcharges from another cellular network for downloading an MMS message, follow these steps:

1. **Open the phone's text messaging app.**

   See Chapter 9 to find out what the app may be named, though often it's Text Messaging.

2. **Ensure that you're viewing the apps' main screen, the one that lists all the conversations.**

   Touch the Back icon or the app icon in the upper-left corner of the screen until the app's main screen is displayed.

3. **Touch the Action Overflow icon or Menu icon.**

4. **Choose the Settings or the Messaging Settings command.**

5. **Remove the check mark by the Auto-Retrieve or Roaming Auto-Retrieve command.**

   Or if the item isn't selected, you're good to go — literally.

The lock screen may also announce that the phone is roaming. You might see the name of the other cellular network displayed. The text *Emergency Calls Only* might also appear.

Airplane Mode

The rules about flying on an airplane with a cell phone are changing. Where it was once outright forbidden to even look at a cell phone while the plane was aloft, governments around the world have left it up to each airline to determine in-flight usage.

Generally speaking, follow the crew's direction when it comes to using your cell phone. They'll let you know when and how you can use the phone: specifically, whether it needs to be turned off for takeoff and landing and, once in the air, whether you can use it to make phone calls or enable any wireless features, such as Wi-Fi and GPS.

Traditionally, cell phones are placed into what's commonly called airplane mode during a flight. In that mode, it's okay to use the phone and access many of its features, except for cellular network access. So you can listen to music, play games, or use the in-flight Wi-Fi if your bankroll can afford it.

To activate airplane mode on a typical Android phone, follow these steps:

1. **Open the Settings app.**

2. **Choose the More item in the Wireless & Networks section.**

3. **Place a check mark by the Airplane Mode option.**

   Airplane mode is active.

When the phone is in airplane mode, a special icon appears in the status area, similar to the one shown in the margin. You might also see the text *No Service* on the phone's lock screen.

To exit airplane mode, repeat the steps in this section, but in Step 3 remove the check mark.

And now . . . the shortcuts!

Perhaps more shortcuts exist for finding airplane mode than any other Android phone feature. First, the Device Options menu features and Airplane Mode setting; press and hold down the Power/Lock key to see the Device Options menu.

Second, you can find an Airplane Mode icon in the quick actions drawer. See Chapter 3 for information on summoning quick actions.

Finally, you may find an Airplane Mode icon on the Power Lock widget, should your phone feature that widget on the Home screen.

✔ Some Android phones feature sleep mode, in which case you can place your phone into sleep mode for the duration of a flight. The phone wakes up faster from sleep mode than it does when you turn it on.

✔ Bluetooth networking is disabled in airplane mode, as is NFC communications and the Android Beam feature. See Chapter 19 for more information.

Android phone air travel tips

I don't consider myself a frequent flyer, but I travel several times a year. I do it often enough that I wish the airports had separate lines for security: one for seasoned travelers, one for families, and one, of course, for frickin' idiots. That last category would have to be disguised by placing a Bonus Coupons sign or a Free Snacks banner over the metal detector. That would weed 'em out.

Here are some of my cell phone and airline travel tips:

✔ **Charge your phone before you leave.** This tip probably goes without saying, but you'll be happier with a full cell phone charge to start your journey.

✔ **Take a cell phone charger with you.** Many airports feature USB chargers, so you might need just a USB-to-micro-USB cable. Still, why risk it? Bring the entire charger with you.

✔ **At the security checkpoint, place your phone in a bin.** Add to the bin all your other electronic devices, keys, brass knuckles, grenades, and so on. I know from experience that keeping your cell phone in your pocket most definitely sets off airport metal detectors.

✔ **If the flight crew asks you to *turn off* your cell phone for takeoff and landing, obey the command.** That's *turn off,* as in power off the phone or shut it down. It doesn't mean that you place the phone in airplane mode. Turn it off.

✔ **Use the phone's Calendar app to keep track of flights.** The combination of airline and flight number can serve as the event title. For the event time, I insert takeoff and landing schedules. For the location, I add the origin and destination airport codes. Remember to set the proper time zones. Referencing the phone from your airplane seat or in a busy terminal is much handier than fussing with travel papers. See Chapter 17 for more information on the Calendar app.

✔ **Some airlines feature Android apps you can use while traveling.** Rather than hang on to a boarding pass printed by your computer, for example, you simply show your phone to the scanner.

International Calling

You can use your Android phone to dial up folks who live in other countries. You can also take your cell phone overseas and use it in another country. Completing either task isn't as difficult as properly posing for a passport photo, but it can become frustrating and potentially expensive when you don't know your way around.

Dialing an international number

A phone is a bell that anyone in the world can ring. To prove it, all you need is the phone number of anyone in the world. Dial that number using your phone and, as long as you both speak the same language, you're talking!

To make an international call with your Android phone, you merely need to know the foreign phone number. The number includes the international country-code prefix, followed by the number.

Before dialing the international country-code prefix, you must first dial a plus sign (+) when using the Phone app. The + symbol is the *country exit code,* which must be dialed to flee the national phone system and access the international phone system. For example, to dial Finland on your phone, you dial +358 and then the number in Finland. The +358 is the exit code (+) plus the international code for Finland (358).

To produce the + code in an international phone number, press and hold down the 0 key on the Phone app's dialpad. Then type the country prefix and the phone number. Touch the Dial Phone icon to complete the call.

- ✔ Most cellular providers surcharge when sending a text message abroad. Contact your cellular provider to confirm the text message rates. Generally, you'll find two rates, one for sending and another for receiving text messages.

- ✔ If texting charges vex you, remember that e-mail has no associated per-message charge. You also have alternative ways to chat, such as Google Hangouts and Skype, both covered in Chapter 13.

- ✔ In most cases, dialing an international number involves a time zone difference. Before you dial, be aware of what time it is in the country or location you're calling. The Clock app can handle that job for you: Summon a clock for the location your calling and place it on the Clock app's screen.

- ✔ Dialing internationally also involves surcharges, unless your cell phone plan provides for international dialing.

✏ The + character isn't a number separator. When you see an international number listed as 011+20+xxxxxxx, do not insert the + character in the number. Instead, dial +20 and then the rest of the international phone number.

✏ International calls fail for a number of reasons. One of the most common is that the recipient's phone company or service blocks incoming international calls.

✏ Another reason that international calls fail is the zero reason: Oftentimes, you must leave out any zero in the phone number that follows the country code. So, if the country code is 254 for Kenya and the phone number starts with 012, you dial +254 for Kenya and then 12 and the rest of the number. Omit the leading zero.

✏ Know which type of phone you're calling internationally — cell phone or landline. The reason is that an international call to a cell phone might involve a surcharge that doesn't apply to a landline.

Making international calls with Skype

One of the easiest, and cheapest, ways to make international calls on your Android phone is to use the Skype app. If the app isn't supplied on your phone, you have to install it from the Google Play Store.

Because Skype uses the Internet, you can also use Skype to contact overseas Skype users without incurring extra costs (well, beyond your normal data plan). You can, however, use Skype Credit in your Skype account to dial internationally, both from the United States to a foreign country as well as from a foreign country to home.

You need Skype Credit to place an international call (or any call to a real phone). The easiest way to add credit is to visit Skype on the Internet using a computer: www.skype.com. Sign in to your account and surrender a credit card to add a few pennies of credit. Although that may seem disappointing, remember that Skype's rates are far cheaper than placing a call by using your cellular provider.

To make an international call, log in to Skype as you normally would. At the main Skype screen, touch the Call Phone icon to summon the phone dialpad. Punch in the number, including the plus sign (+) for international access. Touch the Call icon to make the call. When you're finished with the call, touch the End icon.

✏ See Chapter 13 for more information on using Skype.

✏ You're always signed in to Skype unless you sign out. Touching the Home or Recent icon to switch to another app doesn't sign you out of Skype.

✔ To sign out of Skype, touch the Action Overflow icon on the main Skype screen and choose Sign Out.

✔ Check with your cellular provider to see whether you're charged connection minutes for using Skype. Even though the international calling with Skype is free, you might still be dinged for the minutes you use on Skype to make the call.

Taking your Android phone abroad

The easiest way to use a cell phone abroad is to rent or buy one in the country where you plan to stay. I'm serious: Often, international roaming charges are so high that it's cheaper to simply buy a temporary cell phone wherever you go, especially if you plan to stay there for a while.

When you opt to use your own phone rather than buy a local phone, things should run smoothly — if a compatible cellular service is in your location. Not every Android phone uses the same network and, of course, not every foreign country uses the same cellular network. Things must match before the phone can work. Plus, you may have to deal with foreign carrier roaming charges.

The key to determining whether your phone is usable in a foreign country is to turn it on. The name of that country's compatible cellular service should show up at the top of the phone, where the name of your carrier appears on the main screen. So where your phone once said *Verizon Wireless,* it may say *Wambooli Telcom* when you're overseas.

✔ You receive calls on your cell phone internationally as long as the phone can access the network. Your friends need only dial your cell phone number as they normally do; the phone system automatically forwards your calls to wherever you are in the world.

✔ The person calling you pays nothing extra when you're off romping the globe with your Android phone. Nope — *you* pay extra for the call.

✔ While you're abroad, you need to dial internationally. When calling home (for example, the United States), you need to use a 10-digit number (phone number plus area code). You may also be required to type the country exit code when you dial.

✔ When in doubt, contact your cellular provider for tips and other information specific to whatever country you're visiting.

✔ Be sure to inquire about texting and cellular data (Internet) rates while you're abroad.

✔ Using an Android phone over a Wi-Fi network abroad incurs no extra fees (unless data roaming is on, as discussed earlier in this chapter). In fact, you can use the Skype app on your phone over a Wi-Fi network to call the United States or any international number at inexpensive rates.

Customize and Configure

Customizing your Android phone doesn't involve sprucing up the phone's case, so put away that Bedazzler™. The kind of customization this chapter refers to involves fine-tuning the way the Android operating system presents itself. You can modify the Home screen, add security, change sounds, and alter numerous other features to truly make your phone your own.

It's Your Home Screen

The typical Android Home screen sports anywhere from three to nine or more pages. It comes preconfigured with an assortment of apps and widgets, some of which you'll never use. That's okay because you can easily replace those items. You can put new wallpaper on the Home screen background, including fancy *live* wallpaper. Truly, you can make the Home screen look just the way you want.

Modifying the Home screen

The key to unlocking the Home screen can be subtly different from phone to phone. The standard method is to long-press a blank part of the Home screen; do not long-press a launcher icon or widget. Upon success, you may see a Home screen menu, similar to those shown in Figure 22-1.

Samsung Home screen menu   Some other phone's Home screen menu

Figure 22-1: The Home screen menu.

After long-pressing, you see a Home screen page overview along with a few icons, as illustrated in the figure.

The standard items controlled by the Home screen menu are

- **Wallpaper:** Change the background image on the Home screen.
- **Apps and widgets:** Add launcher icons (apps) and widgets to the Home screen.
- **Folders:** Create folders for multiple apps on the Home screen.
- **Pages:** Add, remove, or manage multiple Home screen pages.

Later sections in this chapter describe how to use each command.

- You cannot long-press the Home screen when it's full of launcher icons and widgets. Swipe to a screen that's all or partially empty. If such a screen isn't available, remove an item from the screen; see the section "Rearranging and removing apps and widgets."
- Use folders to help organize apps on the Home screen, especially when the Home screen starts to overflow with launcher icons. See the later section, "Building app folders."
- On some Android phones, you can customize the Home screen by touching the Menu icon and choosing the Add to Home Screen command. The menu may also list specific commands, such as those shown in Figure 22-1.
- On some Android phones, the long-press action lets you change only the wallpaper. Refer to other sections in this chapter for information on adding icons and widgets to the Home screen.

Changing wallpaper

The Home screen background can be decorated with two types of wallpaper:

- **Traditional:** The wallpaper is chosen from a selection of still images. These images can be preloaded as wallpapers on the phone, or you can pluck an image from the phone's gallery, such as a photo you've taken.

- **Live:** The wallpaper image is animated, either displaying a changing images or reacting to your touch.

To set new wallpaper for the Home screen, obey these steps:

1. **Long-press the Home screen.**

2. **Choose the Set Wallpaper or Wallpapers command or icon.**

   Refer to Figures 22-1 and 22-2 for examples.

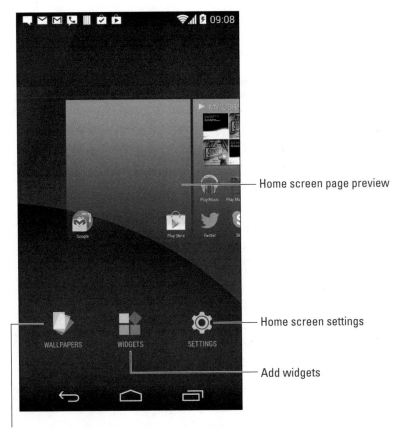

Figure 22-2: The stock Android Home screen menu.

3. **Choose the wallpaper type.**

   For example, choose Gallery to use a photo you've taken or Wallpapers to select a preset wallpaper design.

   You may see a scrolling list of wallpaper options. The Pick Image option lets you use the Gallery or Photo app to choose an image. Live wallpapers may be shown in the list by name.

4. **If prompted, choose the wallpaper you want from the list.**

   For selecting an image from the phone, you see a preview of the wallpaper. A cropping tool may appear, and you can select and crop part of the image.

   For certain live wallpapers, a Settings icon appears. It lets you customize certain aspects of the interactive wallpaper.

5. **Touch the Save, Set Wallpaper, or Apply button to confirm your selection.**

   The new wallpaper takes over the Home screen.

Live wallpaper is interactive, usually featuring some form of animation. Otherwise, the wallpaper image scrolls slightly as you swipe from one Home screen page to another.

✐ You may also be able to change the lock screen wallpaper on some phones. For example, after Step 2 (in the preceding list), you may be prompted to select wallpaper for the Home screen, the lock screen, or both.

✐ The Settings apps may feature a Wallpaper command. Choose Display and then look for a Wallpaper command. Likewise, you might find a Lock Screen command on the Settings app's main screen. Use it to set the lock screen's wallpaper.

✐ The Zedge app has some interesting wallpaper features. Check it out at the Google Play Store; see Chapter 18.

✐ See Chapter 15 for more information about the Gallery, including information on how to crop an image.

Adding apps to the Home screen

You need not live with the unbearable proposition that you're stuck with only the apps that come preset on the Home screen. Nope — you're free to add your own apps. Just follow these steps:

1. **Visit the Home screen page on which you want to stick the app icon, or launcher.**

   The screen must have room for the app icon.

2. **Touch the Apps icon to display the apps drawer.**

3. **Long-press the app icon you want to add to the Home screen.**

4. **Drag the app to the Home screen page, lifting your finger to place the app.**

   A copy of the app's icon is placed on the Home screen.

The app hasn't moved: What you see is a copy or, officially, a *launcher.* You can still find the app in the apps drawer, but now the app is also available — more conveniently — on the Home screen.

- ✔ Not every app needs a launcher icon on the Home screen. I recommend placing only those apps you use most frequently.

- ✔ The best icons to place on the Home screen are those that show updates, such as new messages, similar the icon shown in the margin. These icons are also ideal to place in the favorites tray, as covered in the next section.

- ✔ See the later section "Rearranging and removing apps and widgets" for information on moving an app icon around on the Home screen or from one page to another. That section also covers removing apps from the Home screen.

- ✔ You can add apps to the Home screen also by choosing the Apps command from the Home screen menu (refer to Figure 22-1). Often this command merely skips over Steps 1 and 2 in this section; you still have to long-press the icon and drag it to a Home screen page.

Putting an app in the favorites tray

The line of icons at the bottom of the Home screen is called the *favorites tray.* It includes the Apps icon, as well as other icons you place there, such as the Phone or Dialer app icon, or any app you use most often. The favorites tray icons appear the same no matter which Home screen page is displayed.

Icons are managed on the favorites tray in one of two ways:

- ✔ Drag an icon off the favorites tray, either to the Home screen or to the Remove or Delete icon. That action makes room for a new icon to be placed in the favorites tray.

- ✔ Drag an icon from the Home screen to the favorites tray, in which case any existing icon swaps places with the icon already there.

Of these two methods, the second one may not work on all phones. In fact, the second method may create an app folder in the favorites tray, which is probably not what you want. (See the later section, "Building app folders," for information.)

Slapping down widgets

The Home screen is the place where you can find *widgets,* or tiny, interactive information windows. A widget often provides a gateway to another app or displays information such as status updates, the name of the song that's playing, or the weather. To add a widget to the Home screen, heed these steps:

1. **Switch to a Home screen page that has room enough for the new widget.**

   Unlike app icons, widgets can occupy more than a postage-stamp-size piece of Home screen real estate.

2. **Long-press the Home screen and choose the Widget or Widgets command or icon.**

   If necessary, touch the Widgets tab atop the screen to peruse widgets.

3. **Find the widget you want to add.**

   Swipe the screen to browse widgets. They're listed by name, but you also see a tiny widget preview.

4. **Long-press the widget and drag it to a Home screen page to add that widget.**

   At this point, the operation is similar to adding an app. One major difference, however, is that some widgets can be very big. Room must be available on the Home screen page or you won't be able to add the widget.

Some widgets may require additional setup after you add them, such as setting a few quick options. You might also see a resize rectangle around the widget, similar to what's shown in Figure 22-3. Drag the edges or corners of that rectangle to resize the widget.

- Most phones let you browse widgets from the apps drawer; choose the Widgets tab from the top of the screen or keep swiping the screen left until you start viewing widgets.

- The variety of available widgets depends on the apps you have installed. Some applications come with widgets; some don't.

- A great widget to add is the Power Control widget.

- To remove, move, or rearrange a widget, see the later section "Rearranging and removing apps and widgets."

Figure 22-3: Arranging a widget.

Building app folders

Each Home screen page sports a grid that holds only so many app icons. Even when you can add more pages, an upper limit exists. Although you could use math to calculate the maximum number of Home screen icons, a better choice is to use app folders to avoid any overflow.

An *app folder* is a collection of two or more apps, both in the same spot on the Home screen. Figure 22-4 illustrates an app folder on the Home screen, shown both closed and open.

Folders are created in different ways, depending on the phone. The stock Android method for creating a folder follows:

1. **Place on the same Home screen page the icons that you want to put in the folder.**

2. **Long-press one icon and drag it right on top of the other icon.**

The folder is created. Both icon images show up inside a circle, similar to what's shown on the left in Figure 22-4.

3. **Continue to drag icons into the folder.**

   You can also drag an icon directly from the apps drawer.

Folder name

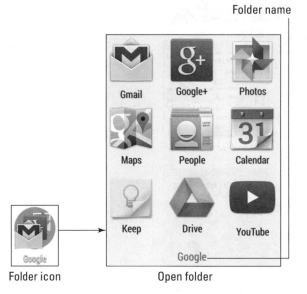

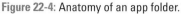

Folder icon   Open folder

Figure 22-4: Anatomy of an app folder.

Other phones may not let you drag two icons together to build a folder, as described in Steps 1 and 2. On those phones, long-press the Home screen and choose the Create Folder or Folder command. Name the folder, and then touch the OK button to create it. At that point, you can drag icons into the folder as described in this section.

Open a folder by touching it. You can then touch an icon in the folder to start an app. Or if you don't find what you want, touch the Back icon to close the folder.

✔ Some phones require that you long-press the Home screen to create a folder. Drag an app icon onto the Create Folder icon to build the folder.

✔ Folders are managed just like other icons on the Home screen. You can long-press them to drag them around. They can also be deleted. See the next section.

✔ Change a folder's name by opening the folder and then touching its name. Type the new name by using the onscreen keyboard.

✔ Add more apps to the folder by dragging them over the folder's icon.

✔ To remove an icon from a folder, open the folder and drag out the icon. When the second-to-last icon is dragged out of a folder, the folder is removed. If not, drag the last icon out, and then remove the folder as described in next section.

Rearranging and removing apps and widgets

Apps, folders, and widgets aren't fastened to the Home screen with anything stronger than masking tape. That's obvious because it's very easy to pick up and move an icon to a new position or remove it completely. The process starts by long-pressing the app, folder, or widget, as shown in Figure 22-5.

Drag here to
uninstall the app

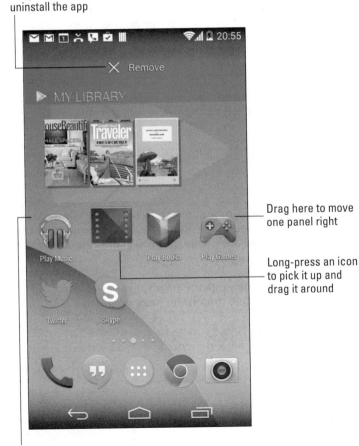

Drag here to move
one panel right

Long-press an icon
to pick it up and
drag it around

Drag here to move
one panel left

Figure 22-5: Moving an icon.

You can drag a free icon to another position on the Home screen or to another Home screen page. To banish the icon, drag it to the Remove icon that appears on the Home screen.

- ✔ The Remove icon might appear as a Trash icon (shown in the margin) instead of an X.

- ✔ Removing an app or a widget from the Home screen doesn't uninstall the app or widget. See Chapter 18 for information on uninstalling apps.

- ✔ When an icon hovers over the Remove or Trash icon, ready to be deleted, its color changes to red.

Managing Home screen pages

The number of pages on the Home screen isn't fixed. You can add pages. You can remove pages. You can even rearrange pages. These features might not be available to all Android phones and, sadly, they're not implemented in exactly the same way.

The stock Android method of adding a Home screen page is to drag an icon left or right, just as if you were positioning that icon on another Home screen page. When a page to the left or right doesn't exist, the phone automatically adds a new, blank page.

Other phones may be more specific in how pages are added. For example, you might be able to choose a Page command from the Home screen menu (refer to Figure 22-1).

Samsung phones feature a Home screen page overview, shown in Figure 22-6. To edit Home screen pages, touch the Menu icon while viewing the Home screen and then choose the Edit Page command. You can then manage Home screen pages as illustrated in the figure.

Generally speaking, to rearrange the pages, long-press a page and drag it to a new spot. When you're done, touch the Back or Home icon.

- ✔ The total number of Home screen pages is fixed. The maximum may be three, five, seven, or nine, depending on your phone.

- ✔ A minimum number of Home screen pages also exists. The fewest I've seen is three.

Drag here to remove a page

Drag pages to rearrange

Main Home screen page

Add page

Figure 22-6: Manipulating Home screen pages.

Android Phone Locks

Your Android phone comes with a *lock,* the simple touchscreen gizmo you slide to unlock the phone and gain access to its information and features. For most folks, this lock is secure enough. For others, the lock is about as effective as using a kitten to frighten an alligator.

Finding the screen locks

All screen locks on the phone can be found in the same location: on the Choose Screen Lock screen. Heed these steps to visit that screen:

1. **Open the Settings app.**

2. **Choose the Security item.**

   This item may have another name, such as Lock Screen. If you see both a Security and Lock Screen item, choose Lock Screen.

On some Samsung phones, you choose the Lock Screen item on the Device tab in the Settings app.

3. **Choose Screen Lock.**

   If you don't see a Screen Lock item, look for the item titled Set Up Screen Lock or Change Screen Lock.

If the screen lock is already set, you have to work the lock to proceed: Trace the pattern, or type the PIN or password. You then get access to the Choose Screen Lock screen, which shows several items:

- **None:** The phone has no lock, not even the basic swipe screen lock. Choosing this option disables all screen locks.
- **Slide:** Unlock the phone by swiping your finger across the screen. This item might also be titled *Swipe*.
- **Pattern:** Trace a pattern on the touchscreen to unlock the phone.
- **PIN:** Unlock the phone by typing a personal identification number (PIN).
- **Password:** Type a password to unlock the phone.

Additional items might also appear, such as the *Face Unlock* as well as any custom unlocking screens added by the phone's manufacturer.

To set or remove a lock, refer to the following sections.

- The locks don't appear when you answer an incoming phone call. You're prompted, however, to unlock the phone if you want to use its features while you're on a call.
- See Chapter 2 for details on unlocking your phone.

Removing a lock

To disable the pattern, PIN, or password screen lock on your phone, choose the None or Slide option from the Choose Screen Lock screen. When None is chosen, the phone has no lock screen. When Slide is chosen, the phone uses the standard slide lock, as described in Chapter 2.

Setting a PIN

The PIN lock is second only to the password lock as the most secure for your Android phone. To access the phone you must type a PIN, or Personal Identification Number. This type of screen lock is also employed as a backup for the less-secure screen unlocking methods.

The *PIN lock* is a code between 4 and 16 numbers long. It contains only numbers, 0 through 9. To set the PIN lock for your Android phone, follow the directions in the earlier section "Finding the screen locks" to reach the Choose Screen Lock screen. Choose PIN from the list of locks.

Use the onscreen keypad to type your PIN once. Touch the Continue button, then type the same PIN again to confirm that you know it. Touch OK. The next time you unlock the phone, you'll need to type the PIN to gain access.

To disable the PIN, reset the security level as described in the preceding section.

Applying a password

The most secure way to lock the phone's screen is to apply a full-on password. Unlike a PIN (refer to the preceding section), a *password* contains a combination of numbers, symbols, and uppercase and lowercase letters.

Set the password by choosing Password from the Choose Screen Lock screen; refer to the earlier section "Finding the screen locks" for information on getting to that screen. The password you create must be at least four characters. Longer passwords are more secure but easier to mistype.

You type the password twice to set things up, which confirms to the phone that you know the password and will, you hope, remember it in the future.

The phone prompts you to type the password whenever you unlock the screen, as described in Chapter 2. You also type the password when you change or remove the screen lock, as discussed in the section "Finding the screen locks," earlier in this chapter.

Creating an unlock pattern

The unlock pattern is perhaps the most popular, and certainly the most unconventional, way to lock an Android phone's screen. The pattern must be traced on the touchscreen to unlock the phone.

To set the unlock pattern, follow these steps:

1. **Summon the Choose Screen Lock screen.**

   Refer to the earlier section "Finding the screen locks."

2. **Choose Pattern.**

   If you haven't yet set a pattern, you may see the tutorial describing the process; touch the Next button to skip merrily through the dreary directions.

3. **Trace an unlock pattern.**

   Use Figure 22-7 as your guide. You can trace over the dots in any order, but you can trace over a dot only once. The pattern must cover at least four dots.

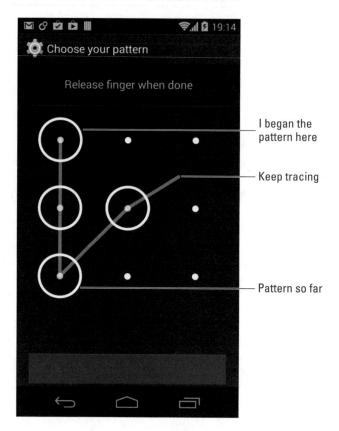

I began the
pattern here

Keep tracing

Pattern so far

Figure 22-7: Setting the unlock pattern.

4. Touch the Continue button.

5. Redraw the pattern again, just to confirm that you know it.

6. Touch the Confirm button, and the pattern lock is set.

Some phones may require you to type a PIN or password as a backup to the pattern lock. If so, follow the onscreen directions to set that lock as well.

Ensure that a check mark appears by the Make Pattern Visible option, found on the Security, Screen Security screen. That way, the pattern shows up when you need to unlock the phone. For even more security, you can disable this option, but you *must* remember how and where the pattern goes.

↳ The unlock pattern can be as simple or as complex as you like. I'm a big fan of simple.

↳ Wash your hands! Smudge marks on the display can betray your pattern.

Delaying the screen lock

Your phone can be configured to automatically lock after a given period of inactivity, as described in this chapter's "Changing various settings" section. Even so, the phone may not lock right away after a screen timeout. Instead, there is a brief delay, which allows you to wake up the phone right away without having to work the screen lock. The setting is called Automatically Lock.

To adjust the automatic lock, open the Settings app and choose the Security or Lock Screen item. Choose Automatically Lock to set how long the touchscreen waits to lock after the phone's touchscreen display has a timeout. The

Automatically Lock item appears only when a secure screen lock is set, so if you don't see it, first set a secure lock. The value can be adjusted from Immediately to 30 minutes. The standard value is typically 5 seconds.

The Automatically Lock setting isn't enforced when you manually lock the phone: Pressing the Power/Lock key always locks the phone, applying whatever lock screen security you've set. But when the screen times out, the Automatically Lock delay value is used, which saves some time should the phone try to snooze on you.

Adding owner info text

Screen locks add security to your Android phone, but what happens when a Good Samaritan finds your phone? My guess is that he'll probably pick up the phone and turn it on. Whether your phone is locked or not, the Good Samaritan would probably appreciate some text right on the lock screen that says who the phone belongs to and how to contact that person. That makes sense.

To add owner info text to your Android phone's lock screen, follow these steps:

1. **Visit the Settings app.**

2. **Choose the Security or Lock Screen category.**

   On some Samsung phones, the Lock Screen category is found on the Device tab.

3. **Choose Owner Info or Owner Information.**

4. **Ensure that there's a check mark by the Show Owner Info on Lock Screen option.**

5. **Type text in the box.**

   You can type more than one line of text, though the information is displayed on the lock screen as a single line.

6. **Touch the OK button.**

   Or touch the Back icon to return to the previous screen.

Whatever text you type in the box appears on the lock screen. Therefore, I recommend typing something useful as the command suggestions: your name, address, another phone number, and e-mail address, for example. This way, should you lose your phone and an honest person finds it, he can get it back to you.

Various Phone Adjustments

Android phones feature a plethora of options and settings for you to adjust. You can fix things that annoy you or make things better to please your tastes. The whole idea is to make your phone more usable for you.

Setting the incoming call volume

Whether the phone rings, vibrates, or explodes depends on how you've configured it to signal you for an incoming call. Abide by these steps to set the various options (but not explosions) for your phone:

1. **Open the Settings app.**

2. **Choose Sound.**

   On some Samsung phones, the Sound option is found on the Settings app's Device tab.

3. **Set the phone's ringer volume by touching Volumes or Volume.**

4. **Manipulate the Ringtone slider left or right to specify how loud the phone rings for an incoming call.**

   After you release the slider, you hear an example of how loudly the phone rings.

5. **Touch OK to set the ringer volume.**

   If you'd rather mute the phone, touch the Silent Mode option on the main Sound settings screen.

6. **To activate vibration when the phone rings, touch Vibrate or Vibrate When Ringing.**

   Some phones have a single Vibration option; others have several settings from which you can choose.

When the next call comes in, the phone alerts you using the volume setting or vibration options you've just set.

      ✔ See Chapter 3 for information on temporarily silencing the phone.

      ✔ Turning on vibration puts a wee extra drain on the battery. See Chapter 23 for more information on power management for your phone.

Changing display settings

The Display item in the Settings app deals with touchscreen settings. Two popular settings worthy of your attention are the Brightness and Screen Timeout options.

To access the Display screen, open the Settings app and choose Display. On some Samsung phones, this item is found on the Settings app's Device tab.

Screen brightness: Choose Display, and then choose Brightness. Use the slider to adjust the touchscreen's intensity. Some phones feature the Automatic Brightness setting. It uses the phone's magical light sensor to determine how bright it is where you are.

Screen timeout: Choose Display, and then choose Screen Timeout. Select a time-out value from the list. This duration specifies when the phone automatically locks the touchscreen.

Maintenance, Troubleshooting, and Help

In This Chapter

▶ Checking the phone's battery usage

▶ Making the battery last

▶ Cleaning the phone

▶ Keeping the system up-to-date

▶ Dealing with problems

▶ Finding support

▶ Getting answers to common questions

Maintenance is that thing you were supposed to remember to do, but you didn't do, and that's why you need help and troubleshooting advice. Don't blame yourself; no one likes to do maintenance. Okay, well, I like maintaining my stuff. I even change the belt on my vacuum cleaner every six months. Did you know that the vacuum cleaner manual tells you to do so? Probably not. I read that in *Vacuum Cleaner Maintenance For Dummies*. This book is *Android Phones For Dummies*, which is why it contains topics on maintenance, troubleshooting, and help for Android phones, not for vacuum cleaners.

∠135553126

↙ Yesterday

Dan Gookin
Mobile
↙ 2 days ago

(202) 555-8888
Washington D.C.
↙ 2 days ago

+1 435-555-2741

Battery Care and Feeding

Perhaps the most important item you can monitor and maintain on your Android phone is its battery. The battery supplies the necessary electrical juice by which the phone operates. Without battery power, your phone is about as useful as a tin-can-and-a-string for communications. Keep an eye on the battery.

Monitoring the battery

Android phones display the current battery status at the top of the screen, in the status area, next to the time. The icons used to display battery status are similar to the icons shown in Figure 23-1.

Battery is fully charged and happy.

Battery is being used, starting to drain.

Battery getting low, you should charge!

Battery frighteningly low, stop using and charge at once!

Battery is charging.

Figure 23-1: Battery status icons.

You might also see the icon for a dead or missing battery, but for some reason I can't get my phone to turn on and display it.

- ✔ Heed those low-battery warnings! The phone sounds a notification whenever the battery power gets low. The phone sounds another notification whenever the battery gets *very* low.

- ✔ When the battery is too low, the phone shuts itself off.

- ✔ In addition to the status icons, the phone's notification light might turn a scary shade of red whenever battery juice is dreadfully low.

- ✔ The best way to deal with a low battery is to connect the phone to a power source: Either plug the phone into a wall socket, or connect the phone to a computer by using a USB cable. The phone charges itself immediately; plus, you can use the phone while it's charging.

✔ The phone charges more efficiently when it's plugged into a wall socket rather than a computer.

✔ You don't have to fully charge the phone to use it. If you have 20 minutes to charge and the power level returns to only 70 percent, that's great. Well, it's not great, but it's far better than a 20 percent battery level.

✔ Battery percentage values are best-guess estimates. Just because you talked for two hours and the battery shows 50 percent doesn't mean that you're guaranteed two more hours of talking. Odds are good that you have much less than two hours. In fact, as the percentage value gets low, the battery appears to drain faster.

Determining what is drawing power

A nifty screen on your Android phone lets you review which activities have been consuming power when the phone is operating from its battery. This informative screen is shown in Figure 23-2.

To view the battery usage screen on your phone, open the Settings app and choose the Battery item. On some Samsung phones, touch the General tab in the Settings app to locate the Battery item.

Touch an item in the list to view its details. For some items, the details screen contains an icon that you can touch to adjust the setting. For example, touch the Wi-Fi icon (shown in Figure 23-2) to turn off Wi-Fi.

The number and variety of items listed on the battery use screen depend on what you've been doing with your phone between charges and how many different apps you've been using. Don't be surprised if an item (such as the Play Books app) doesn't show up in the list. Not every app uses a lot of battery power.

Saving battery life

Here's a smattering of things you can do to help prolong battery life for your Android phone:

Dim the screen. The display is capable of drawing down quite a lot of battery power. Although a dim screen can be more difficult to see, especially outdoors, it definitely saves on battery life. Adjust screen brightness from the Settings app, or choose the Brightness quick action from the quick actions drawer.

Usage and time chart

Touch to view usage and change settings

Current battery charge and state

Items drawing power

Figure 23-2: Battery usage info.

Disable vibration options. The phone's vibration is caused by a teensy motor. Although you don't see much battery savings by disabling the vibration options, it's better than no savings. To turn off vibration, follow these steps:

1. **Open the Settings app.**

2. **Choose Sound.**

    On some Samsung phones, the Sound item is found by choosing the Device tab in the Settings app.

3. **Peruse the vibration options.**

   Most phones lack a single setting for vibration. Instead, you'll find settings such as Vibrate While Ringing, Vibration Intensity, and Vibrate on Touch.

4. **Disable one or all of the vibration settings.**

Additionally, consider lowering the volume of notifications by choosing the Volume option. This option also saves a modicum of battery life, though I've missed important notifications by setting the volume too low.

Deactivate Bluetooth. When you're not using Bluetooth, turn it off. Or when you *really* need that cyborg Bluetooth ear-thing, try to keep your phone plugged in. See Chapter 19 for information on Bluetooth.

Turn off Wi-Fi. The phone's Wi-Fi radio places only a modest drain on the battery. Disable it only when battery life is critical; otherwise don't fret over the Wi-Fi setting.

Get a bigger battery. Most Android phones have larger batteries available as an option. The nice people at the Phone Store will be more than happy to sell you one or more, if you please. Having a larger battery definitely increases the time you can use your phone without having to recharge.

If you buy a larger battery — or any replacement battery, for that matter — ensure that the battery is manufacturer-compatible with your phone. Improper batteries can damage your phone. Heck, they can catch fire. So be careful when choosing a replacement battery.

Manage battery performance. Several Android phones have battery-saving software built in. You can access the software from a special app or from the Battery item in the Settings app. Similar to your computer, battery-performance management involves turning phone features on or off during certain times of the day. Third-party battery management apps are also available at the Google Play Store. See Chapter 18.

Regular Phone Maintenance

Relax. Unlike draining the lawnmower's oil once a year, regular maintenance of an Android phone doesn't require a drip pan or a permit from the EPA. In fact, an Android phone requires only two basic regular maintenance tasks: cleaning and backing up.

Keeping it clean

You probably already keep your phone clean. I must use my sleeve to wipe the touchscreen at least a dozen times a day. Of course, better than your sleeve is something called a *microfiber cloth*. This item can be found at any computer- or office-supply store.

✔ Never use ammonia or alcohol to clean the touchscreen. These substances damage the phone. Use only a cleaning solution specifically designed for touchscreens.

✔ If the screen continually gets dirty, consider adding a *screen protector.* This specially designed cover prevents the screen from getting scratched or dirty while still allowing you to interact with the touchscreen. Ensure that the screen protector you obtain is intended for use with your specific phone.

✔ You can also find customized cell phone cases, belt clips, and protectors, which can help keep the phone looking spiffy. Be aware that these items are mostly for decorative or fashion purposes and don't even prevent serious damage should you drop the phone.

Backing up your phone

A *backup* is a safety copy of the information on your phone. It includes any contact information, music, photos, videos, and apps you've recorded, downloaded, or installed, plus any settings you've made to customize your phone. Copying this information to another source is one way to keep the information safe, in case anything happens to the phone.

On your Google account, information is backed up automatically. This information includes your Contacts list, Gmail messages, and Calendar app appointments. Because Android phones automatically sync this information with the Internet, a backup is always present.

To confirm that your phone's information is being backed up, heed these steps:

1. **Open the Settings app.**

2. **Choose your Google account.**

   It's listed under the Accounts heading.

   On some Samsung phones, touch the General tab, choose the Accounts item, and then choose Google on the Accounts screen.

3. **Touch the green Sync icon by your Gmail address.**

   The Sync icon is shown in the margin.

4. **Ensure that a check mark appears by every item for your account.**

   Where a check mark doesn't appear, touch the square to add one.

Adding the check marks ensures that those items are synchronized (backed up) between your phone and your Google account on the Internet.

Likewise, if you're using Yahoo! or some other account, repeat these steps but in Step 2 choose that account.

Updating the System

Every so often, a new version of your phone's operating system becomes available. It's an *Android update* because *Android* is the name of the phone's operating system, not because your phone thinks that it's a type of robot.

Whenever an update occurs, an alert or a message appears on the phone, indicating that a system upgrade is available. Your choice is to install immediately or put it off. As long as the phone has a decent charge and you don't need to shut it off right away, install the update.

- ✔ Some Samsung phones can be updated only by using the Kies program on a computer. You can attempt to upgrade the phone by itself, but if that fails, connect the phone to a computer running the Kies program to complete the upgrade.

- ✔ You can manually check for updates: In the Settings app, choose About Phone or About Device. Touch the System Updates item and then the Check Now button. I can pretty much guarantee that you won't find an update pending; they're downloaded automatically based on the whims of your phone's manufacturer and cellular service provider. Still, it's fun to touch the Check Now button and dream that you have a modicum of power.

Help and Troubleshooting

Getting help isn't as bad as it was in the old days. Back then, you could try two sources for technological help: the atrocious manual that came with your electronic device or a phone call to the guy who wrote the atrocious manual. It was unpleasant. Today, the situation is better. You have many resources for solving issues with your gizmos, including your Android phone.

Getting help

Some phone manufacturers, as well as cell phone providers, offer more help than others. Some phones come with the Help app, although it's not part of the standard Android operating system. The app may be called Help or Help Center or something similar, and it may not be the kind of avuncular, well-written help you get from this book, but it's better than nothing.

Also look for an e-book in the Play Books app. You may find the old, dratted manual lurking in e-book form, which doesn't make it any better.

A Guided Tour or Tutorial app may also be available, which helps you understand how to work some of the phone's interesting features.

Fixing random and annoying problems

Aren't all problems annoying? A welcome problem doesn't exist, unless the problem is welcome because it diverts attention from another, preexisting problem. And random problems? If problems were predictable, they would serve in office. Or maybe they already do?

Here are some typical problems and my suggestions for a solution:

You have general trouble. For just about any problem or minor quirk, consider restarting the phone: Turn off the phone, and then turn it on again. This procedure will most likely fix a majority of the annoying and quirky problems you encounter when using an Android phone.

Some Android phones feature the Restart command on the Phone Options menu: Press and hold down the Power/Lock key to see this menu. If a Restart command is there, use it to restart the phone and (you hope) fix whatever has gone awry.

When restarting doesn't work, consider turning off the phone and removing its battery. Wait about 15 seconds, and then return the battery to the phone and turn on the phone again. See Chapter 1 for battery removal and insertion directions.

The data connection needs to be checked. Sometimes the data connection drops but the phone connection stays active. Check the status bar. If you see bars, you have a phone signal. When you don't see the 4G, 3G, 1X, or Wi-Fi icon, the phone has no data signal.

Occasionally, the data signal suddenly drops for a minute or two. Wait and it comes back around. If it doesn't, the cellular data network might be down, or you may simply be in an area with lousy service. Consider changing your location.

For wireless connections, you have to ensure that Wi-Fi is set up properly and working. Setup usually involves pestering the person who configured the Wi-Fi signal or made it available, such as the cheerful person in the green apron who serves you coffee.

An app has run amok. Sometimes, apps that misbehave let you know. You see a warning on the screen announcing the app's stubborn disposition. Touch the Force Close button to shut down the errant app.

When you see no warning or an app appears to be unduly obstinate, you can shut 'er down the manual way, by following these steps:

1. **Open the Settings app.**

2. **Choose Apps.**

   On some Samsung phones, touch the General tab atop the Settings app screen, and then choose the Application Manager item.

3. **Touch the Running tab to view only active or running apps.**

   Or you can swipe the screen to the left until the Running tab appears.

4. **Choose the app that's causing you distress.**

   For example, a program might not stop or might say that it's busy or has another issue.

5. **Touch the Stop or Force Stop button.**

   The program stops.

After stopping the app, try opening it again to see whether it works. If it continues to run amok, contact the developer. Choose My Apps from the navigation drawer and then choose the app to open its description screen in the Play Store. Scroll down to the bottom of the description screen and choose the Send Email option. Send the developer a message describing the problem.

The phone's software must be reset (a drastic measure). When all else fails, you can do the extreme thing and reset all software on the phone, essentially returning it to the state it was in when it arrived. Obviously, you should not perform this step lightly. In fact, consider finding support (see the next section) before you start:

1. **Open the Settings app.**

2. **Choose Backup & Reset.**

   On some Samsung phones, this item is found by choosing the General tab in the Settings app.

3. **Choose Factory Data Reset.**

   Nothing scary happens yet.

4. **Touch the Reset Phone or Reset Device button.**

   Still nothing scary.

5. **Touch the Erase Everything or Delete All button to confirm.**

   Scary: All the information you've set or stored on the phone is purged.

Again, *do not* follow these steps unless you're certain that they will fix the problem or you're under orders to do so from someone in tech support.

You can, however, follow these directions should you decide to sell, give away, or return your phone. In that case, erasing all your personal information makes a lot of sense.

Getting support

Never discount two important sources of support for your Android phone: the cellular provider and the phone's manufacturer. Between the two, I recommend contacting your cellular provider first, no matter what the problem.

Contact information for both the cellular provider and phone manufacturer is found in the material you received with the phone. In Chapter 1, I recommended that you save those random pieces of paper. You obviously read that chapter and followed my advice, so you can easily find that information.

Okay, so you don't want to go find the box, or you didn't heed my admonition and you threw out the box. Table 23-1 lists contact information on U.S. cellular providers. The From Cell column has the number you can call using your Android phone; otherwise, you can use the toll-free number from any phone.

Table 23-1		U.S. Cellular Providers	
Provider	*From Cell*	*Toll-Free*	*Website*
AT&T	611	800-331-0500	www.att.com/esupport
Sprint Nextel	*2	800-211-4727	mysprint.sprint.com
T-Mobile	611	800-866-2453	www.t-mobile.com/Contact.aspx
Verizon	611	800-922-0204	http://support.vzw.com/clc

Your cellular provider's help phone number might already be found in the phone's address book app. Look for it there if it's not listed in the table.

In Table 23-2, you can find contact information for various Android handset manufacturers.

Table 23-2	Android Phone Manufacturers
Manufacturer	*Website*
HTC	www.htc.com/www/help
LG	www.lg.com/us/support
Motorola	www.motorola.com
Samsung	www.samsung.com/us/mobile/cell-phones

If you have an issue using the Google Play Store, you can visit its support website at http://support.google.com/googleplay.

Android Phone Q&A

I love Q&A! That's because not only is it an effective way to express certain problems and solutions but some of the questions might also cover topics I've been wanting to write about.

"The touchscreen doesn't work!"

The touchscreen, such as the one used on your phone, requires a human finger for proper interaction. The phone interprets complicated electromagnetic physics between the human finger and the phone to determine where the touchscreen is being touched.

You can use the touchscreen while wearing special touchscreen gloves. Yes, they actually make such things. But wearing regular gloves? Nope.

The touchscreen might also fail when the battery power is low or when the phone has been physically damaged.

"The screen is too dark!"

Android phones feature a teensy light sensor on the front. The sensor is used to adjust the touchscreen's brightness based on the amount of ambient light at your location. If the sensor is covered, the screen can get very, very dark.

Ensure that you aren't unintentionally blocking the light sensor. Avoid buying a case or screen protector that obscures the sensor.

The automatic brightness setting might also be vexing you. See Chapter 22 for information on setting screen brightness.

"The battery doesn't charge!"

Start from the source: Is the wall socket providing power? Is the cord plugged in? The cable may be damaged, so try another cable.

When charging from a USB port on a computer, ensure that the computer is turned on. Computers provide no USB power when they're turned off.

Some phones charge from a special cord, not the USB cable. Check to confirm that your phone is able to take a charge from the USB cable.

"The phone gets so hot that it turns itself off!"

Yikes! An overheating phone can be a nasty problem. Judge how hot the phone is by seeing whether you can hold it in your hand: When the phone is too hot to hold, it's too hot. If you're using the phone to keep your coffee warm, the phone is too hot.

Turn off the phone. Take out the battery and let it cool.

If the overheating problem continues, have the phone looked at for potential repair. The battery might need to be replaced.

"The phone won't do landscape mode!"

Just because an app doesn't enter landscape mode doesn't mean that it *can* enter landscape mode. Not every app takes advantage of the phone's capability to orient itself in landscape mode. On certain Android phones, the Home screen doesn't "do landscape" unless it's placed into a car mount or has a physical keyboard that works in landscape mode.

One app that definitely does landscape mode is the web browser, which is described in Chapter 11.

 Android phones have a setting you can check to confirm that landscape orientation is active. Check the quick actions drawer for the Auto-Rotate setting. That setting might also be found in the Settings app, on the Display screen.

Part VI

The Part of Tens

Enjoy a Part of Tens list online at www.dummies.com/extras/androidphones.

In this part . . .

- Glean ten tips, tricks, and shortcuts.
- Remember ten important things.

Ten Tips, Tricks, and Shortcuts

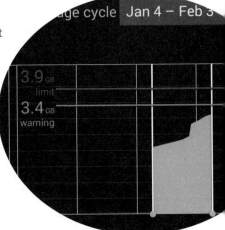

A *tip* is a handy suggestion, something spoken from experience or insight, and something you may not have thought of yourself. A *trick* is something that's good to know, something impressive or unexpected. And a *shortcut* is the path you take through the grave-yard because it's a lot faster — not minding that the groundskeeper may, in fact, be a zombie.

Although I'd like to think that everything I mention in this book is a tip, trick, or shortcut for using your Android phone, I can offer even more information. This chapter provides ten tips, tricks, and shortcuts to help you get the most from your phone.

Quickly Switch Apps

Android apps don't quit. Sure, some of them have a Quit or Sign Out command, but most apps lurk inside the phone's memory while you do other things. The Android operating system may eventually kill off a stale app. Before that happens, you can deftly and quickly switch between all running apps.

The key to making the switch is to use the Recent icon, found at the bottom of the touchscreen. On phones that lack a Recent icon, touch the Home icon twice.

✔ Some phones may feature a Task Manager, in the form of an app or often an icon at the bottom of the recent app list.

✔ The difference between a Task Manager and the recent app list is that the Task Manager lets you kill off running apps. That brutal step isn't necessary, but some people take great satisfaction in the feature.

✔ If your phone lacks a Task Manager, you can view running apps by opening the Settings app and choosing the Apps or Application Manager item. Touch the Running tab to view apps and other activities making themselves busy on your phone.

Add Lock Screen Widgets

Just as you can adorn the Home screen with widgets, you can also slap down a few right on the lock screen. In fact, the time display on your phone's lock screen is most likely a widget.

To ensure that the lock screen widget is active (or even available) on your phone, obey these steps:

1. **Open the Settings app.**

2. **Choose Lock Screen.**

   On certain Samsung phones, the Lock Screen item is found in the Device tab in the Settings app.

   When you can't find a Lock screen item, your phone may not sport this feature. Still, swipe the clock on the lock screen to confirm.

3. **Choose Lock Screen Widgets.**

4. **Mess with the settings.**

   The lock screen settings are not part of the stock Android operating system, so I can't be more specific. Do ensure that the master control icon or check box that enables lock screen widgets is activated. On Samsung phones the setting is called Multiple Widgets.

To add a lock screen widget, touch the large plus icon on the lock screen. If you don't see that icon, swipe the lock screen left or right. From the displayed list, choose a widget to add, such as Calendar, Gmail, Digital Clock, or other widgets.

✔ Multiple widgets can be placed on the lock screen, though you can see only one at a time. Swipe the screen to see others.

✔ To remove a lock screen widget, long-press it. Drag the widget up to the Remove icon and it's gone. You can even remove the Clock widget, in which case only the large plus icon appears on the lock screen.

Choose Default Apps

Every so often, you may see the Complete Action Using prompt on your Android phone, similar to the one shown in Figure 24-1.

Complete action using	
 Amazon MP3	
Google Play Music	
Always	Just once

Figure 24-1: The Complete Action Using question is posed.

The phone has discovered multiple apps that can deal with your request. You pick one, and then choose either Always or Just Once.

When you choose Always, the same app is always used for whatever action took place: listening to music, choosing a photo, navigation, and so on.

When you choose Just Once, you see the prompt again and again.

My advice is to choose Just Once until you're sick of seeing the Complete Action Using prompt. At that point, after choosing the same app over and over, choose Always.

The fear, of course, is that you'll make a mistake. Fret not, gentle reader. The settings you choose can always be undone. For example, if you chose Google Play Music from Figure 24-1, you can undo that setting by following these steps:

1. **Open the Settings app.**

2. **Choose Apps or Application Manager.**

   On some Samsung phones, first choose the General tab in the Settings app to find the Application Manager item.

3. **Locate the app you chose to "always" use.**

   This is the tough step, in that you may not remember your choice. The way I can tell is when the same app opens and I don't really want it to.

4. **Touch the app to display its detailed information screen.**

5. **Touch the Clear Defaults button.**

   The phone immediately forgets to always use that app.

You can't screw up by following these steps. The worst that happens is that the Complete Action Using prompt appears again. The next time you see it, however, make a better choice.

Avoid Data Overages

An important issue for everyone using an Android phone is whether you're about to burst through your monthly data quota. Mobile data surcharges can pinch the wallet, but your Android phone has a handy tool to help you avoid data overages. It's the Data Usage screen, shown in Figure 24-2.

To access the Data Usage screen, follow these steps:

1. **Open the Settings app.**

2. **Choose Data Usage.**

   On some Samsung phones, you'll find the Data Usage item by choosing the Connections tab at the top of the Settings app screen.

The main screen is full of useful information and handy tools. The line chart (refer to Figure 24-2, left) informs you of your data usage over a specific period of time. You can touch the Data Usage Cycle action bar to set that time span, for example, matching it up with your cellular provider's monthly billing cycle.

The orange and red lines are used to remind you of how quickly you're filling your plan's data quota. Warning messages appear when total data usage passes each line, first the orange and then the red.

To set the limits, touch the graph on the screen. Use the tabs that appear to drag the limit lines (orange and red) up or down, and the data usage cycle lines left or right. You do need to activate the Limit Mobile Data Usage item, shown in Figure 24-2, left. This item might also be named Set Mobile Data Limit.

To review access for a specific app, scroll down the Data Usage screen and choose the app from those shown. Only apps that access the network appear. After choosing the app, detailed information shows up, similar to what's shown in Figure 24-2, right. If you notice that the app is using more data than it should, touch the View App Settings button. You may be able to adjust some of the settings to curtail unintended Internet access.

Make the Phone Dream

Does your phone lock or does it fall asleep? I prefer to think that the phone sleeps. That begs the question of whether or not it dreams.

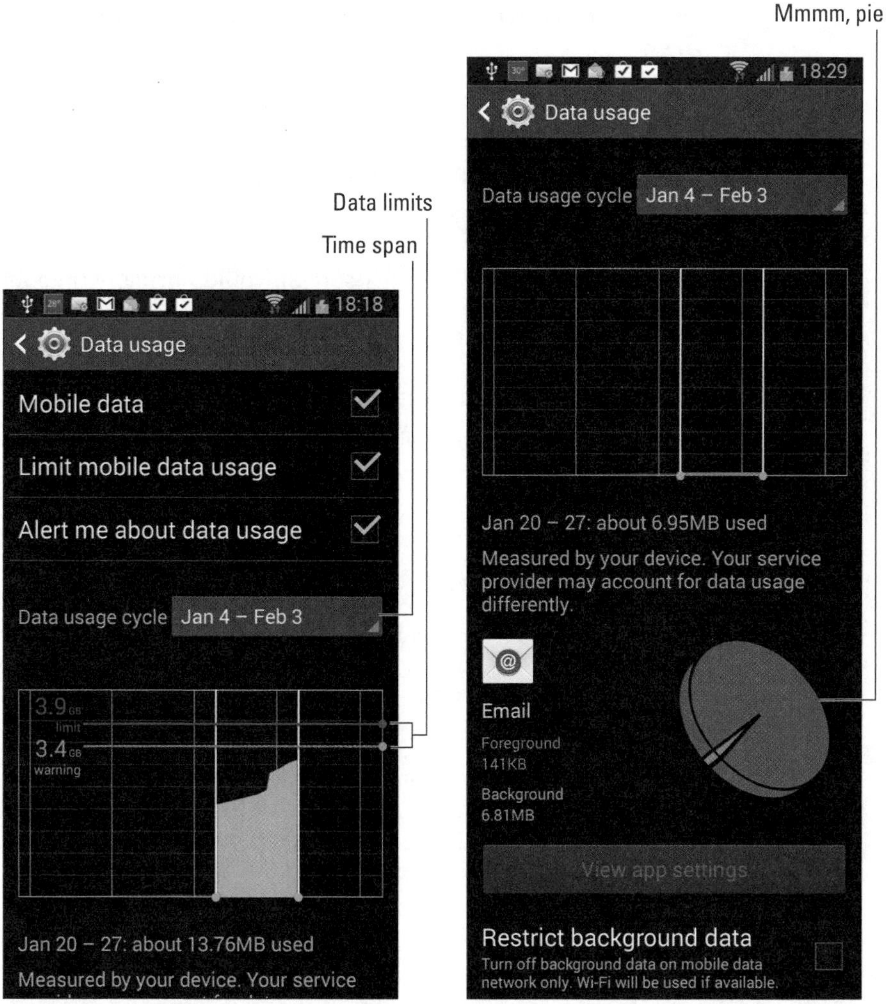

Mmmm, pie

Data limits

Time span

Figure 24-2: Data usage.

Of course it does! You can even see the dreams, providing you activate the Daydream feature — and you keep the phone connected to a power source or in a docking station. Heed these steps:

1. **Start the Settings app.**

2. **Choose Display, then Daydream.**

3. **Ensure that the Daydream master control is in the On position.**

4. **Choose which type of daydream you want displayed.**

The Clock is a popular item, though I'm fond of Colors.

 Some daydreams feature a Settings icon, which can be used to customize how the daydream appears.

5. **Touch the When to Daydream button.**

6. **Choose the Either option.**

The daydreaming begins when the screen would normally timeout and lock. So if you've set the phone to lock after 1 minute of inactivity, it daydreams instead — provided that it's plugged in or docked.

- ✔ To disrupt the dream, swipe the screen.

- ✔ The phone doesn't lock when it daydreams. To lock the phone, press the Power/Lock key.

Get a Wireless Charging Battery Cover

When you want to go truly wireless (I mean, forgo all wires — period), you can get the wireless charging battery cover for your Android phone. Although not every phone may have an official, manufacturer-blessed wireless charging battery cover, many do, and the Phone Store is the first place to look for them.

You get two toys with the wireless charging battery cover. The first is the cover itself. The second is a charging pad. With the cover installed, you simply set the phone on the pad to charge it. A battery inside the back cover lines up the phone for perfect charging.

Voila! No more wires. Ever.

Can you go completely wireless?

When you wave bye-bye to the USB cord for charging purposes, thanks to the wireless charging battery cover, it brings you one step closer to that nirvana of being completely wireless. Is paradise possible?

Beyond charging the phone, other reasons for connecting the phone to something involve exchanging information.

For file transfers, you can use wireless access over the Wi-Fi network. Some file management apps let you easily move files between the phone and computers on the network. The Samsung Kies file exchange utility is completely wireless.

Finally, the HDMI connection between a phone and TV could be obsolete. Google's own Chromecast TV gizmo works with Android phones to share a movie or video playing on the phone's screen, echoing the image on the TV.

Add Spice to Dictation

I feel that too few people use dictation, despite how handy it can be — especially for text messaging. Anyway, if you've used dictation, you might have noticed that it occasionally censors some of the words you utter. Perhaps you're the kind of person who doesn't put up with that kind of s***.

Relax. You can lift the vocal censorship ban by following these steps:

1. **Start the Settings app.**

2. **Choose Language & Input.**

   On some Samsung phones you'll find the Language and Input item on the Controls tab in the Settings app.

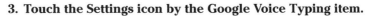

3. **Touch the Settings icon by the Google Voice Typing item.**

4. **Remove the check mark by the Block Offensive Words option.**

And just what are offensive words? I would think that *censorship* is an offensive word. But no. Apparently only a few choice words fall into this category. I won't print them here, because the phone's censor retains the initial letter and generally makes the foul language easy to guess. D***.

Add a Word to the Dictionary

Betcha didn't know that your phone sports a dictionary. The dictionary is used to keep track of words you type — words that it may not recognize as being spelled properly.

Words unknown to the phone are highlighted on the screen. Sometimes, the word is shown in a different color or on a different background or even underlined in red. To add that word to the phone's dictionary, long-press it. You see the Add Word to Dictionary command, which sticks the word in the phone's dictionary.

To review or edit the phone's dictionary, follow these steps:

1. **Start the Settings app.**

2. **Choose Language & Input.**

3. **Choose Personal Dictionary.**

   The command may not be obvious on some phones: Try choosing the keyboard first, and then choose either the Dictionary or User Dictionary command.

When the dictionary is visible, you can review words, edit them, remove them, or manually add new ones. To edit or delete a word, long-press it. To add a word, choose the Add icon.

Employ Some Useful Widgets

Your phone features a wide assortment of widgets with which to festoon your phone's Home screen. Of the lot, I prefer contact and navigation widgets.

For the folks you contact most frequently, consider slapping down some contact widgets. Here's how:

1. **Long-press a Home screen panel that has room for at least one icon.**

2. **Choose the Widgets command.**

3. **If necessary, touch the Widgets tab atop the screen.**

4. **Choose the Direct Dial widget: Long-press that widget and drag it to a position on the Home screen.**

   Specific directions for adding widgets are presented in Chapter 22.

5. **Select the contact you want to direct-dial.**

   Contacts with multiple phone numbers have more than one listing; choose the number you want to dial.

A widget representing the contact's phone number (with the contact's picture, if available) appears on the Home screen. Touching the widget instantly dials the contact.

TIP

- Just as you can create a direct-dial shortcut, you can create an icon to directly text message a contact. The difference is that you choose Direct Message rather than Direct Dial in Step 4.

- See Chapter 9 for more information about text messaging.

- Another handy widget to add is the Directions widget. Follow Steps 1–3, but choose the Directions widget in Step 4. Then type the location where you want to go. At this point, creating the widget works like getting directions in the Maps app. After you save the widget's information, touch the widget to summon the Maps app and get directions from your location.

- See Chapter 14 for more information about using the Maps app.

Find Your Lost Phone

Someday, you may lose your beloved Android phone. It might be for a few panic-filled seconds, or it might be for forever. The hardware solution is to weld a heavy object to the phone, such as an anvil or a rhinoceros, yet that strategy kind of defeats the entire mobile/wireless paradigm. (Well, not so much the rhino.) The software solution is to use a cell phone locator service.

Cell phone locator services employ apps that use a phone's cellular signal as well as its GPS to help locate the missing gizmo. These types of apps are available at the Google Play Store. One that I've tried and recommend is Lookout Mobile Security.

Lookout features two apps; one is free, which you can try to see if you like it. The paid app offers more features and better locating services. As with similar phone-locating apps, you must register at a website to help you locate your phone, should it go wandering.

Ten Things to Remember

In This Chapter

▶ Locking the phone

▶ Switching to landscape orientation

▶ Using Google Now

▶ Saving typing time

▶ Minding the battery

▶ Checking for phone roaming

▶ Using the + key to dial international calls

▶ Obtaining a docking stand

▶ Taking a picture of your contacts

▶ Using the Search command

*I*f only it were easy to narrow to ten items the list of all the things I want you to remember when using your Android phone. Even though you'll find in this chapter ten good things not to forget, don't think for a moment that there are *only* ten. In fact, as I remember more, I'll put them on my website, at www.wambooli.com. Check it for updates about your phone and perhaps for even more things to remember.

Lock the Phone on a Call

Whether you dialed out or someone dialed in, after you start talking, you should lock your phone. Press the Power/Lock key. By doing so, you disable the touchscreen and ensure that the call isn't unintentionally disconnected.

Of course, the call can still be disconnected by a dropped signal or by the other party getting all huffy and hanging up on you. But by locking the phone, you prevent a stray finger or your pocket from disconnecting (or muting) the phone.

Use Landscape Orientation

The natural orientation of the typical Android phone is vertical — its *portrait* orientation. Even so, that doesn't mean you have to use an app in portrait orientation.

Turning the phone to its side makes many apps, such as the web browser app and the Maps app, appear wider. It's often a better way to see things, such as more available items on certain menus, and to give you larger key caps on which to type if you're using the onscreen keyboard.

✔ Not every app supports landscape orientation.

✔ You can lock orientation so that the touchscreen won't flip and flop. The easiest way to do so is by touching the Auto Rotate quick action. Otherwise, open the Settings app and choose Display to find the orientation lock setting.

Enjoy Google Now

Perhaps the most powerful feature on any Android phone is Google Now. You use it for more than just searching for something. Google Now updates you with cards. And the more you use Google Now, the more cards you see and the more relevant they become.

Start Google Now by touching the Google Search widget on the Home screen, starting the Google Now app, or swiping the screen from the bottom up. That swipe works even on the lock screen, as shown in Figure 25-1.

Abuse the Onscreen Keyboard

Don't forget to take advantage of the suggestions that appear above the onscreen keyboard while you type. Choosing a word, or long-pressing a word to see more choices, greatly expedites the ordeal of typing on a cell phone. Plus, the predictive text feature may instantly display the next logical word for you.

Lock screen

Swipe up

Figure 25-1: Starting Google Now.

When predictive text fails you, keep in mind that you can use Google Gesture typing instead of the old hunt-and-peck. Dragging your finger over the keyboard and then choosing a word suggestion works quickly — when you remember to do it.

See Chapter 4 for information on activating these phone features.

Things That Consume Lots of Battery Juice

Three items on your phone suck down battery power faster than an 18-year-old fleeing the tyranny of high school on graduation day:

- Navigation
- Bluetooth
- The display

Navigation is certainly handy, but because the phone's touchscreen is on the entire time and dictating text to you, the battery drains rapidly. If possible, try to plug the phone into the car's power socket when you're navigating. If you can't, keep an eye on the battery meter.

Bluetooth requires extra power for its wireless radio. When you need that level of connectivity, great! Otherwise, turn off your Bluetooth gizmo as soon as necessary to save power.

Finally, the touchscreen display draws a lot of power. You can try using the Auto Brightness setting, but it can get too dark to see or, more frequently, it takes too long to adjust to a high- or low-light setting. So if you avoid the Auto Brightness setting, remember how that bright display can drain the battery.

See Chapter 23 for more information on managing the phone's battery.

Check for Roaming

Roaming can be expensive. The last non-smartphone (dumbphone?) I owned racked up $180 in roaming charges the month before I switched to a better cellular plan. Even though you might have a good cell phone plan, keep an eye on the phone's status bar to ensure that you don't see the Roaming status icon when you're making a call.

Well, yes, it's okay to make a call when your phone is roaming. My advice is to remember to *check* for the icon, not to avoid it. If possible, try to make your phone calls when you're back in your cellular service's coverage area. If you can't, make the phone call but keep in mind that you will be charged roaming fees. They ain't cheap.

Use the + Symbol When Dialing Internationally

I suppose that most folks are careful when dialing international numbers. On an Android phone, you can use the + key to replace the country's exit code. In the United States, the code is 011. So whenever you see an international number listed as 011-*xxx-xxxxxxx,* you can instead dial +*xxx-xxxxxxx,* where the *x* characters represent the number to dial.

See Chapter 21 for more information on international dialing.

Get a Docking Stand

I adore my phone's docking stand. Yes, it was horrifically expensive for what it is: a squat little chunk of plastic that props up the phone to a favorable viewing angle. It comes with a charging cord, so the phone charges while it's docked. Yet the docking stand has no other features to justify the high price, except that it was designed specifically for my phone.

Docking stands make excellent bedside holders for your phone. In fact, most phones recognize the docking stand and run a special Home screen app while they're docked. You can use the Clock app, play music, or watch a photo slideshow while the phone is docked.

Snap a Pic of That Contact

Here's something I always forget: Whenever you're near one of your contacts, take the person's picture. Sure, some people are bashful, but most folks are flattered. The idea is to build up your Contacts list so that all contacts have photos. Receiving a call is then much more interesting when you see the caller's picture, especially a silly or an embarrassing one.

When taking the picture, be sure to show it to the person before you assign it to the contact. Let the person decide whether it's good enough. Or if you just want to be rude, assign a crummy-looking picture. Heck, you don't even have to do that: Just assign a random picture of anything. A plant. A rock. Your dog. But seriously, the next time you meet up with a contact, keep in mind that the phone can take that person's picture.

See Chapter 15 for more information on using the phone's camera.

The Search Command

The Search command is not only powerful but also available all over your Android phone. Just about every app features a Search icon, just like the one shown in the margin.

Touch the Search icon to look for information such as locations, people, text — you name it. It's handy. It's everywhere. Use it.

Once upon a time, the Search icon was part of the basic navigation icons that appeared at the bottom of an Android phone's touchscreen.

Index

• H •

About the Author

Dan Gookin has been writing about technology for over 25 years. He combines his love of writing with his gizmo fascination to create books that are informative, entertaining, and not boring. Having written over 140 titles with 12 million copies in print translated into over 30 languages, Dan can attest that his method of crafting computer tomes seems to work.

Perhaps his most famous title is the original *DOS For Dummies,* published in 1991. It became the world's fastest-selling computer book, at one time moving more copies per week than the *New York Times* number-one bestseller (though, as a reference, it could not be listed on the *Times'* Best Sellers list). That book spawned the entire line of *For Dummies* books, which remains a publishing phenomenon to this day.

Dan's most popular titles include *PCs For Dummies, Word For Dummies, Laptops For Dummies,* and *Android Phones For Dummies.* He also maintains the vast and helpful website www.wambooli.com.

Dan holds a degree in Communications/Visual Arts from the University of California, San Diego. He lives in the Pacific Northwest, where he enjoys spending time with his sons playing video games indoors while they enjoy the gentle woods of Idaho.

Publisher's Acknowledgments

Acquisitions Editor: Katie Mohr

Senior Project Editor: Susan Pink

Copy Editor: Susan Pink

Editorial Assistant: Annie Sullivan

Sr. Editorial Assistant: Cherie Case

Project Coordinator: Patrick Redmond

Cover Image: Front Cover Image: Background ©iStockphoto.com/Studio-Pro; the Android robot is reproduced or modified from work created and shared by Google and used according to terms described in the Creative Commons 3.0 Attribution License. Back Cover Images: Dan Gookin

Math & Science

Algebra I For Dummies,
2nd Edition
978-0-470-55964-2

Anatomy and Physiology
For Dummies, 2nd Edition
978-0-470-92326-9

Astronomy For Dummies,
3rd Edition
978-1-118-37697-3

Biology For Dummies,
2nd Edition
978-0-470-59875-7

Chemistry For Dummies,
2nd Edition
978-1-118-00730-3

1001 Algebra II Practice
Problems For Dummies
978-1-118-44662-1

Microsoft Office

Excel 2013 For Dummies
978-1-118-51012-4

Office 2013 All-in-One
For Dummies
978-1-118-51636-2

PowerPoint 2013
For Dummies
978-1-118-50253-2

Word 2013 For Dummies
978-1-118-49123-2

Music

Blues Harmonica
For Dummies
978-1-118-25269-7

Guitar For Dummies,
3rd Edition
978-1-118-11554-1

iPod & iTunes
For Dummies, 10th Edition
978-1-118-50864-0

Programming

Beginning Programming
with C For Dummies
978-1-118-73763-7

Excel VBA Programming
For Dummies, 3rd Edition
978-1-118-49037-2

Java For Dummies,
6th Edition
978-1-118-40780-6

Religion & Inspiration

The Bible For Dummies
978-0-7645-5296-0

Buddhism For Dummies,
2nd Edition
978-1-118-02379-2

Catholicism For Dummies,
2nd Edition
978-1-118-07778-8

Self-Help & Relationships

Beating Sugar Addiction
For Dummies
978-1-118-54645-1

Meditation For Dummies,
3rd Edition
978-1-118-29144-3

Seniors

Laptops For Seniors
For Dummies, 3rd Edition
978-1-118-71105-7

Computers For Seniors
For Dummies, 3rd Edition
978-1-118-11553-4

iPad For Seniors
For Dummies, 6th Edition
978-1-118-72826-0

Social Security
For Dummies
978-1-118-20573-0

Smartphones & Tablets

Android Phones
For Dummies, 2nd Edition
978-1-118-72030-1

Nexus Tablets
For Dummies
978-1-118-77243-0

Samsung Galaxy S 4
For Dummies
978-1-118-64222-1

Samsung Galaxy Tabs
For Dummies
978-1-118-77294-2

Test Prep

ACT For Dummies,
5th Edition
978-1-118-01259-8

ASVAB For Dummies,
3rd Edition
978-0-470-63760-9

GRE For Dummies,
7th Edition
978-0-470-88921-3

Officer Candidate Tests
For Dummies
978-0-470-59876-4

Physician's Assistant Exa
For Dummies
978-1-118-11556-5

Series 7 Exam For Dumm
978-0-470-09932-2

Windows 8

Windows 8.1 All-in-One
For Dummies
978-1-118-82087-2

Windows 8.1 For Dummi
978-1-118-82121-3

Windows 8.1 For Dummi
Book + DVD Bundle
978-1-118-82107-7

📖 **Available in print and e-book formats.**

Available wherever books are sold. **For more information or to order direct visit www.dummies.com**

Take Dummies with you everywhere you go!

Whether you are excited about e-books, want more from the web, must have your mobile apps, or are swept up in social media, Dummies makes everything easier.

For Dummies is the global leader in the reference category and one of the most trusted and highly regarded brands in the world. No longer just focused on books, customers now have access to the For Dummies content they need in the format they want. Let us help you develop a solution that will fit your brand and help you connect with your customers.

Advertising & Sponsorships

Connect with an engaged audience on a powerful multimedia site, and position your message alongside expert how-to content.

Targeted ads • Video • Email marketing • Microsites • Sweepstakes sponsorship

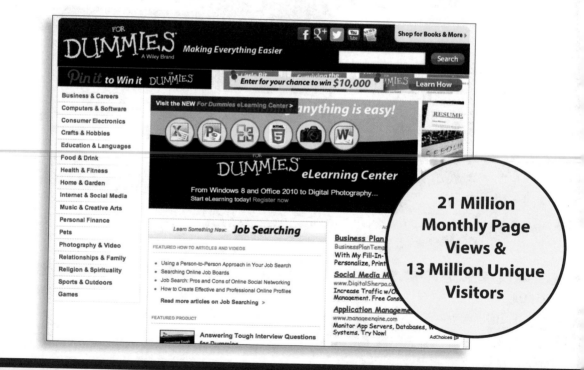

Custom Publishing

Reach a global audience in any language by creating a solution that will differentiate you from competitors, amplify your message, and encourage customers to make a buying decision.

Apps • Books • eBooks • Video • Audio • Webinars

Brand Licensing & Content

Leverage the strength of the world's most popular reference brand to reach new audiences and channels of distribution.

For more information, visit www.Dummies.com/biz

A Wiley Brand

Dummies products make life easier!

- DIY
- Consumer Electronics
- Crafts
- Software
- Cookware
- Hobbies
- Videos
- Music
- Games
- and More!

For more info store by category.

For Dummies is a registered trademark of J

FOR
DUMMIE
A Wiley-B